Craig A. Everett
Robert E. Lee
Editors

When Marriages Fail
Systemic Family Therapy Interventions and Issues

A Tribute to William C. Nichols

Pre-publication
REVIEW . . .

"Children are our future, and children of divorce are a major part of that future. Marriage is a lifestyle where children acquire their lifestyle. Everett and Lee afford us not only their reflections, but systemic family therapy interventions and issues that are part and parcel of failed marriages. This must-have book discusses constructive divorce processes, i.e., alternate dispute resolution and coparenting, all positive divorce preparedness. In addition to the professional literature, there have been many resources written specially for parents and children to assist them with the divorce process. This must-have book affords the professional reader rich resources in an abbreviated form through many research studies. It allows the marriage and family therapist and divorce mediator to know where we've been and the know-how for where we are going."

Peggy W. Fellouris, PhD, MA
Marriage and Family Therapist/
Divorce Mediator

When Marriages Fail
Systemic Family Therapy Interventions and Issues

A Tribute to William C. Nichols

THE HAWORTH PRESS
Divorce and Remarriage
Craig A. Everett, PhD
Editor

Divorce, Family Structure, and the Academic Success of Children by William Jeynes

Divorce, Annulments, and the Catholic Church: Healing or Hurtful? by Richard J. Jenks

When Marriages Fail: Systemic Family Therapy Interventions and Issues edited by Craig A. Everett and Robert E. Lee

When Marriages Fail
Systemic Family Therapy Interventions and Issues

A Tribute to William C. Nichols

Craig A. Everett
Robert E. Lee
Editors

The Haworth Press
New York • London • Oxford

For more information on this book or to order, visit
http://www.haworthpress.com/store/product.asp?sku=5562

or call 1-800-HAWORTH (800-429-6784) in the United States and Canada
or (607) 722-5857 outside the United States and Canada

or contact orders@HaworthPress.com

Published by

The Haworth Press, Inc., 10 Alice Street, Binghamton, NY 13904-1580.

PUBLISHER'S NOTE
The development, preparation, and publication of this work has been undertaken with great care.
However, the Publisher, employees, editors, and agents of The Haworth Press are not responsible
for any errors contained herein or for consequences that may ensue from use of materials or
information contained in this work. The Haworth Press is committed to the dissemination of ideas
and information according to the highest standards of intellectual freedom and the free exchange of
ideas. Statements made and opinions expressed in this publication do not necessarily reflect the views
of the Publisher, Directors, management, or staff of The Haworth Press, Inc., or an endorsement by
them.

Identities and circumstances of individuals discussed in this book have been changed to protect
confidentiality.

Cover design by Kerry Mack.

Library of Congress Cataloging-in-Publication Data

When marriages fail : systemic family therapy interventions and issues : a tribute to William C.
Nichols / Craig A. Everett, Robert E. Lee, editors.
   p. ; cm.
Includes bibliographical references and index.
ISBN-13: 978-0-7890-2862-4 (hard : alk. paper)
ISBN-10: 0-7890-2862-X (hard : alk. paper)
ISBN-13: 978-0-7890-2863-1 (soft : alk. paper)
ISBN-10: 0-7890-2863-8 (soft : alk. paper)
   1. Family psychotherapy. 2. Marital psychotherapy.
   [DNLM: 1. Family Therapy—Festschrift. 2. Marital Therapy—Festschrift. 3. Divorce—
psychology—Festschrift. 4. Family Relations—Festschrift. 5. Marriage—psychology—
Festschrift. WM 430.5.F2 W567 2006] I. Everett, Craig A. II. Lee, Robert E. (Robert Ernest), 1943-
III. Nichols, William C.

RC488.5.W54 2006
616.89'156—dc22
                                                                 2006006815

CONTENTS

ABOUT THE EDITORS

Craig A. Everett, PhD, is in private practice in Tucson, Arizona, and is also the Director of The Arizona Institute for Family Therapy. He was formerly on the faculties of Florida State University and Auburn University where he directed AAMFT Accredited Graduate Programs in Family Therapy. He was also Director of the Pima County Conciliation Court. He is a past president of the American Association for Marriage and Family Therapy and has been Editor of the *Journal of Divorce and Remarriage* since 1984. He is co-author (with Dr. Sandra Volgy) of *Family Therapy with ADHD: Treating Children, Adolescents, and Adults and Short-term Family Therapy with Borderline Patients*; and editor of *Child Custody: Legal Decisions and Family Outcomes*. Dr. Everett is a Fellow and Approved Supervisor with AAMFT and has been in clinical practice for 30 years.

Robert E. Lee, PhD, ABPP, is Professor of Marriage and Family Therapy and Director of the doctoral MFT program at Florida State University. Prior to that he was Professor of Family and Child Ecology at Michigan State University and Clinical Director of the MFT program there. He is co-author (with Craig Everett) of *The Integrative Family Therapy Supervisor, a Primer,* and co-editor (with Shirley Emerson) of *The Eclectic Trainer* and (with Jason Whiting) *The Handbook of Relational Therapy for Foster Children and Their Families*. He is a past president of the Association of Marital and Family Therapy Regulatory Boards, an AAMFT Approved Supervisor, and an ABPP Diplomate in Clinical Psychology. Dr. Lee has been in clinical practice for 35 years.

When Marriages Fail
© 2006 by The Haworth Press, Inc. All rights reserved.
doi:10.1300/5562_a

CONTRIBUTORS

Mary Anne Armour, MA, is a retired faculty member from Mercer University School of Medicine where she started an ongoing Master's degree program in marriage and family therapy (MFT). She taught medical students in the Behavioral Sciences and Clinical Skills programs as well as marriage and family therapists there for sixteen years. Previously she was instrumental in started the American Association for Marriage and Family Therapy (AAMFT) Accredited Masters Program at Auburn University, where she also directed the Family Life Center. She served on AAMFT's national board from 1990 to 1993, and also served on the State MFT boards of both Georgia and Alabama. She is now retired and in part-time private practice in Macon, Georgia.

Derek Ball, PhD, is Senior Marriage and Family Therapist and Director of the Hiebert Institute at the Marriage and Family Counseling Service in Rock Island, Illinois. He earned his doctorate at Purdue University and is a licensed marriage and family therapist in Illinois. He is currently the president-elect of the Illinois Association of Marriage and Family Therapy.

David A. Baptiste, PhD, is a senior psychologist with the New Mexico Corrections Department and a marital and family therapist in private practice, Las Cruces, New Mexico. He has been active in AAMFT for many years and has published in the areas of minority families, gay/lesbian and heterosexual stepfamilies, and single-parent families.

Dorothy S. Becvar, PhD, is an associate professor in the School of Social Service at Saint Louis University, St. Louis, Missouri. She is an LMFT and an LCSW, and has maintained a private practice since 1980. She is also the president/CEO of The Haelan Centers, a not-for-profit organization dedicated to facilitating growth and wholeness in

When Marriages Fail
© 2006 by The Haworth Press, Inc. All rights reserved.
doi:10.1300/5562_b

body, mind, and spirit. She has been involved with AAMFT governance for many years—DAC chair/non-voting board member, AAMFT board member, chair of the Standards Committee, and editor of the *Supervision Bulletin.* For the past nine years she has been secretary of the Missouri Board of Licensed Marital Family Therapists and is currently president-elect of the Association of Marital and Family Therapy Regulatory Boards (AMFTRB).

Jerry J. Bigner, PhD, is Professor Emeritus, Department of Human Development and Family Studies, Colorado State University. He is also the editor of the *Journal of GLBT Family Studies,* and senior editor of the *Haworth Text Series in GLBT Family Studies.* He is a graduate of the doctoral program at Florida State University.

Lee Bowen, PhD, has served in the roles of co-director and director of the AAMFT accredited graduate program in Marriage and Family Therapy, Department of Psychiatry and Behavioral Sciences, Mercer University School of Medicine, for the past fifteen years. He has been chair of the Georgia State Licensing Board for Professional Counselors, Social Workers, and Marriage and Family Therapists. He is a graduate of the Interdivisional Doctoral Program in Marriage and Family Therapy at Florida State University.

Israel Charny, MD, is Professor of Psychology and Family Therapy, and the former director and founder of the Program for Advanced Studies in Integrative Psychotherapy, Magid Center at the Hebrew University of Jerusalem. He also serves as editor in chief of the *Encyclopedia of Genocide,* and executive director of the Institute on the Holocaust and Genocide, Jerusalem.

Frank M. Dattilio, PhD, ABPP, is a clinical psychologist and family therapist who maintains a dual faculty position in the Departments of Psychiatry at both the Harvard Medical School and the University of Pennsylvania. Dr. Dattilio is internationally recognized for his work in the field of cognitive-behavioral therapy and has authored more than 180 professional publications, including eleven books.

Sandra M. Halperin, PhD, has practiced marital and family therapy and supervision for more than thirty years, most of which have been in Auburn, Alabama. She was on the faculty of Auburn's Accredited MFT program. She is a graduate of the Interdivisional Doctoral Program in Marriage and Family Therapy at Florida State University and is a clinical member, approved supervisor, and fellow of the American Association of Marriage and Family Therapy.

Kenneth V. Hardy, PhD, is the director of the Eikenberg Institute for Relationships in New York City and is a professor of family therapy at the AAMFT accredited graduate program at Syracuse University. He has been actively involved in the AAMFT as both a volunteer and a member of the national staff. He has been a member of the Continuing Education Committee, the Membership Committee, the Ethnic Minority Committee, the Minority Task Force, the Ethics Committee, and served as legislative liaison for the NYAMFT. He also served on the national staff, holding several positions including deputy executive director; acting executive director; and executive director of the Commission on Accreditation for Marriage and Family Therapy Education. He is a graduate of the Interdivisional Doctoral Program in Marriage and Family Therapy at Florida State University.

Michele Harway, PhD, ABPP, is on the faculty of the MAP program at Antioch University, Santa Barbara, and is on the consulting faculty at the Fielding Graduate Institute. She is the author and editor of eight books in the areas of domestic violence, family psychology and women's development, including, most recently, the edited work, *The Handbook of Couples Therapy* (John Wiley & Sons, 2005). She is a past president of the Family Psychology Division of APA, current treasurer of the Division on Men and Masculinity and a fellow of several APA divisions. She is board certified in Family Psychology and is licensed as a psychologist and marriage and family therapist.

Toby Sigrun Herman, MA, ECP, is the current president and past recording secretary of the International Family Therapy Association. He also serves as president of the Professionals Practicing Family Therapy in Iceland and chair of the Training Standards Committee and president of the Association of Supervision in Iceland. He is the national delegate for Iceland to the European Association for Psychotherapy. He lives in Reykjavik, Iceland, where he works with the school systems and in private practice.

William Hiebert, STM, Executive Director of Marriage and Family Counseling Service, is an adjunct professor at the University of

Dubuque Theological Seminary and editor of the International Connection, the newsletter of the International Family Therapy Association. He was the founding editor of both *The Family Therapy News* (AAMFT newspaper) and the *Illinois Family Therapist*. He is also co-author of *Pre- and Re-Marital Counseling.*

Sara Ivanir, PhD, is the clinical director of SHINUI Institute Systemic Studies, Israel, and head of the Couples Therapy Program. She is also a faculty member of Magid Institute For Integrative Therapy, Hebrew University, Jerusalem, and Head of the Licensure Committee for Institutes, Israeli Family Therapy Association.

Florence Kaslow, PhD, is in independent practice as a family business consultant and family psychologist. She is board certified in forensic, family, and clinical psychology. Dr. Kaslow has authored or edited twenty-eight books and contributed more than 170 articles to the professional literature on couples therapy, family therapy, divorce therapy and mediation, family business consultation, supervision, and a variety of other topics. She was the founding president of the International Family Therapy Association, is a past editor of the *Journal of Marital and Family Therapy,* and serves on numerous other journal boards in the United States and abroad, including the *Journal of Divorce.*

Marcia Lasswell, MA, is Professor of Psycholgy and Marriage and Family Therapy at California State University, Pomona. She has been in private practice for more than forty years and has taught marriage and family therapy graduate seminars in the AAMFT accredited doctoral program at the University of Southern California. She is the author of numerous journal articles, book chapters, and seven books on marriage and the family. She is a past president of the American Association of Marriage and Family Therapy, the recipient of the California State Marriage and Family Therapy Association Outstanding Clinical Member Award, and California State University Outstanding Teacher Award.

Steve Livingston, PhD, is an assistant professor of counseling in the Adrian Dominican School of Education at Barry University in Orlando, Florida. He is president-elect of the Florida Association for Marriage and Family Therapy (FAMFT) and is a licensed Marriage and Family Therapist. He was formerly on the faculty of the AAMFT accredited graduate program in Marriage and Family Therapy, Department of Psychiatry and Behavioral Sciences, Mercer University School of Medicine. He is a graduate of the Interdivisional Doctoral Program in Marriage and Family Therapy at Florida State University.

David Moultrup, MSW, LICSW, is in private practice in Belmont, Massachusetts. His professional journey has taken him from state hospitals, to university teaching hospitals, to free standing training programs. Enroute he has had the good fortune to learn from Murray Bowen, a host of other bright and caring therapists, and many courageous and thoughtful patients. His current focus is on finding ways to pass on wisdom gained in the field to musicians and performing artists, the general public, and the next generation of mental health providers.

Noga Rubinstein-Nabarro, PhD, is the executive and professional director of the "SHINUI" Institute for Systemic Studies, Israel. She is also the founding director of the International Program for Advanced Family Therapy and Supervision, Israel, a past board member of IFTA, and on the editorial advisory boards of *Contemporary Family Therapy* and the *Journal of Family Therapy.*

Wencke J. Seltzer, PhD, is a professor and researcher at the Unit of Mental Health Research and Clinical Develpment, Division of Psychiatry, Buskerud Hospital, Lier, Norway. She also holds a faculty appointment with the Department of Psychology, University of Trondheim. She is a past president of the International Family Therapy Association and former editor of *The International Connection* (IFTA).

Douglas H. Sprenkle, PhD, is Professor and Director of the AAMFT accredited doctoral program in Marriage and Family Therapy at Purdue University. He is a former editor of the *Journal of Marital and Family Therapy* and has published extensively in the field.

Sandra Volgy Everett, PhD, is the co-director of the Arizona Institute for Family Therapy and is in private practice in Tucson, Arizona. She is a licensed clinical psychologist and a family therapist who was formerly the chief psychologist with the Tucson Child Guidance

Clinic and director of Child Advocacy Services for the Pima County Conciliation Court. She is an AAMFT approved supervisor and was an adjunct faculty member and clinical supervisor with the AAMFT accredited doctoral program in marital and family therapy at Florida State University.

Foreword

When I began my career as a marriage and family therapist in 1970, I may have been especially idealistic or naïve, but I thought of my work with couples as saving marriages. My "awakening" occurred during a postdoctoral year in the Department of Psychiatry at the University of Wisconsin, when, during a session with a couple, an enraged, rejected wife pulled a long, shiny butcher knife out of her purse and lunged at her husband, who had reported he had been engaged in an affair. Fortunately, after a moment of stunned disbelief, I managed to subdue her. She was quickly hospitalized at University Hospital, where her rages continued. Then her husband became suicidal, and he too was hospitalized in the other wing of that psychiatric unit. Over the next several weeks, this pair tried to get access to each other through the locked doors of the two units, and I was looked at somewhat skeptically as the young psychologist whose patients had taken over the energies of an entire inpatient facility.

Working with couples and families is indeed an education for the therapist in the powerful irrationality that prevails when couples are getting married, but especially when marriages are coming apart. The field of marriage and family therapy went through its own early period of naïvete. However, as the wave of divorces has risen to tsunamic proportions, we have had to develop strategies and techniques for dealing with the stormy and often destructive forces in marital dissolution. We also now know just how damaging divorce can be to children; and we as family therapists can mitigate some of those psychological injuries. We have also realized that while particularly the rejected partner in a divorce may suffer long-term psychological harm from the divorce process, divorce can also prompt growth and change in both partners. A skilled and well-informed family therapist can make an important difference in turning a destructive process toward adaptation and growth.

When Marriages Fail
© 2006 by The Haworth Press, Inc. All rights reserved.
doi:10.1300/5562_c

This book, which will become a valuable tool in the hands of the therapist working with marital dissolution and its sequela, was conceived by a group of friends and colleagues of Bill Nichols who wanted to honor him on his retirement, and who also wanted to support his efforts to build an archive for the history and resources of the marriage and family therapy field. Bill's career is a long and distinguished one, and it spans the development of our field from "marriage counseling" and "child guidance" to its multidimensional nature including systemic family therapy today.

What strikes me in reading this book is not only the breadth and diversity of these excellent chapters, but also their specificity. A number of chapters are devoted to the dynamics that precede divorce: Armour, Ball, and Hiebert, with treatments suggested for different patterns. Several chapters deal with the needs and experiences of children: Sandra Everett, Herman, Lee, and Seltzer. Baptiste and Bigner focus on issues that involve lesbian relationships, while Lasswell looks at "gray divorces." Craig Everett explores the rebalancing that must take place when the first partner remarries. Harway treats separation and divorce in families affected by divorce. Two of these chapters would have been especially helpful to me in dealing with my early, tumultuous case: Halperin's treatment of the trauma experienced by the abandoned wife, and Becvar's chapter on working with the spouse for whom the rejection is unanticipated. Frank Dattilio introduces a cognitive-behavioral approach to postdivorce treatment, a helpful addition.

That such an outstanding group of contributors came forward to honor Bill Nichols is hardly surprising. Not only has Bill given a tremendous amount to the development of the field of marriage and family therapy, but he has done much of his work in close relationship with others. As a consequence, he is loved as well as respected; and this network of writers comes out of those long associations.

Even though Bill and I practiced together in Atlanta at The Family Workshop, and co-edited (with Mary Anne Pace-Nichols and Dorothy Becvar) *The Handbook of Family Development and Intervention,* I had not added up—until I began this foreword—the full roster of his national leadership positions. Not only has Bill been president of the American Association for Marriage and Family Therapy, the National Council on Family Relations, the International Family Therapy Association (of which he was a charter member), he also co-founded the Michigan and Florida Marriage and Family Therapy Associations, was president of Georgia's MFT group, and was a charter member of the American Family Therapy Academy. He is the only person to serve as president of both AAMFT and IFTA.

When Bill and I practiced together, he often spoke of helping couples "birth" their marriages and create between them something that was not there before. On an impressive scale, he has helped "birth" the field of marriage and family therapy through his writing, his teaching, and his leadership of its major organizations. Bill is a tall man, with a strong, reserved steadiness. He has a penchant for organization, a logical mind, a quick wit, and a ready smile. He has literally "walked tall" through the history of MFT, leading the whole way.

Bill's work has always been grounded in clinical practice—twenty-five years full-time, and an additional fifteen years part-time. His "integrative" therapy approach draws broadly from a number of therapeutic methods: he pulls together what makes sense, what works; and as marriage and family therapy has changed, he has led some of those changes. But he has always looked at the family system both in its individual parts, and its tangled and convoluted dynamics, and he assumes that what he sees can be understood and talked about honestly and directly with the client family. His relationship with his clients is what guides the work.

Throughout his career, Bill has been deeply committed to the education and training of psychotherapists; in a variety of settings and in a number of modalities, he has taught and supervised therapists for thirty-two years. He has written extensively about so much, but his writings about the education and growth of the therapist are among his best and most deeply-felt contributions. The personal growth of the therapist is a particularly strong thread that unites his approach to supervision.

Bill has worked hard and long to establish the structures and procedures that ensure responsibility and competence in the therapist. He was, for example, the author of the first MFT licensing laws, and the author of the first licensure/certification manual. He rewrote Georgia's MFT laws and included limited licensure for the first time in that state. Bill was deeply involved in the creation and development of our national examination for marriage and family therapists. He was also instrumental in the process of accreditation of MFT graduate and postgraduate programs: he wrote the first accreditation manual, was a site visitor for thirty years, and helped found and was a consultant to the Commission on Accreditation for Marriage and family Therapy Education.

As if all this were not enough, Bill has been a tireless editor and publisher of the works of others: he founded AAMFT's *Journal of Marital and Family Therapy* and continued his editorial work twenty-seven years, including editing *Contemporary Family Therapy* for nineteen years, *Family Relations* for six years, and AAMFT's *Family Therapy News* and IFTA's *The International Connection.* He also served on the editorial or advisory boards of twelve family/family therapy journals.

Several other themes emerge from Bill's writing, most significantly his role in developing integrative family therapy and the field marriage and marriage therapy. Abuse, violence, and victimization are another interest; he has written extensively on childlessness and on divorce and remarriage. In recent years, he has concentrated on family development and his writings have made important contributions to this area. And then there is the world itself: in addition to his involvement in IFTA, he has written about South Africa, Israel, Germany after the Wall, and India.

I do not want to call such a likeable man an institution, but Bill Nichols is a tremendously respected champion, nationally and internationally, of the family. Though Bill's accomplishments might lead one to think of him as "driven," I have never experienced him in this way. He is hard-working, serious, ultimately responsible, but always curious and interested in new thoughts and directions. He seems to enjoy what he is doing, and he has always seemed calm and kind.

I *am* a bit worried about him, though. I know he has many other interests, including his and Mary Anne's beloved retreat in the mountains of north Georgia, a place which must necessitate some hiking and wood-splitting. But I do wonder if he won't have a bit of a struggle with learning to retire. Perhaps we can look forward to a new book: *The Growth Process During Retirement: Special Challenges for Therapists.* I'll be sure to buy it.

Gus Napier, PhD
Ashville, North Carolina

* * *

When I look at the list of distinguished contributors to this book honoring William C. Nichols, I witness a group whose accomplishments mirror Bill's own record. I see presidents of state, national, and international marriage and family therapy associations. I see editors of national newsletters and distinguished journals. I see the founders of professional organizations and individuals whose leadership has shaped the profession. I see major international authors in family therapy. What makes Bill Nichols' record so remarkable is that he is all of these in one person (and more).

The United States may never know again a single individual who becomes a division president, president of the National Council on Family Relations (NCFR), president of the American Association for Marriage and Family Therapy (AAMFT), and president of the International Family Therapy Association (IFTA). This is not only a tribute to his indefatigable work ethic, but to Bill's concern for people and issues at all levels of the profession. When I also realize this one scholar founded what is now the AAMFT's prestigious *Journal of Marital and Family Therapy;* edited the *Family Therapy News,* IFTA's the *International Connection,* and what is now NCFR's *Family Relations*; and still edits *Contemporary Family Therapy: An International Journal*; I also wonder if another family therapist will ever match his record as an editor. I could wax about Bill Nichols' professional record for much more space than is allotted me. Suffice it to say that he wrote the first manual on accreditation for training programs (Nichols, 1975) and also authored the outstanding and definitive history of the profession of MFT (Nichols, 2002). These are enduring legacies by someone who has both made history and recorded it.

What unites all of the contributors of this volume and me, however, is that we are personal friends of Bill's and have deep affection for him. I am confident that each of us has our favorite Bill Nichols stories which testify to his warmth, to the personal interest he has taken in us, or to his remarkable memory. Even as a "lowly" graduate student I remember vividly that Bill, then a journal editor, took the time to offer me sage advice. At our next encounter years later, he asked about my spouse by name! I also remember wandering into the AAMFT business meeting when he was president. Every time a hand went up, he called on the member personally. Bill has been a friend and mentor to at least three generations of MFTs—and these relationships are perhaps his greatest legacy.

Finally, the contributors to this book represent a potpourri of race, gender, sexual orientation, nationality, and theoretical persuasion. The interventions they describe demonstrate both breadth and depth. This comprehensiveness is also fitting for a work in Bill's honor, for he has been the quintessential integrative therapist. Consider that three of his textbooks (Nichols, 1988; Nichols and Everett, 1986; and Nichols, 1996) include the word "integrative" in the title. His writings, like those in this current book, integrate systems, psychodynamic, and behavioral principles in the service of working with couples and families. That such a group of diverse authors are friends and colleagues of Bill's is also a warm testimony to the universality of his ideas.

I invite you to chew and digest these creative papers on working with divorcing families. As does the work of William C. Nichols, they have the flavor of deep clinical wisdom. As Bill's friends, we hope this feast in his honor will be a fitting way of expressing our thanks and honoring all that he has brought to the table of our lives.

Douglas H. Sprenkle
Purdue University

REFERENCES

Nichols, W. C. (1975). *Marriage and family counseling: A manual on accreditation.* Claremont, CA: American Association of Marriage and Family Counselors.

Nichols, W. C. (1988). *Marital therapy: An integrative approach.* New York: Guilford Press.

Nichols, W. C. (1996). *Treating people in families: An integrative framework.* New York: Guilford Press.

Nichols, W. C. (2002). *The AAMFT: Fifty years of marital and family therapy.* Washington, DC: American Association for Marriage and Family Therapy.

Nichols, W. C., & Everett, C. A. (1986). *Systemic family therapy: An integrative approach.* New York: Guilford Press.

Preface

Tribute to William C. Nichols Jr., EdD

This book is compiled as a tribute to William C. Nichols Jr., who is recognized as a consummate clinician and pioneer in defining the early field of marital and family therapy. This is not written in the traditional Festschrift format. Rather, in order to model Nichols' career-long focus on the integration of theory and practice, we decided to focus this book on a specific clinical concern—*divorcing families*—and to ask the contributors to address this subject from the orientation of integrative family therapy. Nichols has defined and championed the integrative model for more than fifty years as the core of family therapy theory and practice.

From his modest roots in north Alabama to Columbia University to the Merrill-Palmer Institute to Florida State University to the University of Georgia, Bill's career has spanned the education and supervision of at least three generations of emerging family therapists. As the founding editor of *The Journal of Marital and Family Therapy* (1974), he defined the earliest scholarly expectations and criteria for the growing literature, for its theory and research, for the emerging field and for the ensuing generations of family therapy scholars. As the author of the first *Manual on Accreditation* (Nichols, 1975) for family therapy education, he set the earliest standards that defined not only the educational and training requirements for the field, but also the "profession and practice of marital and family therapy." As one of the earliest contributors to writing the legislative model for licensure and certification of marital and family therapists (1974) nationally, he helped set the earliest standards again.

In addition, Bill is also viewed as the keeper of the field's history. In 1992 he wrote *The AAMFT: Fifty Years of Marital and Family Therapy* (Nichols, 1992). Often he was the sole voice addressing the need for the profession to claim and protect its documents and history. When many in the field believed that the primary professional organization, AAMFT, should have taken the lead in creating archives to save the early documents reflecting the field's development, Bill took matters into his own hands and began collecting and cataloguing a major portion of this historical material and data.

In the 1960s and 1970s, when the relatively new family therapy field was rather fragmented by the competing loyalties of practitioners to the theoretical models proposed by the field's pioneers (i.e., Bowen, Jackson, Haley, Minuchin, Nagy, Satir, Whitaker, etc.), Bill's voice advocating the integration of clinical approaches was the first and the loudest. During a period when many early family therapists had been trained in only one model and practiced this model on all of their clients, Bill pushed the field for the implementation of integrated models of assessment and treatment to better meet the needs of couples and families in therapy.

As a doctoral student studying with Bill at Florida State University from 1974 to 1976, I was at first overwhelmed watching the intensity and dedication that he brought to his commitment to define, nurture, and protect the then fledgling field of marriage and family therapy. Many of my fellow graduate students fell by the wayside, claiming that he "demanded perfection." That was not the case at all; he demanded a commitment to a professional identity and, quite simply, to professional and clinical competence. I went to Florida State to learn to be a capable family therapist, but I learned and was challenged by Bill's commitment to the profession, to also become an educator, supervisor, politician, sometimes rebel, and caring therapist.

I left Florida State to direct the marriage and family therapy graduate program at Auburn University. This was a very new role for me, but Bill challenged those of us who were directors of AAMFT accredited programs from around the country to join him in a new struggle. During the tumultuous decade of the 1980s, we were urged to fight in the mental health "trenches" to define and defend the growing profession of marriage and family therapy amid challenges from practically every other established clinical discipline. These were battles for territory and political standing that occurred in meetings and confrontations with other mental health organizations and even with lobbyists and lawmakers in the halls of Congress. These battles, with Bill Nichols as perhaps the clearest and most outspoken of the voices for the new marital and family therapy profession, shaped the early definition of the marital and family therapy field. They also marked its boundaries with lines drawn forever in the sand. All of us who practice now as licensed or certified marriage and family therapists have this privilege, recognition, and secure professional identity thanks to the early work and contributions of Bill Nichols.

During this decade of the 1980s Bill wrote, with Tom Clark (then director of the marriage and family therapy program at Wake Forest University), the clearest early definition of the marriage and family therapy profession. This was adopted by AAMFT in 1983:

> Marital and family therapy is defined as the professional application of marital and family systems theories and techniques in the diagnosis and treatment of mental and emotional conditions in individuals, couples, and families. Marital and family therapy is distinguished from marriage and family counseling by the presence of a mental or physical disorder in standard diagnostic nomenclature in at least one member of the family or couple being treated. (AAMFT, 1983, p. 1)

This definition became controversial immediately in the larger mental health community. It was one of our "lines drawn in the sand" that identified marriage and family therapists as trained and competent to *diagnose and treat mental and emotional conditions.* The ensuing battle for this position in the mental health field—that is, would marriage and family therapists be allowed into the "private" clinical circle of those who could "diagnose"—would last and be fought in state licensure committees and legislatures across the country for the next decade or more.

This book is an acknowledgement of the "bigger-than-life" contributions that Bill Nichols has made to the development and present standing of the marriage and family therapy profession. A summary of his career activities and publications may be found in the Appendix.

As second generation family therapists, Robert Lee, my co-editor, and I have carried the mentoring, cajoling, and training we received from Bill into our years of directing graduate programs and training marriage and family therapists: Bob at Michigan State University and now Florida State University; and I, Craig, at Auburn University, Florida State University, and the Arizona Institute for Family Therapy. Our careers, and those of the several generations of marriage and family therapists that we have trained, carry the clear influences from Bill's commitment to the field and to professional excellence.

In this work we have invited some of the more experienced systemic family therapy practitioners and authors from around the world, who have worked with and been influenced by Bill Nichols, to present aspects of their work in each chapter. The clinical topic of divorcing families is one to which Bill has made major contributions. It also focuses the reader on more practical clinical and treatment issues. The subjects will range from pure systemic family therapy interventions to broader theoretical and policy discussions. We also asked each contributor to offer a brief personal reflection on their experiences and relationship with Bill Nichols.

We hope this book will be seen as a fitting tribute to the career, work, and contributions of Bill Nichols.

On an accreditation site visit with Bill in 2004, I kidded with him that, in writing this introduction and tribute, I felt as if I were preparing a eulogy for his funeral. In typical fashion, he replied, "Well, I hope you get it right!"

Bill and his wife, Mary Anne, are "retired" in Athens, Georgia. He is the recent past president of the International Family Therapy Association, editor of the *Contemporary Family Therapy* journal, and he continues to write prolifically.

REFERENCES

AAMFT. (1983). *Manual on accreditation.* Washington, DC: American Association for Marriage and Family Therapy.

Nichols, W. C. (1975). *Marriage and family counseling: A manual on accreditation.* Claremont, CA: American Association of Marriage and Family Counselors.

Nichols, W. C. (1992). *The AAMFT: Fifty years of marital and family therapy.* Washington, DC: American Association for Marriage and Family Therapy.

PART I:
AN OVERVIEW

The evolving knowledge base of marriage and family therapy has included a substantial body of literature that deals specifically with divorce and remarriage from a family and larger systems perspective. In Part I, this literature is summarized. In addition, therapists and their clients are given tools to explore their internal and dyadic processes in considering whether to divorce. Finally, policies are recommended to ensure the well-being of children involved in divorce.

Chapter 1

Treating Divorcing Families in Family Therapy: A Literature Review

Steve Livingston
Lee Bowen

Tributes to William C. Nichols

It has been an honor to have met, known, and worked with Bill Nichols over the past twenty years. He has had a profound effect on my career as a marriage and family therapist through his research, writing, and fellowship. I enjoyed interacting with Bill during his time in Tallahassee, Florida, and our continued interaction at conferences over the years. Bill, thank you for your hard work, wisdom, and friendship. You are greatly appreciated. SL

It is with pleasure that I have the opportunity to thank Bill publicly for his contribution and influence. I have had the pleasure of knowing Bill since my days in graduate school in the late 1980s. For the last fifteen years as director of the MFT program, Mercer University School of Medicine, I have had the privilege of an ongoing relationship with him. During these years I have enjoyed his support of the MFT program and have frequently sought his wise counsel on numerous issues. I can always count on the soundness and wisdom of his responses. Bill, thanks for your contribution to the field, your personal encouragement, and for your support of the program! —LB

Divorce in the Unites States continues to be a significant social event with serious consequences experienced by a number of American families each year. In response, the family therapy field has evolved over the past forty years with regard to recognizing the systemic nature of the divorce and remarriage experience for families. While there has been considerable family science literature published over the past four decades regarding the broad field of divorce, in this introductory chapter we will review the literature that has been directed primarily toward clinicians treating various aspects of divorcing families. Tracing this literature from the earliest contributions to the present provides a clear summary of the developments in the field as well as the resources systemic family therapy.

Divorce is a complex phenomenon that affects all aspects of the intergenerational family system. It has even replaced death as the single most common reason for the end of marriages (Pinsof, 2002). It has become so common in our culture that we now define it as a component in the family's developmental life cycle. Family therapy can be crucial in helping divorcing systems negotiate the potential dysfunctional elements that can arise throughout the divorce process.

Divorce evolved as a significant social issue in the 1960s. Although, Gottman and Notarius (2002) reflected that divorce did not become an object of serious scientific study until the last quarter of the 20th century, census data indicated a steady rise in the number of divorces in the United States from 1963 to 1978. Moreover, early clinical and sociological studies tended to focus on independent causes and consequences of divorce, with therapeutic interventions focused on individual adjustment. This early literature failed to look at the basic systemic nature of divorce—the interactive roles between the parent, child, sibling, and intergenerational subsystems.

EARLY LITERATURE ON THE STAGES OF DIVORCE

The focus of theory began to shift in the 1970s, when divorce began to be viewed as a process within a broader systemic perspective. The first studies began to address the *stages* of the divorce process. For example, Bohannan (1970) suggested that there were six smaller divorces ("stations") within the larger divorce process divorce, namely, the emotional, legal, economic, coparental, community, and psychological divorces. The implication was that some of these separations would take place soon and be more complete than others. Kessler (1975) suggested seven stages ranging from disillusionment to hard work, and Weiss (1975) explored the broader transition and recovery phases of divorce. Other clinical papers followed. Weisman (1975) introduced crisis theory to elaborate on the stages and process of divorce, and Froiland and Hozman (1977) offered a counseling model based on the loss of self-esteem accompanying rejection. Enough progress was made by the late 1970s that Salts (1979) could provide a comparative analysis of the initial models of the divorce process. Finally, Carter and McGoldrick (1980) asked family therapists to reconsider their ideas about the family life cycle. They observed that normal life-cycle tasks are interrupted and altered by the divorce and remarriage processes. They indicated four phases that a family must navigate if the family system is to successfully restabilize and continue its expected developmental life cycle.

Despite all of this attention given to the process of divorce, the majority of the divorce and remarriage clinical literature has continued to focus on individual adjustment. However, Kaslow (2000) reviewed seven aspects of divorce and offered a "dialectic" model of the divorce stages. Finally, most recently, Everett, Livingston, and Bowen (2005) reviewed what clinically competent practitioners needed to know about the processes of separation, divorce, and remarriage.

THE INTRODUCTION OF DIVORCE THERAPY AND SYSTEMIC TREATMENT MODELS

By 1980, *divorce therapy* was becoming recognized as a systemic intervention focusing on helping couples and families negotiate the stages of the divorce process (Kaslow, 1981). Although there was some debate at this time regarding whether divorce therapy was an independent mental health practice specialty, most clinicians working with divorcing families viewed it as a component of systemic family therapy. (See Kaslow, 1981; Nichols & Everett, 1986.)

Kaslow (1981) presented an early review of the existing divorce literature and introduced her dialectic model of divorce therapy. This model identified major tasks to be accomplished during the various stages of the divorce process, similar to the Carter and McGoldrick work (1980). Kaslow also was one of the first clinicians to offer systemic family therapy recommendations which clearly addressed children's needs in the divorcing system.

Nichols and Everett (1986) presented another systemic model that described preambivalent, ambivalent, and postambivalent stages of the divorce process. This was also one of the earlier efforts to define clinical issues and interventions associated with specific divorce stages for families. Later, Everett and Volgy Everett (1991) offered a comprehensive systemic map of the divorce process. Their fourteen stages (steps) is the most comprehensive to date. Specific family therapy interventions were recommended for each stage that the family experiences. Sprenkle and Gonzalez-Doupe (1996) also addressed treatment recommendations for the family system at each stage of their three-stage model.

As we look back on the literature focused on stages, consensus seemed to be that there were three major stages, with substages, that defined the clinical divorce process (see Sprenkle & Gonazalez-Doupe, 1996; Everett & Volgy Everett, 1991; Kaslow & Schwartz, 1987): (1) predivorce issues, (2) the decision to divorce, and (3) postdivorce restructuring and remarriage.

This developing body of literature on the stages and process of divorce led to a more systemic focus on family therapy interventions and treatment recommendations. Some literature focused on the decision to divorce and the process whereby one partner wants to leave the marriage and the other does not. (See Crosby, 1989; Everett & Volgy Everett, 1989; Nichols, 1989.) A major professional journal, *The Journal of Divorce* (now the *Journal of Divorce & Remarriage*, Haworth Press), specializing in research and clinical literature on divorce was begun in the late 1970s. Major texts, ranging from the specifics of divorce therapy to treating divorcing families in the context of recognized family therapy techniques, began appearing in the 1980s. These included the following:

- Sprenkle (1985) provided a comprehensive treatment text with clinical recommendations for the different stages of divorce.
- Kressel (1985) addressed the process of divorce and looked at the nature of treatment.
- Rice and Rice (1986) provided a developmental clinical approach for divorce therapy.
- Isaacs, Montalvo, and Abelsohn (1986) presented a systemic treatment approach for working with couples and children through divorce.
- Everett (1987) edited a handbook for clinicians dealing with the divorce process.

- Textor (1989) provided a comprehensive text on varying aspects of divorce and clinical interventions.
- Pam and Pearson (1998) examined the emotional process of divorce and provided clinical techniques for therapists dealing with divorce.
- Gurman and Jacobson (2002) edited a clinical handbook on couples therapy that included a section on addressing separation and divorce issues.

Clinical issues relating to divorce also were further explored in a number of marriage and family therapy texts, including Nichols and Schwartz (2004).

RECOGNIZING CHILDREN'S EXPERIENCES IN DIVORCE

Children experience a wide range of emotions in response to their parents' divorce. Working with and consideration of children in the divorce process is critical to their emotional adjustment. Common reactions reported by children experiencing divorce range from anger, fear, sadness/depression, guilt, rejection, regression to school and physical problems. Most of the clinically identified problems for children in the divorce process revolve around issues of emotional security, safety, protection, and family continuity (Everett & Volgy Everett, 1991; Kaslow & Schwartz, 1987; Nichols, 1984).

A review of the early literature on children's issues and clinical interventions for children relating to divorce began with Gardner (1976), who was one of the first clinicians to write about treating children of divorce. Wallerstein and Kelly (1980) described a longitudinal study of children of divorce, while Kaslow (1981) suggested systemic clinical interventions directed at children's needs within a divorcing system. Hetherington, Cox, and Cox (1986) described the effect of divorce on parents and children. Francke (1983) interviewed children and therapists about the effects of divorce on children and offered a review of clinical interventions. Nichols (1984, 1985) addressed the therapeutic needs of children of divorce, while Ahrons (1994) presented a model for helping divorcing families rebalance by providing clinical suggestions for the stages of the divorce process. Everett (1989,

1992, 1994) edited a series of texts that focused on the economic, developmental, and clinical impacts of divorce on children. The area of single-parent families, the systemic issues and implications for treatment were addressed by Everett and Volgy Everett (2000).

In addition to the professional literature, there have been many resources written specifically for parents and children to assist them with the divorce process. Among the most well known were Gardner's (1971, 1977) work which presented guidelines for children and parents dealing with divorce, Everett's and Volgy Everett's (1994) work which outlined a "healthy" divorce guide for parents and children, and Ahrons (1994) who produced the "good" divorce guide. Brown and Brown (1988) also offered an illustrated guide, using figures of dinosaurs to help children of divorce. Winchester, Beyer, and Verdick (2001) presented a "survival" guide for children that was reflective of the numerous self-help books available for parents and children.

LITERATURE ON THE LEGAL AND TECHNICAL ASPECTS OF DIVORCE

Constructive Divorce Processes

Alternative Dispute Resolution

Upon deciding to divorce, a couple moves into a new phase in the divorce process in which they must decide on how to proceed with legal issues. These practical and serious issues range from dealing with financial matters, the division of personal property, the division of assets and debts, disposition of the family house to custody and access of the children, and financial support of the children.

Divorce mediation emerged in the 1970s as a constructive method for helping couples to resolve their various legal issues and potential disputes associated with divorce. Most notably it offered parents an alternative to the adversarial process of hiring attorneys and going into a court to fight over children and finances. The earliest works and models in this field were presented by Haynes (1981) and Kressel (1985).

The success of this alternative led to the emergence of new resources related to the process of mediation. Folberg and Taylor (1984), in their comprehensive guide to mediation, suggested that divorce mediation was beneficial to couples in many significant ways. Everett (1985) provided an introduction and overview to the field of mediation with recommendations for beginning mediators. Folberg and Milne (1988) edited a text that explored the legal and emotional aspects of divorce and the role of mediation. Marlow and Suber (1990) guided beginning mediators through the process of mediation using a sample case, while Emery (1994) used a variety of case examples to suggest effective techniques. Folberg, Milne, and Salem (2004) presented a comprehensive guide to family and divorce mediation in their update of their original divorce mediation text.

A divorcing couple's choice of a mediated settlement allows the family system to rebalance with as little disruption as possible. Following a divorce, spouses begin a process of systemic restructuring necessary to stabilize the postdivorce family system. This can be a difficult transition, especially in relation to parenting. Everett and Volgy Everett (1991) referred to this period as "postdivorce coparenting."

Coparenting

To enhance parents' postdivorce coparenting, the 1990s provided a growing literature on the needs for and models to provide divorce education programs. These were intended to enhance the resources available to families coping with the consequences of divorce. Many of these were initiated and supported by court-related programs and community counseling agencies. These divorce education programs were designed to assist both children and parents, and offered psychoeducational approaches to improve coparenting and well as personal adjustment (Kirby, 1998). Many states now require divorcing parents to participate in these divorce education programs prior to the finalization of a divorce (Geasler & Blaisure, 1999).

Policy

As our nation and its mental health providers have been acquiring experience with the process of divorce, family therapists have been attempting to influence how legislators, officers of the family court, and government officials think about this institution. Specifically, they have shared insights with regard to how society should structure the divorce process to encourage the well-being of those involved. Some of their vehicles have been state and federal Family Impact Seminars, such as ones at the University of Wisconsin (Policy Institute for Family Impact, 2005) with published proceedings (e.g., Trzcinski & Genheimer, 2000), publications in family law journals (e.g., Lee, 1990, 2000), textbooks with an eye toward members of the family bar (e.g., Gardner, 1982, 1989), and meta-analyses in refereed journals (e.g., Whiteside & Becker, 2000).

Finally, William Doherty (1995) wrote compellingly to America's therapists in general, they who counsel families pre-, during, and post-divorce and who serve as expert witnesses in matters of family law. He asked them to think about their roles as therapists, evaluators, and advisors through the lens of moral responsibility to clients and communities.

LITERATURE ON REMARRIAGE AND BLENDED FAMILIES

In directing attention to the changing demographics associated with divorce and remarriage, Cherlin and Furstenburg (1994) asserted that nearly one-third of all Americans will marry, divorce and remarry. Concurrently, those who choose to cohabit rather than remarry are also increasing, leading to greater difficulty in collecting reliable data on remarriage and stepfamily functioning. Among those who are the most likely to remarry, according to Cherlin and Furstenburg (1994), are women who first marry in their teens or early twenties, women who divorce younger, and women who have fewer than three children. Their data regarding children in remarried families indicated that 11.2 percent of children lived with one biological parent and one stepparent in 1992.

Pinsof (2002) observed that approximately one-half of the children born after 1960 in the Western world experienced parental divorce. Visher and Visher (1996) noted that 60 percent of first marriages ended in divorce. However, Marano (2000) asserted that even though one of every two marriages ended in divorce, 90 percent of Americans continued to marry. In fact, surveys consistently revealed that marriage continues to be a valued institution and a highly held status. Furstenberg and Spanier (1984) stated that more than 40 percent of marriages in the United States involved at least one spouse who had been married at least once before. In hindsight, Pinsof (2002) acknowledged that society was not equipped legally, socially, and emotionally to deal with this experience.

With regard to remarriage, Marano (2000) noted that, in spite of the numbers of first marriages that ended in divorce, society continues to view marriage through optimistic lenses and this optimism extends through remarriage. Despite the disappointment and conflict associated with divorce, most individuals will choose to marry again. An astonishing 75 percent of those who divorce marry again and do so within three to four years (Visher & Visher, 1996). If the number of individuals who choose to forego the legal status of marriage and cohabit instead are added to the remarried data, this rate would be even higher. However, U. S. Census Bureau data show that sixty percent of remarriages fail, and they do so even more quickly than do first marriages. At the ten-year mark, 37 percent of remarriages have ended in divorce in contrast to 30 percent of first marriages.

Elaborating on this remarriage phenomena further, Ahrons (1994) observed that one-half of the marriages that occurred in 1993 in the United States were remarriages in which one or both partners had been divorced. Clinicians who work extensively with divorcing and remarrying couples often wonder why individuals are willing to try marriage again and again. Sager, Brown, Crohn, Engel, Rodstein, and Walker (1982) postulated that individual motives to remarry on the part of men and women play a significant part. Such personal motives may include: electing to live with someone they love in order to bear and raise children; the desire for emotional and financial security; or the desire to build a system of support around them. Additional motives may include: fear of being alone; revenge toward former spouse; feeling abandoned; having unrealistic dreams and fantasies that the former mate was simply bad and the new spouse will be loving, kind, and considerate; having the desire to have a family; and marrying someone who is younger thinking he or she will be a revitalizing force, among others.

As described previously, the early literature that addressed the process of divorce did so in terms of stages. These early formulations directed little attention toward the experience or process of remarriage (Kaslow, 1981). In the mid-1980s, Crosbie-Burnett and Ahrons (1985) asserted that the bi-nuclear family form was so new that not enough information existed on the process of providing therapy for these families. Due to the lack of reliable information, they encouraged therapists to

assume an individualized approach with each family. Their suggestions for working with remarried families included: (1) therapists
should take a facilitative role and help family members reach their
own conclusions; (2) therapists must be alert to normative biases that
may have been emphasized in their own training; and (3) when an individual, couple, or family who is a part of a stepfamily system, the
therapist must visualize those present within the office as part of a
larger family system.

Emphasizing the differences between first marriages and subsequent marriages, Ahrons and Rodgers noted (1987) that the transition
from divorce to remarriage for one or both spouses was different than
that which occurs in first marriages. They suggested that each new
spouse brings his or her family of origin into the marriage as well as
their former biological spouses and her/his family of origin. The issues associated with negotiating the integration of a remarried and
blended family are immense and complex.

Hartin (1990) conceptualized remarriage in terms of a process that
moves through four stages: (1) marriage and its dissolution, (2) the
divorced family, (3) repartnering, and (4) achieving family solidarity.
Clinicians serving this population were told to expect children's behavioral problems, complaints about the partner's parenting, conflicts about having a mutual child, conflicts about access arrangements, and conflicts about money.

William Nichols and Craig Everett (Nichols, 1996; Nichols &
Everett, 1986) identified specific clinical issues in working with remarried couples. These included the presence of "ghosts from the
past" for remarried couples in which reactive relational patterns from
former relationships may be triggered in the newly formed remarriage.
A spouse needs time to grieve the loss of his or her former partner and
the lack of fulfillment of the hopes and dreams that were once attached
to that relationship. Nichols and Everett (1986) also identified the fact
that the children from one or both parents' prior marriages are present
from the very beginning of the couple's new relationship. This remarriage relationship begins with children and the couple has little time
to bond or settle into the marital relationship, as occurs typically in
first marriages. They also identified the task for these remarried parents in establishing rules for managing property, money, and inheri-
tance-related issues. Preexisting debt or financial obligations may

exert not only financial pressure, but also issues related to anxiety, trust, and loyalty.

One of the most critical issues that must be addressed by clinicians working with remarriages and stepfamilies is the issue of role ambiguity. Fine (1996) suggested that this occurs because there are so few established guidelines and models for stepparents. He suggested that developing clear communication with the spouse who is the biological parent about roles and expectations can help establish complementary roles between the stepparent and the biological parent. This may minimize the systemic experiences of splitting and triangulation in remarried families and often involve the children.

The Vishers, historic leaders in identifying and reporting the dynamics in stepfamilies, stated that the greatest problem experienced by adults who remarried when a partner had children was the unrealistic expectations that the household would integrate and settle down quickly (Visher & Visher, 1990). They enumerated several areas that were most likely to pose difficulties in the process of stabilizing and reintegrating stepfamilies: change and loss, unrealistic beliefs, insiders and outsiders, life-cycle discrepancies, loyalty conflicts, boundary problems, power issues, and closeness and distance. They also identified specific tasks that remarried and blended families must accomplish to further the process of integrating the new roles in a stepfamily: dealing with losses and change, negotiation of different developmental needs of members of the stepfamily, establishing new traditions, developing a solid couple bond, forming new relationships, creating a parenting coalition, accepting continuing shifts in household composition, risking involvement despite little support from society.

For clinicians working with blended families, the Vishers recommended the need to focus on strengthening a couple's relationship before issues related to the stepparenting and stepchild(ren) are addressed (Visher & Visher, 1988). Since the central issue for the remarried couple is integration, Hartin (1990) suggested that the primary goal of treatment would be strengthening, supporting, and defining boundaries for their relationship. A second goal would consist of helping these parents become a collaborative parenting team and consolidate their authority over biological children and stepchildren. A third goal of treatment would be assisting the couple in dealing with disruptive contact from former spouses.

An additional stressful family transition occurs when the first ex-spouse remarries. Such an announcement made by the biological parent can produce shock waves that reverberate throughout the family system (Everett & Volgy Everett, 1994). This may trigger a reaction from the former spouse who may have been holding onto fantasies of reconciling or who reacts to another parent entering his or her children's lives. These reactions may include attempts directed toward sabotaging the children's visitation schedule with the remarrying parent, efforts directed toward turning the children against the parent who is remarrying and/or toward the new partner, and even the return to court to prevent the ex-partner from having access to the children. This latter issue may involve serious issues of parental alienation. (See Gardner, 2001; Everett, in press.)

Ahrons (1994) observed that it is the male who typically remarries first and does so within the first year after the divorce. She noted that 50 percent of divorced males remarry within a year of the divorce and will most often marry women who are atleast four years younger than their prior partner. Additional effects of remarriage were highlighted in a study conducted by Christensen and Rettig (1996). They reported that remarriage of one or both spouses was associated with less frequent coparent interaction, less reported parenting support from the former spouse, more negative attitudes about the other parent for both women and men, less parenting satisfaction, and lower levels of involvement in children's activities for the married men.

In the initial phase of integrating members of a blended family, the stepparent may be viewed as an "outsider." Premature attempts on the part of the stepparent to become an "insider" may actually exacerbate and perpetuate the role of being an "outsider." It is necessary that a stepparent display respectfulness, sensitivity, and the recognition that inclusion into a parenting role may take several years to achieve. The role of stepfather may actually be easier to achieve in many blended families because a vacuum exists due to the frequent departure of the biological father. Stepmothers, on the other hand, may have to struggle with attempting to fulfill a role that remains occupied by the biological mother (Cherlin & Furstenburg, 1994).

Children of all ages are also affected by the family transition of remarriage. Young children experience anxiety and fearfulness with new environmental surroundings, new adults, and new children entering/intruding into their lives. Many will cling to their biological parent for security and nurturance while others may refuse visits to a new and uncertain setting. Somewhat older children may experience and express anger and depression when the remarriage of one of their parents occurs. Adolescents may engage in actions designed to reunite their biological parents. They may engineer circumstances, such as getting in trouble or reporting false physical symptoms, to bring their parents together.

Visher and Visher (1996) conducted a survey of 267 clients who were asked to identify the most helpful interventions that they received from their therapists. Their responses included the following:

1. validating and normalizing stepfamily dynamics;
2. supplying important psychoeducation on stepfamilies;
3. reducing the sense of helplessness; and
4. strengthening the couple relationship.

We have presented an overview and discussion of the primary literature and contributions from the family therapy field for clinical work with divorcing families. We hope they will provide a foundation for the contributions that follow.

REFERENCES

Ahrons, C. (1994). *The good divorce.* New York: Harper Collins Publishers, Inc.

Ahrons, C., & Rodgers, R. (1987). *Divorced families.* New York: W.W. Norton & Company.

Bohannan, P. (1970). The six stations of divorce. In P. Bohannan (Ed.), *Divorce and after.* Garden City, NY: Doubleday.

Brown, M., & Brown, L. (1988). *Dinosaurs divorce.* New York: Little, Brown.

Carter, A. E., & McGoldrick, M. (1980). The family life cycle and family therapy: An overview. In E. A. Carter & M. McGoldrick (Eds.), *The family life cycle: A framework for family therapy* (pp. 3-20). New York: Gardner Press.

Cherlin, A., & Furstenburg, Jr., F. (1994). Stepfamilies in the United States: A reconsideration. *Annual Review Sociology, 20,* 359-381.

Christensen, D., & Rettig, K. (1996). The relationship of remarriage to post-divorce co-parenting. In C. A. Everett (Ed.), *Understanding stepfamilies: Their structure and dynamics* (pp. 73-88). New York: Haworth Press.

Crosbie-Burnett, M., & Ahrons, C. (1985). From divorce to remarriage: Implications for therapy with families in transition. In D. Sprenkle (Ed.), *Divorce therapy* (pp. 121-137). New York: Haworth Press.

Crosby, J. F. (Ed.) (1989). *When one wants out and the other doesn't: Doing therapy with polarized couples.* New York: Brunner/Mazel.

Doherty, W. J. (1995). *Soul searching: Why psychotherapy must promote moral responsibility.* New York: Basic Books.

Emery, R. E. (1994). *Renegotiating family relationships: Divorce, child custody, and mediation.* New York: Guilford Press.

Everett, C. (Ed.) (1985). *Divorce mediation: Perspectives on the field.* New York: Haworth Press.

Everett, C. (Ed.) (1987). *The divorce process: A handbook for clinicians.* New York: Haworth Press.

Everett, C. (Ed.) (1989). *Children of divorce: Developmental and clinical issues.* New York: Haworth Press.

Everett, C. (Ed.) (1992). *The consequences of divorce: Economic and custodial impact on children and adults.* New York: Haworth Press.

Everett, C. (Ed.) (1994). *The economics of divorce: The effects on parents and children.* New York: Haworth Press.

Everett, C. A. (in press). Treating Parental Alienation Syndrome in family therapy. In R. Gardner, R. Sauber, & D. Lorandos (Eds.), *Handbook of Parental Alienation Syndrome.*

Everett, C. A., Livingston, S. E., & Bowen, L. D. (2005). Separation, divorce, and remarriage. In R. C. Coombs (Ed.), *Family Therapy Review: Preparing for comprehensive and licensing examinations* (pp. 257-275). New Jersey: Lawrence Erlbaum Associates, Publishers.

Everett, C. A., & Volgy Everett, S. (1989). The assessment and treatment of polarizing couples. In J. F. Crosby (Ed.), *When one wants out and the other doesn't: Doing therapy with polarized couples* (pp. 67-92). New York: Brunner/Mazel.

Everett, C. A., & Volgy Everett, S. (1991). Treating divorce in family therapy practice. In A. S. Gurman & D. P. Kniskern (Eds.), *Handbook of family therapy,* Vol. II (pp. 508-524). New York: Brunner/Mazel.

Everett, C. A., & Volgy Everett, S. (1994). *Healthy divorce.* San Francisco: Josey-Bass.

Everett, C. A., & Volgy Everett, S. (2000). Single parent families: Dynamics and treatment issues. In W. C. Nichols, M. A. Pace-Nichols, D. S. Becvar, & A. Y. Napier (Eds.), *Handbook of family development and intervention* (pp. 323-340). New York: John Wiley & Sons.

Fine, M. (1996). The clarity and context of the stepparent role: A review of the literature. In C. A. Everett (Ed.), *Understanding stepfamilies: Their structure and dynamics* (pp. 19-34). New York: Haworth Press.

Folberg, J., & Milne, A. (Eds.) (1988). *Divorce mediation: Theory and practice.* New York: Guilford.

Folberg, J., Milne, A., & Salem, P. (2004). *Divorce and family mediation: Models, techniques, and applications.* New York: Guilford Press.

Folberg, J., & Taylor, A. (1984). *Mediation: A comprehensive guide to resolving conflict without litigation.* San Francisco: Jossey-Bass.

Francke, L. B. (1983). *Growing up divorced.* New York: Simon and Schuster.

Froiland, D. J., & Hozman, T. L. (1977). Counseling for constructive divorce. *Personnel and Guidance Journal, 55,* 525-529.

Furstenberg, F. F., & Spanier, G. B. (1984). *Recycling the family: Remarriage after divorce.* Beverly Hills, CA: Sage.

Gardner, R. A. (1971). *The boys' and girls' book about divorce.* New York: Bantam Books.

Gardner, R. A. (1976). *Psychotherapy with children of divorce.* New York: Jason Aronson.

Gardner, R. A. (1977). *The parents' book about divorce.* New York: Bantam Books.

Gardner, R. A. (1982). *Family evaluation in child custody litigation.* Cresskill, NJ: Creative Therapeutics.

Gardner, R. A. (1989). *Family evaluation in child custody: Mediation, arbitration, and litigation.* Cresskill, NJ: Creative Therapeutics.

Gardner, R. A. (2001). *Therapeutic interventions for children with parental alienation syndrome.* Cresskill, NJ: Creative Therapeutics.

Geasler, M. J., & Blaisure, K. R. (1999). 1998 Nationwide survey of court-connected divorce education programs. *Family and Conciliation Courts Review, 37*(1), 36-63.

Gottman, J., & Notarius, C. (2002). Marital research in the 20th century and a research agenda for the 21st century. *Family Process, 41,* 159-198.

Gurman, A. S., & Jacobson, N. S. (Eds.) (2002). *Clinical handbook of couple therapy.* New York: Guilford Press.

Hartin, W. (1990). Re-marriage: Some issues for clients and therapists. *Australian & New Zealand Journal of Family Therapy, 11*(1), 36-42.

Haynes, J. M. (1981). *Divorce mediation: A practical guide for therapists and counselors.* New York: Springer Publishing Company.

Hetherington, E. M., Cox, M., & Cox, R. (1986). Long-term effects of divorce and remarriage on the adjustment of children. In S. Chess & T. Alexander (Eds.), *Annual progress in child development* (pp. 407-429). Philadelphia, PA: Brunner/Mazel.

Isaacs, M. B., Montalvo, B., & Abelsohn, D. (1986). *The difficult divorce: Therapy for children and families.* New York: Basic Books.

Kaslow, F. (1981). Divorce and divorce therapy. In A. Gurman & D. Kniskern (Eds.), *Handbook of family therapy* (pp. 662-696). New York: Brunner/Mazel.

Kaslow, F. (2000). Families experiencing divorce. In W. C. Nichols, M. A. Pace-Nichols, D. S. Becvar, & A. Y. Napier (Eds.), *Handbook of family development and intervention* (pp. 341-368). New York: John Wiley & Sons.

Kaslow, F., & Schwartz, L. (1987). *The dynamics of divorce: A life cycle perspective.* New York: Brunner/Mazel.

Kessler, S. (1975). *American way of divorce: Prescription for change.* Lanham, MA: Rowman & Littlefield.

Kirby, J. (1998). Court-related parenting education divorce interventions. *Human Development and Family Life Bulletin, 4*(2), 52-60.

Kressel, K. (1985). *The process of divorce: How professionals and couples negotiate settlements.* New York: Basic Books.

Lee, R. E. (1990). Parenting after the smoke clears. *The Family Advocate, 13* (Summer), 18-21.

Lee, R. E. (2000). Managing the difficult ex-spouse. *Family Advocate, 22*(1), 2-5. Reprinted in W. DaSilva (Ed.), The never-ending divorce: A handbook for clients (pp. 2-5). Chicago, IL: American Bar Association.

Marano, H. (2000). Divorced? *Psychology Today, 33*(2), 56-62.

Marlow, L., & Suber, S. R. (1990). *The handbook of divorce mediation.* New York: Plenum Press.

Nichols, M., & Schwartz, R. (2004). *Family therapy: Concepts and methods.* Needham Heights, MA: Allyn & Bacon.

Nichols, W. C. (1984). Therapeutic needs of children in family system reorganization. *Journal of Divorce, 7*(4), 23-44.

Nichols, W. C. (1985). Family therapy with children of divorce. *Journal of Psychotherapy and the Family, 1*(3), 55-68.

Nichols, W. C. (1989). Polarized couples: Behind the façade. In J. F. Crosby (Ed.), *When one wants out and the other doesn't: Doing therapy with polarized couples* (pp. 1-21). New York: Brunner/Mazel.

Nichols, W. C. (1996). *Treating people in families.* New York: The Guilford Press.

Nichols, W. C., & Everett, C. A. (1986). *Systemic family therapy: An integrative approach.* New York: Guilford Press.

Pam, A., & Pearson, J. (1998). *Splitting up: Enmeshment and estrangement in the process of divorce.* New York: Guilford Press.

Pinsof, W. (2002). The death of "till death us do part": The transformation of pair-bonding in the 20th century. *Family Process, 41*(2), 133-134.

Policy Institute for Family Impact. (2005). Retrieved April 29, 2006, from http://www.uwex.edu/ces/flp/impact/index.cfm.

Rice, J. K., & Rice, D. G. (1986). *Living through divorce: A developmental approach to divorce therapy.* New York: Brunner/Mazel.

Sager, C., Brown, H., Crohn, H., Engel, T., Rodstein, E., & Walker, L. (1982). *Treating the remarried family.* New York: Brunner/Mazel.

Salts, C. J. (1979). Divorce process: Integration of theory. *Journal of Divorce, 2,* 233-240.

Sprenkle, D. H. (Ed.) (1985). *Divorce therapy.* New Yok: Haworth Press.

Sprenkle, D. H., & Gonzalez-Doupe, P. (1996). Divorce therapy. In F. Piercy, D. H. Sprenkle, & J. L. Wetchler (Eds.), *Family therapy sourcebook* (2nd ed.) (pp. 181-219). New York: Guilford Press.

Textor, M. (1989). *The divorce and divorce therapy handbook*. Northvale, NJ: Jason Aronson.

Trzcinski, E., & Genheimer, E. (2000). *Children and divorce: Michigan Family Impact Seminars briefing report*. East Lansing, MI: Michigan State University Institute for Children, Youth, and Families.

Visher, E., & Visher, J. (1988). *Old loyalties, new ties*. New York: Brunner/Mazel.

Visher, E., & Visher, J. (1990). Dynamics of successful stepfamilies. *Journal of Divorce & Remarriage, 14*(1), 3-12.

Visher, E., & Visher, J. (1996). *Therapy with stepfamilies*. New York: Brunner/Mazel.

Wallerstein, J., & Kelly, J. (1980). *Surviving the breakup: Coping with divorce*. New York: Basic Books.

Weisman, R. (1975). Crisis theory and the process of divorce. *Social Casework, 56*, 205-212.

Weiss, R. S. (1975). *Marital separation*. New York: Basic Books.

Whiteside, M. F., & Becker, B. J. (2000). Parental factors and the young child's postdivorce adjustment: A meta-analysis with implications for parenting arrangements. *Journal of Family Psychology, 14*, 5-26.

Winchester, K., Beyer, R., & Verdick, E. (2001). *What in the world do you do when your parents divorce? A survival guide for kids*. Minneapolis: Free Spirit Publishing.

Chapter 2

Staying Together or Separating and Divorcing: Helping Couples Process Their Choices

Israel W. Charny

Tribute to William C. Nichols

I have had a long association with Bill. I like him because although he has been both "president for life" (AAMFT, NCFR, and IFTA—wow!) as well as "editor for life" (CJMFT, CFT, and Family Relations), he is plain "Bill." He is a regular, straight-talking, fair, fun guy, and also someone on whose very good sense I can rely on consistently in the petty and other nonsense of our organizational lives. Mazel tov on a heroic career, Bill, and for being you.

For a long time in the field of psychotherapy, as in the prevailing Western culture, the idea that divorce was fostered by personal neuroticism and immaturity, especially with regard to the spouse more responsible for the divorce, was widely accepted. Often the cause of divorce was fixed on one having neurotically selected an inappropriate mate. In any case, divorce was largely treated as a shame that exposed the weaknesses of the divorcing persons, so that many people who needed to divorce were caught up in painful concerns about their honor over and above their regret and grief over the end of their marriage. Then there came a cultural revolution and the mental health pendulum swung to a point where many willing therapists not only willingly gave automatic approvals to divorce but perhaps looked askance at any person who had *not* divorced at least once. The superficiality and rigidity of either way of thinking is unacceptable for therapists who are careful not to subscribe to fads or absolutes. The

When Marriages Fail
© 2006 by The Haworth Press, Inc. All rights reserved.
doi:10.1300/5562_02

choice of whether to divorce is a profound and powerful drama that many couples must face. Either decision can be right or wrong. What matters is that we therapists develop a language of concepts that help us think about the alternatives meaningfully, so that we can help our clients process their choices in terms of the best possible interests of all concerned in each marital drama.

An existential/dialectical conception of marriage and divorce needs to include a deep respect and affection for marital permanence and continuity as a desired goal for couples. However, there also must be a genuine respect for the right of every married person to process his or her choice as to whether to stay married. Long-term continuity and an expectation of permanence are vital security needs of the human spirit, but people also need to experience themselves as choosing and rechoosing their direction in life and feel that they are in charge of shaping their destinies. These two necessities of human experience are, like so many others, contradictory, and the tension between them is yet another source of dialectical creativity in our lives.

AN EXISTENTIAL-DIALECTICAL VIEW OF "SUCCESS" AND "FAILURE" IN MARRIAGE AND MARITAL THERAPY

Whenever a glib and certain position is taken about divorce and separation, so that there is an automatic judgment that only a given status (marriage or divorce) means that one is successful and the opposite status means that one is a failure, the dialectical tension between continuity and renewed choice is avoided. Obviously, a price is paid by those people for whom the given fixed position is in fact the wrong one, but not only for them. The very elimination of the dialectical tension of having to deal with the uncertainty of whether to put more weight on the value of continuity of marriage or more weight on being free to choose and rechoose whether or not to stay married also weakens couples. The absence of this tension also weakens the overall cultural process around marriage for all of us.

Our profession of psychotherapy tends to become a captive of whatever is the current fad in society at large. Many times seeming professional truths about what is best for peoples' mental health are nothing more than codified statements of current cliches that are in vogue in the culture—some of which our mental health professions in fact helped to create. The preconceived notion that divorce meant failure early in the history of family therapy led to a conception of marital therapy that judged the outcome of all couple treatment on the basis of whether the couple stayed together. Since the early 1980s, there has been a long overdue correction of this simplistic conception of marital therapy outcomes. However, to the best of my knowledge there is no research project in which therapists have undertaken to evaluate *early* in the treatment of a group of couples which would be the more desirable outcome for a given couple—continuation of the marriage or ending it—followed by an evaluation of the outcome of treatment in response to that desired goal. Here is a case example in which we can specify early on the desired outcome against which to evaluate the result of treatment.

A couple with three children comes in for marital counseling because the wife has decided she will no longer tolerate being beaten by her husband. There are times when their original attraction to each other still shines through, but much of their marriage is a gruff indifference alternating with bursts of derisive remarks by him and her mounting hatred of him. He also is chronically enuretic. That in itself doesn't bother the wife so much. She accepts that all people have weaknesses. This is one of his that she could live with. She is also able to live with the fact that her husband does not speak to her very often. But she hates his periodic bursts of cursing her and calling her "a stupid shit." Most of all she can no longer tolerate the fact that her husband gets drunk and beats her up. For a while she had endured these episodes by going to her mother's home for a period of protest before returning to him. But now a decision is welling up inside of her to refuse to be beaten ever again.

What should be the goal of therapy for this couple? It seems to me fairly clear that the first goal should be to stop the husband from hitting his spouse, both from the point of view of his accepting the truth that it is wrong to beat her and from the point of view of his own self-interest in order not to lose her. Optimally, he could learn in therapy how he has been "peeing both on himself and on her"; i.e., he should use therapy to get in contact with how he humiliates her, and how he himself is intensely babyishly angry. However, failing the essential requirement that all beating of the wife must stop, and close behind it the next requirement that demeaning of her also stop, the wife needs to walk out on him and mean it. At that point her husband will have the opportunity to decide whether he wants to grow emotionally and win her back. If not, she needs to divorce him. Moreover, if earlier in the process of her walking out she reaches a point at which she stops loving him and loses the desire to repair their relationship, even if he does advance in therapy, it will be too late and she has the right to choose divorce. If marital therapy ends in either of the outcomes—continuation of the marriage because they have corrected their major problems, or divorce because the repair did not come sufficiently or in time—the therapy has been successful. Continuation of the present pattern will mean that therapy has failed.

We therapists need to know how to think *differentially* about the desirable outcomes of each specific marital case, and our evaluations of those outcomes of marital therapy must be based on appraisals of each specific case. The statistical end product should be in terms of how many cases that should have remained married did stay together, and how many cases that should have divorced were divorced. As in the preceding illustration, in many cases there should first be a conditional statement that *if* treatment does not take place successfully, *then* the desired outcome would be that the couple should divorce, so that there is room both for a hoped-for positive outcome of treatment and for divorce as a no less desirable though regrettable outcome if there is no growth from the present unacceptable situation.

Clinicians actually have been thinking and talking in these terms for a long time in the flow of collegial conferencing, e.g., when a therapist remarks that so-and-so should have divorced because she or he or their marriage was too neurotic. But what is suspect is the fact that these remarks generally are made *after* the fact that a couple's destiny was set, and often in pejorative tones regarding the couple. Sometimes, one has the feeling that such remarks are self-serving for the therapists in their defensiveness about the outcome of cases rather than serious judgments of the couples and what would really have been best for them. I suggest that therapists take responsibility for making prognostic judgments systematically and early in their work with a couple.

The trap in traditional marriages is that miserable couples stayed together out of obligation to each other, or to their children, or to their parents, and even out of obligation to their extended community and/or to their tradition—in some cultures even to their ancestors. Accompanying these obligations are also serious fears of social loss, shame, fears of coping by oneself, and fears of aloneness which are avoided by resigning oneself to chronically bitter marriages. All of these are very human concerns, but they are poor reasons for staying together. Marriages that are continued on the basis of such fears are most likely miserable, deadening experiences. It was right that there was a strong backlash and that the taboos against divorce were lifted for many people. However, it is sad that the backlash in turn sponsored a runaway process, namely, "contagion of divorce." Divorce became a new nostrum for too many people.

Where staying in bad marriages was a trap, the opposite side of the coin is a premature, escapist, or fetishistic use of divorce by couples who *could* work through the difficulties they are experiencing and might transform their conflictual process into individual and couple growth. Instead, they take a quick and easy way out. Some couples flee any tension or drawn-out process by seeking instant, total solutions. They do not trust talking, discussing, and sharing feelings to arrive at new perspectives. When the level of discomfort in their marriage becomes high, they utilize the solution of divorce without hesitation much in the way that one goes to a dentist to remove dental pain.

Another group of people who utilize divorce prematurely are couples who, paradoxically, have a great deal going for them as an attractive and interesting couple. However, when they encounter any major problem in their marriage they cannot cope with it because for them anything less than perfection is insufferable. Often they are "outstanding couples," but when they begin having big troubles in their marriage it is difficult for them to acknowledge their troubles straightforwardly and ask for help in time.

AN EXISTENTIAL-DIALECTICAL VIEW OF THE DECISION TO DIVORCE

An existential-dialectical view (Charny, 1992) of divorce looks at the decision to divorce from the two poles of meanings. On the one hand, a divorce that ends a bad marriage in which people cannot grow any more is an honest step. On the other hand, every divorce is a failure of a marriage and its dream, and there are also many cases in which divorce initiates periods if not lifetimes of subsequent misery for one or both mates.

It is important that our clients include the potential negative consequences of divorce in their decision-making process. Nonetheless, such information still does not change the fact that ending a genuinely bad marriage has an inherent validity. My own observations, like those of Nichols (1988), are that a considerable number of divorced individuals go on to develop excellent subsequent marriages. There are also many people who develop wholesome lifestyles for themselves as singles following divorce. My own conclusion is that divorce is *both* desirable and undesirable, wise and unwise. It is a marvelous solution for disastrous marriages. But it is always a loss—even when one has every reason to be extraordinarily happy about being rid of a bad partner. These losses may include the effects of the divorce on the couple's children. The children may not experience what is best for their parents as being best for them, now and in the future. Furthermore, researchers continue to explore the influence of conflictual marriages on children and what pre- and postdivorce factors have deleterious effects on the children of divorce (e.g., Booth & Amato, 2001; Hetherington & Kelly, 2002; Kelly, 2000; Wallerstein, Blakeslee, & Lewis, 2000). Later we will discuss how thinking about the children's needs should enter into the therapist's thinking.

When Does the Therapist Advise or Encourage Divorce?

Since therapists are often consulted at a point where final decisions are being processed about whether to have a divorce, the therapist's opinion becomes an important contributor to the decision. Many books on therapy have taken the position that the therapist does not have an opinion about divorce, but guides the couple to arrive at "their own decision." My judgment is that therapists cannot help but form opinions, judgments, and preferences, wisely and unwisely, and that they cannot help but convey these judgments inadvertently. Inevitably therapists have a great deal of influence on their clients' movement toward their decision, even if it is all through unconscious communication. So I much prefer that therapists learn to think and formulate clearly and responsibly what their opinion is, make professional decisions about how they are going to use and convey their opinion to their clients, and monitor the impact of their influence on couples. In so doing, therapists should be cautious lest they overwhelm their patients' decision making with their own ideas. More-over, therapists must be aware of their own biases—for example, the desire to maintain "professional impartiality," or fondness for one spouse—and aware of how they are exerting influence.

When does a therapist actually encourage divorce? Marriages de-serve to be ended when:

- the marriage has been chronically destructive, demeaning, or humiliating, cheating people of their natural entitlements to se-curity, friendship, and affection;
- the relationship has been chronically devoid of joy and dignity;
- arrogance and unavailability to simple fairness rule the roost. In-vitations to conciliation and consideration are automatically rejected;
- equality and dignity are trampled;
- the marital system is inherently murderous of the spirit of per-son(s);
- marriages that once were positive no longer are, and do not ap-pear ever again to be able to provide a couple with security based on respect, entitlement, grace, pleasure, warmth, and life.

However, exceptions exist even in situations in which a marriage is very bad. It may be right to defer the divorce on ethical grounds when a member of the family will suffer deeply because of the divorce. For example, there may be concerns about youthful or elderly members of the family and occasions when catastrophic or serious chronic ill-ness, or other misfortunes suffered by one spouse, have led the other spouse to reconsider the marriage.

An Optimal Checklist for Making the Decision to Divorce

Ideally, the decision to divorce comes after a long and serious pro-cess of trying to learn how to improve one's marriage, and taking re-sponsibility for one's own part in the unhappy story of the marriage that has failed. There then comes a time to take a decision coura-geously for oneself. An ideal checklist of steps for a person taking a decision to divorce might look something like this:

Don't divorce until:

1. You see in your own self a similar weakness or personality qualities that have bothered you the most in your spouse.
2. You have learned how to be fair and take responsibility for correcting your own weaknesses as much as possible.
3. You have tried a great deal to encourage your spouse to grow and change: You have told him/her fairly what your complaints and needs are, and have put yourself forward to try to be understanding, empathetic, and supportive.
4. You have tried very hard to put the marriage back on a positive direction.
5. You have considered earnestly the welfare of your children and what will be in their best interests.
6. You have told your spouse that you are thinking of divorce and have expressed your wish that this outcome be avoided.
7. You have gone with your spouse to couple therapy—as well as to individual counseling in conjunction with the couple therapy. If your spouse refused to go to therapy, you yourself have gone for individual therapy, but to a therapist who is also trained in treating couples and therefore worked with you from a point of view of the best interests of the marriage as well as in relation to your personal needs.
8. You have come to a conclusion that your mate is not able to develop and grow further.
9. You have prepared for separation, including facing your realistic vulnerabilities in the short- and long-run of your changing status to a divorced single person.
10. You have mourned the "death" of your marriage for a period of time with appropriate intensity, and you have mourned the loss of your mate as you once dreamed she or he was going to be.

Empirical studies of the relationship between the degree to which people complete the emotional tasks of such a divorce process and their subsequent ability to form healthy new marital relationships would be helpful. The theory that guides me in clinical work is that the best preparation for a remarriage is first to complete the emotional tasks of one's divorce. The most neglected or least completed of these tasks is generally the first one listed previously. It derives most directly from an existential/dialectical point of view, namely, that while our choices of mates are based a good deal on complementary contrasts between us, behind these contrasts there also await "identical" or very similar weaknesses in both mates. Virtually all of us have problems and failings (Charny, 1980; Ellis, 1987), all our marriages are in some part problem- and conflict-filled, and solving tensions and conflicts is one of the challenges of intimacy as well as personal growth (Charny, 1972a,b; Wile, 1981, 1988). Moreover, spouses are surprisingly similar in their basic psychological faults (Willi, 1982, 1984). Our weaknesses, including those that we are least aware of and deny the most, then attach to our spouse's weaknesses to create the kind of locked-in pattern that characterizes so many if not most marriages (Charny, 1992). Since it is typical of us human beings to blame and project on to others our unrecognized weaknesses, when a marriage is going poorly it is unfortunately common that most spouses tend to experience the *other* as the failing one. So even when it is altogether true that one's mate is seriously problematic in some important respect, it is highly likely—perhaps *inevitable*—that a similar if not the very same flaw is present in us. This situation deserves corrective attention before we might be morally justified in leaving our mates for their weaknesses.

Nonetheless, I do want to clarify my opinion that many times it is objectively true that one spouse plays a more definitive role in creating and maintaining the seriously problematic and failing qualities of the marriage. In this respect I differ from some systems theorists who only look at the interaction in the couple system and do not leave any room for identifying individual responsibilities and roles. It is not that I disavow the systemic principle that marital difficulties derive from a meshing of mutual contributions of the two spouses, but for me the contributions are not necessarily equal. Consider this clinical example which illustrates both the neurotic marital complementarity but also the definitive role of the wife in creating the divorce:

They had fallen in love in a classic storybook way. Both were college graduates, ambitious for their own selves and the other, and they made a very beautiful couple together. Both enjoyed the finer sides of life in their admiration of aesthetics, arts, sports, and good living. When their two children were born, they joyed together in these new lives and both proved devoted parents. If asked about their marriage, each one said it was just wonderful.

However, below the surface there were serious emotional difficulties in each of them. He had been raised an only child largely by his mother after his scoundrel father had gone to jail because of a business scam and then abandoned his wife and child after his release from jail. As a mother's boy, he was devoted, indebted, and ever attentive. The pride of a suffering woman's soul, but unknown to himself, he was inwardly disdainful of her neediness, angry at her, and somehow unable to exercise a legitimate selfishness and assertiveness. His wife sensed all of these things that he did not know in himself, not only in respect of his feelings toward his mother, but in the fact that much of the love and devotion that he heaped on her were in continuation of his childhood-long obligation to be loving rather than a genuine love of her for the person she was.

His wife in turn did not feel deep inside of herself that she deserved to be loved. She had been the rebellious black-sheep daughter of parents who used every guilt-provoking technique to tell their children how much they were doing for them. Her mother was openly mean in her demandingness. Her father was a counterpoint of effusive goodness, but he also relentlessly demanded "payment" from the children and invasively tracked their every thought and action. Somehow as a child she had not fallen for the deal, and something both angry and alive in her had spurned the offers of their possessive love to the point where she became the bad child of the family.

In choosing her as his wife, this man was choosing somebody who carried the muted, unexpressed rebellion in him against parental possessiveness. In choosing this man as her husband, the wife was choosing a person who showered on her love and confirmation that she was lovable despite the fact that she had become the obviously unliked child of her parents.

Now some ten years after they married, something changed in the wife. She became critical, querulous, and brittle, and pushed her husband away emotionally and sexually. Soon she was holding him captive to long lectures about his not being a real person and how she did not feel good with him. There was a kernel of truth to her complaints that too much of his personality derived from a compulsion to perform lovingly. But she was relentlessly persecutory, negativistic, and provocative. On his part, he tried everything to find a way to correct what was going on. He did it using his own ways of being pleasing and attentive. He also took them to marital therapy and participated conscientiously. On her end, however, something hardened rapidly and she spurned all overtures and invitations to meet him halfway or to learn about herself. As if to make sure that the outcome would be a breakup, she also went into a series of affairs including cheap sorties with macho men with whom she would engage in mutual sado-masochistic rituals. Altogether, she made life so bitter that divorce became a necessity.

The wife's deep psychiatric disturbance, which proved inaccessible to the effort to treat her, in effect overwhelmed the marital problem and made its possible treatment untenable.

Accounting for Children's Needs in the Decision to Divorce

The issue of how a couple's children figure in decision making about divorce deserves some thought beyond the accepted shibboleths of our time that one does not keep a marriage together for the sake of the children, or that it is better for children to have happy divorced parents than to have miserable parents living together. (See Isaacs, Montalvo, & Abelsohn, 1986.) I believe that children deserve their parents' consideration when they are thinking about a divorce. I also believe there are times that one does stay married, or strenuously tries to stay married, for the sake of a child or children. In some cases a marriage headed for divorce can be transformed into one that is sufficiently supportive and fulfilling for all of the family members. (See Everett, Halperin, Volgy, & Wissler, 1989, on treating a borderline family.)

THE STAGES OF DIVORCE

The processes of ending a marriage and separating from it are complex. There are the various psychological, legal, economic, coparental, and social tasks of divorce (Bohannon, 1971). There are also emotional stages of divorce, namely shock and disbelief, loss, detachment, and feigned indifference or euphoria, anger, ambivalence, depression, acceptance of loss, mourning, separation, reorganization and reorientation, and, finally, hard work toward achieving and maintaining a new level of functioning (Kaslow & Schwartz, 1987). Ability to complete the various tasks adequately depends on how well the family members progress through the emotional stages. Then, too, there are situations in which a divorcing couple may succeed in completing most and possibly all of the *tasks* of divorce, but one or both of them may not have been able to keep step in regard to the *emotions* of divorce. Many divorced individuals never complete the full process; and there are many divorced couples who develop collusions to ensure that the divorce process is never completed. A couple may complete all but one of the stages of divorce such as leaving themselves economically entwined with each other. More commonly, one or both fail to complete the emotional tasks of separating from each other, and even many years afterward divorced persons can feel powerful emotional involvement with their "husband" or "wife" long after they and their divorced mates have remarried. Divorcing couples who agree that they will not finish one or more stages of divorce retain powerful ties. There are cases of such collusions that lead a new spouse of one of the divorced couple to object strenuously to the "continuation" of the former marriage. "Whenever she calls, you jump," says the second wife to her husband about his responses to his former wife. "I know you have the excuse of your relationship with her about your children, and I appreciate that is important. But what I see is that you're still afraid of her, and how do you think that make me feel?"

Sometimes the emotional divorce is more apparent than real. There is a culture-supported form of denial—which can be more pronounced in certain subcultural groups than in others—which encourages people to get on with their divorce, and not let it bother them so much, and just concentrate on making a good new adjustment. Consider:

> He had succeeded in everything in his life. He decided to leave his wife because she bored him. She had nothing interesting to say and aroused no passion in him as she went about life in a tried and true style of being everything he had asked her to be, namely devoted and accommodating. He already had a substitute lined up for himself who was the exact opposite, emotional, tempestuous, and assertive. When the time came to end his current marriage, he insisted that the children be spared all hurt. They were to be told only at the last minute. Any crying, upset, or anger were greeted with immediate efforts to compensate the child. The handling of all issues by the adults was similar: all matters of conflict were to be resolved amicably, and the divorcing couple intended to remain good friends. The therapist's warnings that too many aspects of the divorce were being made to look and feel good was pushed aside as unwelcome. The divorce proceeded according to a storybook script until the man woke up one day shaking with totally unexpected anxiety and indecision, and also with florid psychosomatic gastrointestinal symptoms.

ENCOURAGING DESIRABLE PAIN
IN THE TREATMENT OF DIVORCING COUPLES

There is often confusion about what needs to be done in therapy for a couple who is getting divorced because we are accustomed to think of treatment in terms of reducing pain. It has sometimes been observed that the pain associated with divorce is like no other. It is experienced as totally engulfing. Nothing else seems to matter. Some people are understandably frightened by the overwhelming dimensions of these experiences and turn to professional help. The clinician can certainly comfort and counsel them that their suffering is normal and even desirable, and that ultimately they will recover. Intriguingly, the pain of divorce also has an unusual quality in that it can lift with a suddenness that is not quite familiar in other areas of great pain in people's emotional lives, and I sometimes allow myself to tell the people who are suffering with their divorce about this phenomenon as a way of saying that things can get better.

However, the best thing a divorcing person can do is yield to and, if necessary, even seek a period of deep upset, shock, ambivalence, rage and so forth in order to move through the emotional stages of the difficult process of disconnecting. The task of the therapist is to maximize the process as much as possible. This means whenever people attempt to defend against the tides of the emotions that should accompany the divorce process, the therapist steers them in the direction of feeling more upset rather than less, and help them yield to disorganization rather than to fight it off too quickly. Needless to say, this point of view understandably puzzles those therapists and certainly those patients who are accustomed to think that all psychotherapy is supposed to bring relief from mental suffering and simply make people feel better. While such therapeutic work is occurring both spouses need to alert themselves to the possibility that virtually everyone going through this process functions far below their normal standard with regard to day-to-day responsibilities. However, the other side of the coin is no less important. We need to help those people who are flooded with the pain of their divorce keep their lives going and overcome their pain.

AUTHOR'S REFLECTIONS

A decision to divorce that is based on a regretful conclusion that one's mate can no longer grow and participate in a mutual growth process is different than a decision to divorce based on accusations of one's mate as being all bad and the source of all the trouble in the marriage. The decision is even more trustworthy when it includes a sad acknowledgment of one's own failure to have been sufficiently inspiring to one's mate to have helped him or her over their obstacles to personal growth. The therapist's role in working with divorcing couples ultimately is to help people complete the ending of their defunct marriage in as full a way as possible, and to launch the next phase of their relational lives at the highest level of adjustment and functioning that will be possible.

This is a different way of thinking about treatment than was the case for many years when the goal was to avoid divorce. It is also different from what became the contemporary or modern goal of many therapists to help people divorce with as little pain as possible. Neither remaining married nor getting divorced in themselves guarantee growth or maturity. The therapist's responsibility is to help process the best possible choice, and in either case to promote as much emotional growth in each partner as may be possible. In addition, the larger goal is to help as many people as possible be meaningfully involved in authentic and loving relationships with other human beings.

REFERENCES

Bohannan, P. (Ed.) (1971). *Divorce and after: An analysis of the emotional and social problems of divorce.* Garden City, NY: Doubleday.

Booth, A., & Amato, P. R. (2001). Parental pre-divorce relations and offspring post-divorce well-being. *Journal of Marriage and the Family, 63,* 197-212.

Charny, I. W. (1972a). Injustice and betrayal as natural experiences in family life. *Psychotherapy: Theory, Research & Practice, 9,* 86-91.

Charny, I. W. (1972b). *Marital love and hate.* New York: Macmillan. Original paper: Charny, Israel W. (1969). Marital love and hate. *Family Process, 8,* 1-24.

Charny, I. W. (1980). Why are many (if not really all) people and families disturbed? *Journal of Marriage and Family Therapy, 6* (1), 37-47.

Charny, I. W. (1992). *Existential/dialectical marital therapy.* New York: Brunner/Mazel.

Ellis, A. (1987). The impossibility of achieving consistently good mental health. *American Psychologist, 42* (4), 364-375.

Everett, C., Halperin, S., Volgy, S., and Wissler, A. (1989). *Treating the borderline family: A systemic approach.* Saddlebrook, NJ: Psychological Corp.

Hetherington, E. M., & Kelly, J. (2002). *For better or for worse: Divorce reconsidered.* New York: Norton.

Isaacs, M. B., Montalvo, B., and Abelsohn, D. (1986). *The difficult divorce: Therapy for children and families.* New York: Basic Books.

Kaslow, F. W., and Schwartz. L. L. (1987). *The dynamics of divorce: A life cycle perspective.* New York: Brunner/Mazel.

Kelly, J. B. (2000). Children's adjustment in conflicted marriage and divorce: A decade review of research. *Journal of the American Academy of Child and Adolescent Psychiatry, 39,* 963-973.

Nichols, W. C. (1988). *Marital therapy: An integrative approach.* New York: Guilford.

Wallerstein, J. S., Blakeslee, S., & Lewis, J. M. (2000). *The unexpected legacy of divorce: The 25 year landmark study.* New York: Hyperion.

Wile, D. B. (1981). *Couples therapy: A nontraditional approach.* New York: Wiley.

Wile, D. B. (1988). *After the honeymoon: How conflict can improve your relationship.* New York: Wiley.

Willi, J. (1982). *Couples in collusion.* New York: Jason Aronson.

Willi, J. (1984). *Dynamics of couples therapy: The uses of the concept of collusion and its application to the therapeutic triangle.* New York: Jason Aronson (originally published in London in 1978).

Chapter 3

An Ecosystemic Look at the Rights of Children in Divorce

Robert E. Lee

Tribute to William C. Nichols

Between 1969 and 1973 Bill Nichols successively became my first family therapy teacher, supervisor, and private practice colleague. Over these years and the decades following he became legitimately celebrated for many things involving character and scholarship. I would like to highlight one of these things which to me epitomizes Bill's complex blend of intelligence, humility, integrity, and scholarship. At a time dominated by "gurus" and their disciples, Bill taught that family therapists should use instead a systemic, integrative approach in which knowledge about any family and its constituent members is based on empirical family science, and is a blend of historical/ developmental, interactional, and existential perspectives. Subsequently, Urie Bronfenbrenner, Margaret Bubolz, Richard Lerner, and others would write eloquently about the "ecosystemic orientation" and "applied developmental science." But Bill, with that high intellect, acuity of thought, and capacity to envision complex things, was there first and brought it to many of us.

Since the 1990s, many family therapists have offered advice about the process of coparenting during the immediate and long-term process of divorce (e.g., Ahrons, 1994; Everett & Everett, 1994; Hamilton & Merrill, 1990; Lasswell, 2000; Lee, 1990; Rothman, 2000). They pointed to the alleged effects of divorce on children, and the debate about these effects (e.g., Hetherington & Kelly, 2002; Kelly, 2002; Wallerstein, Blakeslee, & Lewis, 2000). They pointed out that parents might divorce each other, but not their children. Since they would go on being parents to their children forever (coparents one way or another), they and the children would benefit to the extent that the parents could

- declare the marriage over in their hearts and let go of it,
- choose cooperative parenting over some kind of adversarial or competitive process,
- make long-term commitment to be there for the children,
- separate their own needs and feelings from the children's, and
- see the other parent as "good enough" to provide coparenting.

I wince as I think about how facilely such advice is given when it is so hard to follow, especially early in the separation/divorce process. No matter how deeply divorcing parents care about their children, they nevertheless may find it very difficult to deal with their children's emotional circumstances and needs for nurture at a time when they themselves are in crisis. And then professionals like us easily tell them how to adequately navigate as parents and imply that, if they fail at it, they will have dealt their children a grievous blow. In retrospect I have wondered whether some parents feel that they have been violated twice—first by their ex-spouse, and then by Oprah's media shrink du jour.

Self-conscious about such musings, and with an eye toward policy, several of us (Lee, Stollak, Walker, & Senger, 2003) decided to move from the micro to a more macro level. We thought that if we could compile a list of those things all children need, and within that list, those things required by children of divorce, we would specify the parameters within which policy makers, family law officials, and mental health professionals should operate.

Initially we looked at United Nations documents specifying the basic rights of children. Children's rights were generally stated in the *Declaration of the Rights of the Child* proclaimed by the General Assembly in 1959.

> The child shall enjoy special protection, and shall be given opportunities and facilities, by law and by other means, to enable him to develop physically, mentally, morally, spiritually and socially in a healthy and normal manner and in conditions of freedom and dignity. In the enactment of laws for this purpose, the best interests of the child shall be the paramount consideration.

(Office of the United Nations High Commissioner for Human Rights, 1997-2000, p. 1)

Specific rights of children were articulated in a later document, the United Nations Convention on the Rights of the Child, adopted by the U.N. General Assembly on November 17, 1989 (pp. 7-12). It affirmed the following rights for children:

- A right to be cared for by parents (Article 7)
- A right to family ties (Article 8)
- A right to live with parents unless this is deemed incompatible with the child's best interests, and a right to maintain contact with both parents (Article 9)
- A right to have their viewpoints heard and taken into consideration in all judicial and administrative proceedings affecting their futures (Article 12)
- A right that their ethnic, religious, and linguistic heritage will be taken into account when providing alternative family care for the child (Article 20)
- A right that, if victims of abuse, neglect, exploitation, or torture, they will receive physical and psychological rehabilitation and social reintegration (Article 39)

We believed that, if the Untied Nations specified these as the basic rights of all of the world's children, we should recognize these for children of divorce. However, the United Nations was addressing what must be done by major government institutions. We knew that children are psychological systems embedded in larger social systems: sibships, parentships, families, neighborhoods, communities, and nations. We decided to revisit the above rights of children, informed by the empirical and clinical data from divorce and remarriage literature, using an ecosystemic orientation.

THE ECOSYSTEMIC ORIENTATION

Theoretical orientations potentially are both useful and hindrances. They can be useful to the extent that they alert us to the phenomena under their purview. They may be problematic to the extent that using their lenses damps awareness of data and perspectives that would be highlighted by an alternative model. For example, a psychodynamic lens alerts us to the potential influence of intrapsychic phenomena, but does not pay much attention to interpersonal and family dynamics. Conversely, preoccupation with family structure may diminish our awareness of individual psychological differences. Each child's experience of the process of divorce is to some extent unique. It depends on who the child is, and who the parents are, to be sure. But it also depends on the larger world in which the divorce is situated. In this chapter we are using an ecosystemic orientation because it is a good way to recognize, understand, and address such complex phenomena.

Ecosystemic models look at individuals' experiences in the context of their environment. In so doing these models alert us to immediate proximal and more distant contextual influences, and the interaction of these to shape that which occurs and how it is perceived and experienced. Ecosystemic models appreciate that families systems are environments embedded within increasingly larger environments, namely neighborhood, community, state, and nation. Some theories (e.g., Bronfenbrenner, 1992; Lerner, 2001) appreciate that these environments, the systems that comprise them (e.g., school, occupational, medical, court, economic, and political systems), and the attitudes that characterize these systems (e.g., sexism, racism, and socioeconomic prejudices) continuously influence one another. Bubolz and Sontag's (1993) model additionally remind us that these environments differ, person to person, family to family, in terms of their natural, social, and human-built resources. For example, children of differing capacities live in families with diverse social, financial, and other coping resources, in communities differing in how they view and what they have to offer families in distress. These ecosystemic views are important when looking at children in families undergoing divorce. They give us a checklist with which to consider the complex entity compiled as "children's rights."

For some children, a bill of rights includes the right to be heard relative to what is occurring, the right to make various choices, and the right to be protected from parental crisis. For other children, even in a nation of overall affluence, that bill may also include the right to be physically safe, nurtured, and educated. An ecosystemic orientation—a broader view—also gives us guidelines for comprehensive interventions with the potential of being most suitable for the individual case.

RIGHTS OF CHILDREN IN DIVORCE

The basic rights of all children compiled by the United Nations certainly seem applicable to children in divorce (e.g., to have their viewpoints heard, to have access to both parents, and to have family ties maintained). In fact, in our own country each state and even local jurisdictions have written (and continually amended) procedures to guide court officers involved in child custody and visitation considerations. In recent times these guidelines have been based on an evolving view of the "best interests of the child." These are a compilation of theoretically based assertions and/or "best guesses" about the needs of children from birth through adolescence. They are sometimes, but not always, supported by empirical research and they may or may not be in conflict with the needs—and rights—of their parents. Officers of the court have been in agreement with the spirit of the "best interests" statutes, but many, if not most, have experienced significant dissatisfaction in their implementation (Lee et al., 2003). Moreover, with the growing popularity of alternate dispute resolution (Nurse & Thompson, 1999; Tesler, 1999), children may again be thought of as part of the property settlement, and thus their rights less central to the divorce processes. Therefore the time seems ripe to consider an ecosystemically drawn "Bill of Rights for Children in Divorce" informed by ethical considerations (Willemsen & Willemsen, 2000), child development research (e.g., Davies, 1999), and the experiences of disparate professionals working in family law.

A Bill of Rights for Children in Divorce (Lee et al., 2003)

Children have the right to be raised in an environment conducive to their physical, emotional, social, and moral well-being and growth.

Such environments are loving, nurturing, stable, and predictable. They reduce conflict and tension whenever possible. Children in divorce have the right to have a life apart from the parental divorce. Adult conflicts and injustices must not be visited upon the children, directly, or indirectly, if those children are to develop well. Children have the right to seek and achieve a happy environment in which they love and are cherished, are allowed to explore and learn about their world, and are allowed to grow.

Children in divorce have the right to be respected,
including having their views heard and considered.

Children of divorce have the right to share their perspectives with
the people making decisions, and to expect that decision makers will
seriously consider their views and opinions. Children in divorce have
the right to expect that decisions will be made by persons knowledgeable in child development and divorce dynamics.

Children in divorce have the right to be protected
as individual persons.

Because children may be the most vulnerable parties in divorces,
their best interests must be central to the court. They often may be not
able to adequately represent their own best interests. Children are
limited in experience, education, and wisdom. Some may be also limited by developmental level, personality, or intellect. Some would argue that concern about the best interests of young and adaptively
challenged children supercede the rights of the adults.

Children in divorce have the right to be children.

Children in divorce have the right to be treated as children and not
as "little adults" who are able to cope and who perhaps are expected
to hold one or both parents together during and after the marital crisis.
They have the right to express their anger, sadness, and fear in ways
appropriate to their age and circumstances and to expect nurture and
support from society's established institutions.

Children in divorce have the right to adequate parenting
during and following the marital crisis.

Children are at risk to the extent that the adults' response to divorce
conflicts with their ability to consistently and appropriately meet the
legitimate needs of their children. One tragedy of divorce is that the
children may need the most comforting, guidance, and protection at a
time when the parents are least able or willing to provide this assistance.

Children in divorce have the right to develop and sustain relationships with both parents and with members of their extended family.

The children are not divorcing their parents. They have the right to be raised by both parents under circumstances optimal for their positive growth. They have the right to settlements regarding their welfare that take into account the psychological security afforded through enduring relatedness with both parents. Although the scientific literature supports the view that very young children, in particular, need to bond with at least one "psychological parent" or primary caretaker, that person may be either mother or father. Moreover, during the "tender" years most children bond with both parents. These bonds are not likely to diminish and they are necessary to optimal growth.

Children of divorce have the right to stable, long-term living plans.

These plans should meet their rapidly changing developmental needs and other (less predictable) challenges that occur. Children of divorce have the right to expect that these living arrangements will, in most cases, foster meaningful and sustained relationships with both parents, in an atmosphere in which legal and physical custody are clearly defined. They also have the right not to be put in the middle or have to choose sides.

Children in divorce have the right to protection from toxic relationships.

Children of divorce have the right to protection from adults who have not adequately accomplished the psychological divorce and who express it with and through the children. They have the right not to live with or visit parents who maltreat them physically, sexually, or emotionally. Such parents include those who are chronically unavailable psychologically, and those the children have seen maltreat others. Children have the right to expect that divorce deliberations involving them will be confidential and nonadversarial.

*Children in divorce have the right to speedy and fair
determinations with regard to arrangements regarding
their welfare.*

Children need stable and predictable living circumstances, arrived at in as expeditious a way as possible. They also should experience the process, at least in retrospect, as fair. Moreover, children in divorce also have the right to periodic review by knowledgeable personnel when their circumstances change.

*Children in divorce have the right
to their own counsel.*

Children in divorce have the right to a guardian ad litem, or to representation from counsel provided by an office of child advocacy. Legal counsel for the child can advocate specifically for the child's best interests without the conflict inherent in simultaneously representing a parent during the divorce proceedings.

COMPLICATING FACTORS CONSIDERED
BY ECOSYSTEMIC LEVEL

To ask whether divorce helps or hinders a child depends on what child, in what family, at what time, and in what place. Likewise, to adequately address the basic rights of children of divorce, these same factors must be appreciated. According to many experts (e.g., Everett & Everett, 1994; Wallerstein & Kelly, 1980) children of divorce initially are preoccupied with four basic questions: "Who will take care of me?" "How will I be able to be with both of you?" "Will my mom or dad be all right?" "Will I still have all the things I'm used to around me?" Those of us who are concerned about the basic rights of children in divorce do well to focus on those same questions.

Factors Unique to Each Child

Variables that affect children's responses to divorce include their age at the time of severe parental conflict and at the time of the breakup. Age and developmental stage determine children's cognitive, emotional, and social maturity, and how they may typically deal with potentially distressing circumstances (Davies, 1999). Developmental precocity or delays are relevant for the same reason, as well as for the additional stresses these talents and challenges may offer in and of themselves. It also matters whether the children see the marital breakup as constructive or negative, whether they expect a failure to thrive on their part to rescue their parents' marriage, and the extent to which they blame themselves for the marital rupture.

When physical and emotional violence exists between their parents, the research shows that how much children are damaged by this fighting depends on the kind of violence, its intensity, how long it occurs, and the age of the child when it happens. The older the child, the more coping mechanisms available. These include language, understanding, and counteracting and compensatory life experiences. (See summaries in American Psychological Association, 1996; Booth & Amato, 2001; Davies, 1999.) Parental emotional and physical violence during infancy can be catastrophic to children (Perry, 1997). Because of the compound effect of biological (e.g., Perry, 1997) and emotional problems, children with early exposure to emotional and physical marital violence are likely to exhibit developmental delays, including poor cognitive abilities, language deficiency, poor school performance, and difficulties in personal and social relationships (Booth & Amato, 2001; Herrenkohl, Egolf, & Herrenkohl, 1997; Leiter & Johnsen, 1994). These children typically lack the ability to cope with severe stress and are at increased risk for later behavior problems, including hostility in the classroom, aggressive behavior with peers, and ambivalence with regard to dependent relationships

Children's resiliency may also be a function of their past histories of successes and failures, the qualities of their relationships with caretakers, and how they make sense of such things. The amount of energy and optimism children may bring to the divorce process may also be a function of their individual personalities, their adaptive styles, and the number and size of nonnormative life events in their ken including geographic moves, sickness, death, problems in daycare or school, and so on (Davies, 1999).

Another crucial factor may be children's capacities to elicit nurture from others. However, it is not enough that resources are available in a child's proximity. Children need to be aware of these resources, want to use them, and be able to. (See Nadler, 1991.)

Sibling Subsystem

When families are under stress, *sibling* relationships may be protective or destructive (Gnaulati, 2002). Variables involved in this include child gender (Abramovitch, Corter, & Lando, 1979), child temperament interactions (Brody, Stoneman, & Gauger, 1996), the nature of the bonds between the siblings (Abbey & Dallos, 2004), and the children's collective personal and social resources (Parke, 2004), the extent to which the siblings idealize one another and their parents, positive and negative mimicry, and subsystem aggression (Gnaulati, 2002). Siblings may or may not protect one another from stress. Indeed, some may be drawn into alliances with parents that produce stress between the siblings (Everett & Everett, 1994). Another practical consideration is the number of children in a household and their developmental stages. Older children hold the possibility of parental role supplementation (e.g., Boyd-Franklin, 1989). Finally, the amount of relational resilience (see "Family System," later in this section) may be an important subsystem variable.

Parental Subsystem

Parental energy available to the children may vary from family to family and over time in any one family (depending on current events). Moreover, parents have diverse capacities and ways of being involved with their children, not only times of crisis, but in general. These are informed by their overall values, attitudes, and motives. Parents, of course, differ in their personality traits and adaptive styles. Indeed, resiliency in individuals has been associated with social competency, problem-solving skills, autonomy, optimism, and the ability to recruit social support (e.g., Cicchetti & Garmezy, 1993).

We are assuming that in most contemporary divorces both parents are involved in the work force on a relatively full-time basis (Lee & Smith, 2000). Another important factor with regard to parental availability and adequacy is the extent to which the adults are distressed by the impending and actual breakup. Ultimately each parent must acknowledge the reality of the marital breakup, grieve, and move on. Acceptance and hope must come to replace denial, anger/outrage, grief, fear, and chronic insecurity about oneself and one's children (Everett & Everett, 1994). Individuals differ in the extent to which they experience and stand up to stress, and the speed with which they can move through the emotional processes of separation and divorce. Relevant in this regard may be each individual's cognitive, emotional, and social maturity, and how he or she typically deals with potentially distressing circumstances (Lee, 2004; Silverman, 1969). This may not only be a function of personal developmental level and coping resources, but the marriage's place in the marital life cycle (Nichols, 1995). Just as with their children, the parents' individual and congregate experiences of successes and failures are germane as is the financial and social capital of each.

Parental violence experienced directly or witnessed before, during, and after the physical separation can be very detrimental to children's immediate and long-term adjustments (Booth & Amato, 2001; Vandewater & Lansford, 1998). How much toxic emotion is present in a divorce may not be as important as how the adults express it. The bigger it is (physical violence is worst), and the longer it lasts, the more it hurts the children's growth. There is ample evidence that children who live in families characterized by overt intense, chronic, and unresolved marital conflict demonstrate greater emotional insecurity than those from families in which there is more adult agreement or in which toxicity is expressed behind closed doors. The former are being stressed at the same time that they are not being taught appropriate social interaction skills.

Even though the war may be between the adults, marital conflict often undermines the quality of the relationship between the parents and their children. Mothers in such families are found to be less warm to their children, more rejecting, more erratic and harsh in discipline, and to use more guilt and anxiety-inducing disciplinary techniques. Fathers are found to be more withdrawn. Insecure and upset, some of these children are withdrawn. Others tend to mimic their parents. Many develop academic and social difficulties.

Overall, the frequency and intensity of marital conflict, relative to the cognitive, emotional, and social resources of the child, make a difference. Severity perhaps is more influential than frequency. In contrast, where marital conflict is managed well, children accelerate in their social development throughout elementary school. Marital tranquility is thought to provide role modeling, emotional warmth, and a safe climate in support of the growth of social competencies by the children. In contrast, sustained spousal battering is known to gravely erode the battered parent's self-esteem and personal agency (e.g., Browne, 1993; Goodman, Koss, Fitzgerald, Russo, & Keita, 1993).

A related issue is how much of the marital conflict gets focused on the children. This adds self-blame and shame to the toxic mix, or perhaps outrage. But even when the conflict is directed away from the children, the children are upset by what is going on and fear being drawn into it. Parents may involve their children in the marital discord in less overtly destructive ways. Children may be used as confidantes, counselors, and sources of affirmation. Parents differ in the extent to which they do this, as well as the extent to which they support or hinder loyalty conflicts, adequately address financial and logistic obligations, and even take care of themselves.

Parents differ in the extent to which they have and use activities to distract themselves from their distress, discharge anxiety, and replenish their self-esteem. They differ in the extent to which they are aware of and are willing and able to use outside help. Some parents engage in destructive activities with the promise of quick relief (e.g., risk-taking behavior, substance use, sexual promiscuity, and other forms of self-indulgence), even if they in fact feel worse later. Finally, individuals differ in their capacity to accept and to perform the role of single parents.

Family System

Families differ in the extent to which they can deal with external stresses and some may even thrive. Family systems models of resilience view this quality in terms of the process of interdependent relationships (Walsh, 1996; Lee & Lee, 2005). On the whole, families are found to be hardy to the extent that they are able to maintain warm, cohesive, and nurturing family ties, experience themselves as active agents in the face of novel circumstances, review their past with an eye to appreciating adaptive successes, revision positive images of the present and future, and identify and be able to use social and community resources. In this regard, we may ask to what extent a family as a unit is enmeshed as opposed to disengaged, and how permeable the boundaries are between family subsystems and between the family and its community (Imber-Black, 1988). Families, like their constituent members, may exist in relative social isolation. Family researchers have also highlighted effectiveness of communication, especially in addressing problems, and flexibility with regard to problem solving (Minuchin & Fishman, 1981; Olson, Russell, & Sprenkle, 1989). Others have pointed to individual family differences with regard to shared activities, openness to affective expression, and rules (Jacob & Windle, 1999).

The literature tells us that where the individual family members are in their developmental trajectories will influence how they transact with stressors. This also is true of the life-cycle stage of the family of procreation (McGoldrick & Carter, 1998).

Extended Families

In these days of the mobile nuclear family, extended families may or may not be geographically present and able to offer respite and other kinds of hands-on care (Lee & Smith, 2000). We also may assume that family financial, physical, and social capital, along with unique family ways and values, may determine what kinds of help are offered, and the extent to which various offers are accepted (Bubolz & Sontag, 1993). Families have simultaneous memberships in diverse subcultures, such as religious and ethnic memberships, and participate in multiple contexts (Falicov, 1995). Families' subcultural identities and involvements, then, cannot be ignored. Aspects of these can be positive or destructive in that they involve social constructions of what is good and bad, acceptable and unacceptable, with regard to families' circumstances, help-seeking, and the acceptance of help.

Neighborhoods and Communities

Social capital is not just a function of families and their constituent members. Neighborhoods and communities may have various degrees of support services, including alert and altruistic neighbors, drop-in respite care centers, and schools (e.g., Goldman & Beuthin, 1997) attuned to the emotional and social stresses of divorce. Workplaces may differ in the extent to which they recognize and support family needs (Hochschild, 1990; Kamerman, 2004). Employment prospects may be diverse, and so may be the availability of day care. Medical systems may understand the transient stresses of families and childhood and take a contextual approach, or they may perceive problems as existing in people and rely too much on psychotropic medications (Sparks, 2002). In many geographic areas mental health care may be quite limited in amount and kind. District courts systems differ in the extent to which personnel are sensitive to all of the issues articulated in this chapter. Moreover, even specialized family law courts may or may not appreciate the importance of maintaining family, extra-family, and geographic ties (Drapeau, Simard, Beaudry, & Charbonneau, 2000; Kaplan, 1990).

State and National Climates

There has been a move to encourage national and international uniformity in many aspects of divorce law. It is difficult to separate the welfare of the child from the many areas of family divorce law: divorce determination, property division, custody determination, shared parenting time, child support, separation agreements, remarriage, and even adoption. Regions differ in their attitudes and beliefs, sensitivities, and action tendencies with regard to the institution of marriage, common law relationships, same-gender relationships, single parenthood, "family values," parental roles, and divorce.

Sexism, racism (Woldeguiorguis, 2003), and socioeconomic fascism (Lott, 2002) are part of the national climate. Within this climate we have the growing plight of female single-parent households—a plight that may not encourage national sympathy and redress (Boney, 2002). For example, the move of large numbers of women into the work force has also led many policy and decision makers to think less about mothers' preexisting quality of life and to focus instead on their capacity to support themselves (Baer, 1991). This is compounded by the large number of men who do not adequately fulfill their post-divorce financial obligations (Buehler, 1989), the difference between women's and men's salaries (e.g., Joy, 2003) and occupational trajectories (O'Campo, Eaton, & Mutaner, 2004), and the national move toward part-time and temporary employment (Ahlberg & DeVita, 1992).

AUTHOR'S REFLECTIONS: WHAT DOES
THIS MODEL HIGHLIGHT FOR US?

The ecosystemic view is one in which the quality of any human life is a continuous function of both biological and contextual (environmental) processes over time. More specifically, it incorporates the following (Brownell, Kloosterman, Kochka, & VanderWal, 1999):

- a holistic framework that views the relationship between successes and challenges at one level and the resources and constraints operating at other levels,
- the view that interventions that influence only one level are likely to provide lesser and/or shorter-lived benefits, and
- appreciation of the roles of individuals as they interact across multiple levels, and the circular and reciprocal effect of such interactions.

A cynical view of such a model is its implication that the basic rights of children in divorce primarily are held hostage by national attitudes—and the emotions and action tendencies that spring from them—about families and their constituent members. However, an ecosystemic orientation also highlights the many transacting factors, directions, and dynamics characteristic of families within larger systems. In so doing, it allows consideration of the complexity of the contexts in which children and interventions for their welfare are situated. Our vision needs to be expanded to this level if we are to effectively address the welfare of children.

REFERENCES

Abbey, C., & Dallos, R. (2004). The experience of the impact of divorce on sibling relationships: A qualitative study. *Child Clinical Psychology Psychiatry, 9*, 241-259.

Abramovitch, R., Corter, C. M., & Lando, B. (1979). Sibling interaction in the home. *Child Development, 50*, 997-1003.

Ahlberg, D., & DeVita, C. (1992). *New realities of the American family*. Washington, DC: Population Reference Bureau, Inc.

Ahrons, C. (1994). *The good divorce*. New York: HarperCollins Publishers.

American Psychological Association (1996). *Violence and the Family: Report of the American Psychological Association Presidential Task Force of Violence and the Family*. Washington, DC: The American Psychological Association. (ERIC Document Reproduction Service No. ED 399 073).

Baer, J. A. (1991). *Women in American law*. New York: Holmes & Meier.

Boney, V. M. (2002). Divorced mother's guilt: Exploration and intervention through a postmodern lens. *Journal of Divorce and Remarriage, 37*, 61-83.

Booth, A., & Amato, P. R. (2001). Parental pre-divorce relations and offspring post-divorce well-being. *Journal of Marriage and the Family, 63*, 197-212.

Boyd-Franklin, N. (1989). Five key factors in the treatment of black families. *Journal of Psychotherapy and the Family, 6*, 53-59.

Brody, G. H., Stoneman, Z., & Gauger, K. (1996). Parent-child relationships, family problem-solving behaviour, and sibling relationship quality: The moderating role of sibling temperaments. *Child Development, 67*, 1289-1300.

Bronfenbrenner, U. (1992). Ecological systems theory. In R. Vasta (Ed.), *Six theories of child development* (pp. 187-249). London: Jessica Kingsley.

Browne, A. (1993). Violence against women by male partners: Prevalence, outcomes, and policy implications. *American Psychologist, 48*, 1077-1087.

Brownell, J., Kloosterman, D., Kochka, P., & VanderWal, J. (1999). Training in context: A ecosystemic model. In R. E. Lee & S. Emerson (Eds.), *The eclectic trainer* (pp. 197-205). Galena, IL: Geist & Russell.

Bubolz, M. M., & Sontag, S. M. (1993). Human ecology theory. In P. G. Boss, W. J. Doherty, R. LaRossa, W. R. Schumm, & S. K. Steinmetz (Eds.), *Sourcebook of family theories and methods: A contextual approach* (pp. 419-450). New York: Plenum.

Buehler, C. (1989). Influential factors and equity issues in divorce settlements. *Family Relations, 38*, 76-82.

Children's Charter of the Courts of Michigan (2000). *Promoting Positive Relationships Between Parents and Young Children When There Are Two Homes*. 324 N. Pine Street, # 1, Lansing, MI 48933.

Cicchetti, D., & Garmezy, N. (1993). Prospects and promises in the study of resilience. *Development and Psychopathology, 5*, 497-502.

Davies, D. (1999). *Child development: A practitioners guide*. New York: Guilford.

Drapeau, S., Simard, M., Beaudry, M., & Charbonneau, C. (2000). Siblings in family transitions. *Family Relations, 49*, 77-85.

Everett, C. A., & Everett, S. V. (1994). *Healthy divorce*. San Francisco, CA: Jossey-Bass.

Falicov, C. (1995). Training to think culturally: A multidimensional comparative framework. *Family Process, 34*, 373-388.

Gnaulati, F. (2002). Extending the uses of sibling therapy with children and adolescents. *Psychotherapy: Theory, Research, Practice, Training, 39*, 76-87.

Goldman, R. K., & Beuthin, K. M. (1997). Separation and divorce. In T. M. Fairchild (Ed.), *Crisis intervention strategies for school-based helpers* (Second Edition) (pp. 20-59). Springfield, IL: Charles C Thomas.

Goodman, L. A., Koss, M. P., Fitzgerald, L. F., Russo, N. P., & Keita, G. P. (1993). Male violence against women: Current research and future directions. *American Psychologist, 48,* 1054-1058.

Hamilton, G., & Merrill, T. S. (1990). How to survive divorce: Finding your way through hell. *Family Advocate, 13*(1), 15-21.

Herrenkohl, R. C., Egolf, B. P., & Herrenkohl, E. C. (1997). Preschool antecedents of adolescent assaultive behavior: A longitudinal study. *American Journal of Orthopsychiatry, 67*(3), 422-432.

Hetherington, E. M., & Kelly, J. (2002). *For better or for worse: Divorce reconsidered.* New York: Norton.

Hochschild, A. M. (1990). *The second shift.* New York: Avon.

Imber-Black, E. (1988). *Families and larger systems: A family therapist's guide through the labyrinth.* New York: Guilford.

Jacob, T., & Windle, M. (1999). Family assessment: Instrument dimensionality and correspondence across family reporters. *Journal of Family Psychology, 13,* 339-354.

Joy, L. (2003). Salaries of recent male and female college graduates: Educational and labor market effects. *Industrial and Labor Relations Review, 56,* 606-621.

Kamerman, S. B. (2004). *Glossary: Family-friendly work place policies.* New York: The Clearinghouse on International Developments in Child, Youth, and Family Policies, Columbia University.

Kaplan, L. W. (1990). Stay out of court. *Family Advocate, 13*(1), 8-10.

Kelly, J. B. (2000). Children's adjustment in conflicted marriage and divorce: A decade review of research. *Journal of the American Academy of Child and Adolescent Psychiatry, 39,* 963-973.

Lasswell, M. (2000). Emotional uncoupling. *Family Advocate, 22*(4), 6-8.

Lee, M. M., & Lee, R. E. (2005). The voices of accepting and supportive parents of gay sons: Toward an ecosystemic and strengths model. *Journal of GLBT Family Studies, 2*(2), 1-27.

Lee, R. E. (1990). Parenting after the smoke clears: How to stop the fighting. *Family Advocate, 13*(1), 18-21.

Lee, R. E. (2004). Parenting under duress. In N. R. Robbins (Ed.), *A guide-book for the newly divorced person* (pp. 24-26). Lansing, MI: Family Law Section, State Bar of Michigan.

Lee, R. E., & Smith, C. J. (2000). The times they are a'changing: The "American family" and family law. *Michigan Family Review, 5*(1), 53-64.

Lee, R. E., Stollak, G. E., Walker, N. E., & Senger, J. M. (2003). A bill of rights for children in divorce. In N. R. Robbins, S. Bassett, & R. E. Lee (Eds.), *Children's rights* (pp. 8-9). Lansing, MI: Family Law Section, State Bar of Michigan.

Leiter, J., & Johnsen, M. C. (1994). Child maltreatment and school performance. *American Journal of Education, 102,* 154-189.

Lerner, R. M. (2001). *Concepts and theories of human development* (3rd ed.). Mahwah, NJ: Erlbaum.

Lott, B. (2002). Cognitive and behavioral distancing from the poor. *American Psychologist, 57*(2), 100-110.

McGoldrick, M., & Carter, B. (Eds.) (1998). *The expanded family life cycle* (3rd, classic ed.). Boston: Allyn & Bacon.

Minuchin, S., & Fishman, H. C. (1981). *Family therapy techniques*. Cambridge, MA: Harvard University Press.

Nadler, A. (1991). Help-seeking behavior: Psychological costs and instrumental benefits. In M. S. Clark (Ed.), *Prosocial behavior: Review of personality and social psychology*, Vol. 12 (pp. 290-311). Thousand Oaks, CA: Sage.

Nichols, W. C. (1995). *Treating people in families*. New York: Guilford.

Nurse, A. R., & Thompson, P. (1999). Collaborative divorce: A new, interdisciplinary approach. *American Journal of Family Law, 13,* 226-234.

O'Campo, P., Eaton, W. W., & Mutaner, C. (2004). Labor market experience, work organization, gender inequalities, and health status: Results from a prospective analysis of U.S. employed women. *Social Science and Medicine, 58,* 585-594.

Office of the United Nations High Commissioner for Human Rights. (1997-2000). *Declaration of the rights of the child*. Geneva, Switzerland: Author.

Olson, D. H., Russell, C. S., & Sprenkle, D. H. (Eds.) (1989). *Circumplex model: Systemic assessment and treatment of families*. New York: Haworth Press.

Parke, R. (2004). Development in the family. *Annual Review of Psychology, 55,* 365-399.

Perry, B. D. (1997). Incubated in terror: Neurodevelopmental factors in the "cycle of violence." In J. D. Osofsky (Ed.), *Children in a violent society*. New York: Guilford.

Rothman, B. (2000). Put your kids first. *Family Advocate, 22*(4), 11-13.

Silverman, H. (1969). Determinism, choice, responsibility, and the psychologist's role as an expert witness. *American Psychologist, 24,* 5-9.

Sparks, J. (2002). Taking a stand: Challenging the medical discourse. *Journal of Marital and Family Therapy, 28,* 51-59.

Tesler, P. H. (1999). Collaborative law: What it is and why family law attorneys need to know about it. *American Journal of Family Law, 13,* 215-225.

Vandewater, E., & Lansford, J. (1998). Influences of family structure and parental conflict on children's well-being. *Family Relations, 47,* 323-330.

Wallerstein, J. S., Blakeslee, S., & Lewis, J. M. (2000). *The unexpected legacy of divorce: The 25 year landmark study*. New York: Hyperion.

Wallerstein, J. S., & Kelly, J. B. (1980). *Surviving the breakup: How children and parents cope with divorce*. New York: Basic Books.

Walsh, F. (1996). The concept of family resilience: Crisis and challenge. *Family Process, 35,* 261-281.

Willemsen, E., & Willemsen, B. (2000). The best interests of the child. *Issues in Ethics, 11,* 1.

Woldeguiorguis, I. M. (2003). Racism and sexism in child welfare: Effects on women of color as mothers and practitioners. *Child Welfare, 82,* 273-285.

PART II:
MODELS AND ISSUES

In Part II, two systemic models are presented that explore the dynamics of conflicted couples moving toward divorce. Such models aid family therapists in assessing a couple's potential for divorce and provide a conceptual frame for interventions. In addition, specific family circumstances that include predivorce, the divorce process, and postdivorce are considered: family violence, disclosure of gender orientation, the unhappiness experienced by a family's children, and the distancing of grandparents from grandchildren.

Chapter 4

Systemic Dynamics and Interventions for Selected Marital Conflicts

Mary Anne Armour

Tribute to William C. Nichols

Marriage and family therapy and Bill Nichols are almost synonymous. His contributions to the field are numerous and invaluable. My introduction to Bill was as a graduate student at Auburn University thirty years ago where he presented a series of MFT lectures. In recent years he has been most support-ive of Mercer University's annual MFT lecture series. His contributions wherever he goes are creative, innovative, and life-giving to the profession. His founding of the Journal of Marital and Family Therapy *is major among those. In earlier years, when I served as an AAMFT board member, I often sought him out to discuss troublesome issues with him as a sounding board. When licensure was an issue at the state level, his wisdom and insight were crucial.*

This tall, wise gentleman, an intellectual giant, has been able to foresee the needs of this growing profession for decades. He has organized, con-fronted, pushed, and dealt with the "powers that be" to get MFT recognized as a viable and productive mental health profession. He is not only an accom-plished professional, he is my friend. I am proud to be invited to honor him as an author in this tribute to him and his contributions.

Marriages can be fraught with conflict, even under ideal condi-tions. The focus of marriage for most couples is the joining together of two people who have found common goals and ideals, and whose affection for each other can often override reason. Each person usu-ally enters a marital relationship with plans for success. However, when a couple comes for therapy, the therapist must deal with two people who lost their dreams and goals for their futures. In addition, the couple's expectations for romance and companionship have been colored by the lenses of their cultural heritages, families of origin's roles, and personal resources. Many differences may be evident. The therapist recognized that these differences may lead, on the one hand to divorce, or on the other hand to possible solutions. Both directions will be explored by the couple in marital therapy (Nichols, 1988).

UNDERSTANDING MARITAL CONFLICTS FROM A FAMILY SYSTEMS PERSPECTIVE

Couples often describe themselves as being very different from their families of origin. However, when one looks at genograms, which have collected historical data from both partner's families of origin, one can see similarities and parallel dynamics in each partner that have been passed down from their respective families of origin. In my practice I have learned to look for certain important dynamics that point to the makeup of marital interactions: personality traits, patterns of dealing with relationships, parental support, and significant traumas and their resolution. Family systems concepts related to understanding marital conflicts include family strengths and weaknesses, family values and how they are expressed, family resources, and the dynamics of how the system handles conflict and its resolution. Other systemic dynamics will emerge as therapy progresses. The therapist should not be surprised when one of the partners seeking marital help exhibits the same or similar symptoms to those identified in her or his parents at about the same time in their marriage relationship. Experienced therapists have learned to recognize that patterns of behavior are often the same as those present in previous generations (Nichols & Everett, 1986).

Some marital problems can also represent, unconsciously, the result of unresolved issues with one's parent of the same or opposite sex. I have learned to recognize that partners who may be unwilling, or unable, to work on certain issues may be struggling with unconscious behaviors from their families of origin. Identifying these issues and resolving them within the therapy context can be very helpful to further progress. In some cases I will help the partner with the family-of-origin issue to make contact with their family members and work out the problem face to face. These family-of-origin interventions are particularly helpful in working with issues of sexual or physical abuse, desertion, jealousy, divorce, and unresolved anger.

Awareness of overt behaviors in one's family of origin can also result in marital problems, e.g., punishment, being overly criticized or yelled at, never being allowed to express angry feelings, and unmet basic needs for support and nurturance (Napier, 1988).

SITUATIONS THAT UNDERLIE
MARITAL CONFLICTS

There are several specific clinical situations that I have observed over the years that can lead to serious marital conflicts. The following are the ones that I will review and give examples of here:

1. Prolonged, unresolved mourning, e.g., over the death of a child
2. Triangles in families, particularly those related to adultery
3. The presence of divergent personal goals and expectations which detract from a relationship, e.g., matters of parenting or careers
4. Differing cultural heritages, e.g., religions or gender roles
5. Family-of-origin loyalties, i.e., when the vertical loyalties outweigh the spousal loyalties
6. Growing apart, when partners pursue independent and parallel interests

Unresolved Mourning

An example of how grief can damage a marriage is seen in the case of Tom and Susan who had been married for fourteen years. The couple had two children, Jamie, who was eleven years old, and Angela, who was nine. Tom was director of the local YMCA and Susan was secretary to a physician in their small town. Jamie was a healthy young man and loved playing Little League baseball. Angela was a fourth grader who took piano lessons and enjoyed reading. The parents were active in sports and the family had an active social life.

Angela became very sick and was diagnosed with childhood leukemia. After an unsuccessful schedule of medical treatment over a period of several months, Angela died. Tom and Susan were both well loved in their town. During the first six months following Angela's death, they received much support from the community. As the months went by, Tom spent more and more time at his office and began writing a book for children on grief. Susan became more and more involved as a Little League mom. Conversation and communication between Tom and Susan was less and less until Tom found himself getting home just at bedtime. Susan and Jamie would go out to eat, then come home and watch television. Angela was never mentioned during this period in the family. When the couple presented at the therapist's office it was three years after Angela's death and there was very little to hold the marriage together.

I spent many years of my career teaching MFT graduate students in a university medical school and setting. I learned that family life can flow very smoothly when both parents and children are meeting their life goals. However, a sudden reversal of family life expectations occurs with the illness and death of a child. Following the events surrounding the illness, death, and funeral, the parents often find themselves unprepared for such a severe loss. The time and energy of the parents become focused on communication necessary to carry out the activities preceding the funeral and burial. Support from extended family and friends or community may be present for a few weeks or months.

As life moves on and becomes more routine, *the loss of the child can become the silent focus of the couple's attention and thoughts.* However, in some families the loss may never be discussed openly again. Unresolved grief, focus on career issues, neglect of feelings and communication, refusal to talk about the absent child and his/her value to the family, and not mourning their mutual loss can make dysfunctional inroads into the family structure and system. The therapist must recognize that *the dead child remains as a silent member of the family.* Unless the child's death is recognized and confronted, months or years of silence may lead to separation and divorce. The sudden loss of a significant family member may create the dysfunctions described earlier but it may also intensify already present or underlying dysfunctional dynamics within the family system (Guerin et al., 1987).

Adulterous Triangles

John, an attorney, and Carolyn, a pediatrician, had been married for ten years. They could not have children and decided six years ago to adopt Janie as an infant. She was a very loved little girl and both parents were extremely proud of her. After three years of being a stay-at-home mom, Carolyn decided to go back into the practice of medicine with her friend, Margie, another pediatrician. They were very successful in their practices. Soon Margie decided that she wanted to join the practice of her husband in a different city. Carolyn was left to conduct her practice alone and felt that she had to take over Margie's patients as well as her own. This doubled her practice.

John objected, but Carolyn was clear that she felt obligated to take care of those patients until they could find another doctor. She hired a caretaker for Janie when John was not available to be at home with her. John said his law practice was growing as well and he began to stay away from home more and more. After two years, John became involved with another woman at his office; she was also an attorney who was a good friend of John and Carolyn. When John and Carolyn presented at the therapist's office, John had been in the affair for three years. After Carolyn found out about the affair, rather than divorcing, they made a decision that they wanted to save their marriage.

It has been my experience that when individuals try to resolve their pain or discomfort they may often seek partners who offer them comfort or respite. When marital conflict is stressful and cannot be resolved, one or both partners may look for alternate sources to get their needs met. This process creates the dynamic of triangulation in the family system. In addition to affairs, some couples will triangle other persons or family members, their jobs, or other activities in an effort to meet their marital needs. In some cases the involvement with an extramarital partner may be a natural response to unfulfilled needs or it may be an expression of anger and an attempt to get even with their other partner. In either case it becomes a substitute for their inability to confront and work out their pain. The realization that one's partner has been having an affair and may be considering leaving the marriage may be discovered too late to repair the relationship. The couple's fear of confronting the anger and sense of rejection only serves to create further distance in the relationship.

Adulterous triangles are major sources of conflict in marriages (Pittman, 1989). Abandoning the third person is often difficult and is only the beginning of potential resolution. The therapist working with these marital situations is tasked with helping the couple repair a number of areas, including

- restoring trust,
- learning to value oneself again,
- finding common areas of enjoyment in the relationship,
- improving patterns of expressed endearment, and
- reconnecting emotionally and behaviorally.

Working with these clinical tasks may require many months of therapy and personal commitment. Months and even years of work may be necessary to restore faith in the relationship.

Differing Personal Expectations

Matt and Dottie worked together in Matt's family business. Matt managed the workers and kept up with the inventory. Dottie worked in the office as a bookkeeper and secretary. Dottie had a son, Shawn, by a previous marriage. Two years into this new marriage she and Matt had their own son. Earlier in their marriage Dottie had noticed Matt's tendency to become melancholy and to fall back into his old habit of drinking alcohol excessively. She also noticed that Matt was working longer hours and taking pills which had been prescribed for one of their sons. However, she had been advised by her pastor not to "hound" him.

Soon the couple decided to build a new house in the country. In order to find an emotional place where she could feel good about herself, Dottie decided that she could direct the building of the house, including all contacts with the building contractor. She checked every weekend on the progress of the building project. She took the boys with her when she needed to conduct business regarding the house. Then she decided to apply her skills at painting and decorating when the house project was far enough along. Meanwhile, Matt's drinking habits became more and more evident. He was coming to bed later into the mornings. He was less involved in the building of their new home and he was staying at work longer hours. When Dottie realized that she was seeing less of her husband and that he was drinking excessively, she called the therapist. By this time it was too late for Matt. He was already trapped in an ongoing pattern of alcoholism. He said that Dottie had more interest in the house than he ever would. The marriage was in serious trouble when they decided to examine their goals and look at the sources of their conflict in therapy.

Marital conflict can often erupt when couples become aware of having "grown apart" (Stuart, 1980). Each partner may have focused on different pursuits and/or issues, i.e., careers, health, children, travel, leisure, reading, family of origin, building a new house, or other interests. Conflict arises when one partner realizes that she or he has not been receiving support or expressions of caring from the other partner. The partner is then accused of "not loving, not caring about me, not being sensitive to who I am." In many cases the couple's distance has resulted from their focusing on an aspect of their life which at one time had meaning to both of them. However, when their communication stopped they could no longer reach out to the other.

Differing Cultural Heritages

Sami and Laura met when Sami was in medical school in St. Louis. He was Egyptian and she was from rural Missouri. She was a nurse at the hospital where he was doing his internship. Laura was from a Southern religious culture which valued family togetherness, taking care of others, and respect for education. Sami's religious heritage was Muslim. He had come to the United States when he was in college. His parents had been very unhappy at his decision to marry an American and a non-Muslim. However, Sami saw the marriage as one in which they shared many of the same values and similar interests in medicine. In addition, Sami "was ready to get married."

The couple began to have conflict when Laura wanted to start a family, but Sami kept saying they had plenty of time. His attempt to placate her was to say that he would make that decision when the time was right. Five years later, after he had completed his education and had a thriving practice, Laura again approached him about having a child. He said he had made a decision that there would be no children from their marriage and that in his country the male made that choice. Laura was adamant that they should see a therapist. She wanted children and at age thirty-five time was an issue for her. Culturally, their differences were "too deep" for her to accept Sami's decision without her feeling that her opinion had been considered.

Family backgrounds provide a setting for relationships which should be as comfortable, familiar, and supportive as possible. Cultural differences which reflect a totally different lifestyle can be challenging, stressful, and lead to dysfunctional patterns. However, for a marriage with differing cultural backgrounds to be successful, each spouse must understand intellectually and respect the differences that are brought to the relationship and family system (McGoldrick, Pearce, & Giordano, 1982).

The therapist will need to recognize a broad range of potential areas of conflict for these couples, some are subtle and others are quite explicit. These may include the following: expressions of affection, sexuality, management of finances, choice of church or religion, the decision to have children, parenting issues regarding child rearing and discipline, the roles of husbands and wives, lifestyle expectation and where the family will live. Each person is the product of her or his rearing and models in their families of origin.

Cultural diversity can be both stimulating and challenging, as well as dysfunctional. The couple's ability to negotiations may often relieve the immediacy of some of these problems. However, understanding the social, philosophical, and/or intellectual tenets of the partner's religious beliefs and country of origin are essential for a culturally diverse marriage to survive. Recognizing these factors is also critical for the family therapist to provide useful resources for these couples. I always try to remember that *patience is a major virtue* when working with cultural issues.

Loyalties to Families of Origin

David and Nancy had been married for five years when they decided that they needed to see a therapist. David was a building contractor and Nancy was a nurse. Both were very successful in their chosen careers. They had grown up in the same small town where David was known as the "builder of the most beautiful homes" in their community. He worked long hours and said he did not have time to care for their son, Damon, who was three years old. Nancy drove to her job at a neighboring city hospital five days a week. She took Damon to her parents' home where they cared for him all day until she returned at 7:00 p.m. She often visited with her mother until bedtime and then went home to find David asleep. On Sundays the couple went to her parent's home for dinner and to spend the afternoon.

Nancy reported to the therapist that she was dependent on her parents to help her with Damon. When there was a problem, she always discussed it with her mom and admitted that she hardly saw David alone except on the weekends. However, that was her time to grocery shop, clean house, and pay bills. David was willing to take care of Damon during that time. He complained that Nancy spent more time at her mom's house than she did with him, even though he was always at home in the evenings. David's parents were divorced. His mother lived out of town, but he saw his dad at family gatherings on occasion. When asked what they would like to change in their relationship, David said he wished he could have more time with his family. He also commented that he thought Nancy had more loyalty to her mom and dad than to him, and that they certainly saw more of her than he did. She expressed a need for David not to be so angry with her and to make time for her when they could be together.

Younger couples, who have been away from the families of origin for shorter periods of time, tend to express their parental loyalty more readily in the midst of conflict than mature couples. Often these young adults feel financially more dependent on their own parents. If there are young children in the family, grandparents may be more involved on a day-to-day basis helping with child care.

Family therapists need to recognize that years of closeness to the previous generations creates a loyalty which may cause parents of the younger couple to intervene and/or intrude more readily into daily life circumstances. I have observed that when there is marital conflict, the daughter who is now a mother or the son who is now a father may feel greater loyalties to their respective parents than they do to their marital partners. When the spouse's family-of-origin members are intrusive and become involved, dysfunctional patterns are more common and resolution is more difficult. I have found that family therapy with the entire extended families can be very effective. Resolution comes only when these issues of loyalties and intrusive behaviors can be confronted. Developmentally we expect that dedication to one's family of origin should begin to wane as young couples find more distance and when they can shift their emotional loyalties to each other.

Growing Apart

Mark and Jean had been married twelve years and had two children. Mark was a successful business man and traveled daily to a city fifty miles away. He had started the business as a young man and it had grown to be financially far more successful than he had dreamed. He often got home late at night, but tried to spend as much time as possible with his wife and children. Jean had many social interests outside the home and often chose to spend her evenings with her girlfriends rather than staying at home with the family. According to Mark, Jean thought that these roles were part of an "unwritten contract" made by them as a young couple. Keeping a clean house was not one of her strong interests. Jean enjoyed spending the money, living in a large home, and being the wife of a successful husband. She was not very interested sexually in the relationship, and complained that it was because Mark was gone all the time and doing what pleased him. She felt that she had a right to have her friends and her social life independent of the marriage. She insisted that she was doing nothing out of the ordinary and expected him to understand.

When they came to the therapist together it was clear that the marriage expectations had changed over the years. Mark had focused entirely on creating a successful business which had taken him away from home and family. Jean's disappointment and anger was being critically acted out by her neglect of family life and refusal to relate to her husband.

When the marriage becomes the lesser focus of one or both of the partners boredom, indifference, and disinterest can set in. This causes more distance between the couple. Lack of sexual interest occurs and resultant sexual problems often are the presenting problems in therapy (Guerin et al., 1987). These couples reach a place where their time with each other is no longer valued. Social activities are entered into separately and their lives become parallel. To meet their own needs and interests, one partner begins to establish a focus to which he or she can dedicate more and more time, leaving the other behind. At the point where commonalities no longer exist or are diminished, the marriage is in serious trouble. The family therapist must determine the relative desires of each person for the relationship, their common goals, and the depth of their affection for the other. The therapist will discover that for many of these couples the option of "staying together for the sake of the children," or for other practical or financial reasons may no longer provide the stability needed to rehabilitate the relationship.

THREE CLINICAL STAGES OF MARITAL CONFLICT

It is important for family therapists to be able to recognize certain progressive stages that reflect the growing levels of dysfunction and conflict that couples may experience (Nichols & Everett, 1986). Here are the three stages that I tend to use to organize my clinical assessments.

The Early Stage

In the early stages of disagreement and strife in a relationship, there can be relative openness and recognition of the other person's rights to be different. Indications of strife often occur initially at an unconscious level. For example one spouse may stay away from home more or an offended spouse refuses to talk about what she or he sees that is distressing. There is less communication between the partners for fear of offending the other. One may focus more on work and staying at work for longer periods of time as a way of reducing tension and/or confrontations. The sexual relationship may become boring and less frequent. The inner conflict which reflects unresolved pain may be expressed overtly by shouting, withdrawing, or denying. One partner may become secretive and unwilling to talk about relationship issues, while the other begs and pleads for communication.

The Middle Stage

During this stage more ambivalence is present in the relationship. At some point the partner who has worked hard at trying to identify and confront relationship issues becomes ready to finally give up. Following prolonged feelings of failure, she or he may refuse to go out in public with the partner. At home, the couple will have more frequent disagreements. If no progress is made more distance will set into their relationship. In some cases, where there is no resolution to these ongoing marital and family conflicts, one of the partners may seek out another person either for the purpose of having someone with whom to talk and develop a friendship, or simply to meet sexual needs. When this occurs the other partner becomes suspicious and angry which leads to withdrawal and even early grieving.

The Later Stage

When couples in conflict reach an impasse that cannot be resolved, the next step is often separation or divorce. However, in cases in which affection and hope are still alive, family therapy can be effective. A thoughtful and planned separation can bring reality to both partners. This may be a therapeutic plan that can prolong the marriage and reduce the day-to-day conflict, and perhaps allow time for therapy to create some changes.

However, refusal to seek help by one partner is often a sign of the deterioration of the marriage relationship and perhaps that partner's having given up. When these couples enter therapy they often bring an expectation that the "other" will have to change or correct his or her behaviors. By this time in the deteriorating marriage there has been a history of anger and blaming the other partner. Many spouses in this stage have been so hurt that they often find it very difficult to consider change for themselves.

REACHING THERAPEUTIC SOLUTIONS

Realization that the primary relationship in one's life, "our marriage," is deteriorating and may not be beyond repair may cause major emotional distress and can be devastating to both partners (Nichols & Everett, 1986). Making the call to the therapist may actually open old wounds, usually ones that the couple has been unable to confront in the past. In marriages of five years or less, I have found that the partners are still learning about each other's personalities, their likes and dislikes, areas of strong feelings and beliefs, as well as their values and prejudices.

The role of the family therapist is to collect information and plan interventions that will lead to solutions. Many systems therapists use the genogram to collect information and history as well as to understand the family's interactions. The therapist's understanding of the basic underlying rules for each marriage is crucial to connecting information given at each succeeding session. The couple's understanding of the basic principles and themes on which their relationship operates helps them to see the need for change when their interactions become problematic. Understanding these systemic dynamics and rules by which the overall family system has been formed helps the therapist ask questions in a manner which respects those principles and informs the therapist in making effective interventions.

After gathering family history, and recording facts and insights on the genogram during the first session, the next step is to find out what has brought the couple to therapy. Listen to the answers of each partner as they describe their unhappiness and reflect their feelings to help them experience your empathy and grasp of the problems. The material gathered on the genogram may reveal several patterns being repeated from their families of origin. The therapist can draw parallels, for example, by pointing out, "What you are describing in your marriage sounds a lot like what you described for your parent's marriage."

The therapist needs to explore the interactional patterns of the marital system in the first sessions to help identify underlying dynamics and expectations of the relationship:

- What is the basis of the relationship?
- Is there genuine affection for each other?
- Is there an agreement that equality will be exercised or is one of the partners expected to give more of self and emotions than the other?
- Does one partner spend more time focusing on career, while the other focuses on home and children?
- Are those roles agreeable to both?
- How well does the couple resolve disagreements?
- Where are the sources of income and who controls it?
- Who makes the decision where the family will live?
- What is the division of labor in the home?
- How does the couple handle leisure time?
- How does each partner assess his or her level of intimacy and sexual satisfaction?
- Are their belief systems alike or different?

Next the systemic therapist may alternate between asking pointed questions, e.g., "How did your mom and dad get along before they divorced?" or "Did your parents ever show much anger while you were growing up?" with more general questions, e.g., "What was your position in your family of origin?" "How do think that might have influenced your role in your family today?" With an understanding of the basic underlying dynamics of the relationship, the therapist can proceed to work on the presenting problem. Additional questions will focus on areas of the couple's recognition of each other's pain, have the partners discussed these problems with other friends or family members, what are their unresolved issues, what weaknesses do they have in admitting mistakes, is there mutual respect, can they accept individual differences, do they still have hopes and dreams for their future?

I have found it important to urge the couple's continued expressions of caring for each other, even when they experience high levels of conflict. I may ask them to try to identify similar goals for their family. I also focus on their need to respect and accept each other's beliefs, behaviors, and idiosyncrasies and the fact that the partner is a unique human being. If the therapist can reinforce these issues while dealing with other serious problems the underlying resources of the couple may appear. This may support the couple's expressions of love and provide the sustenance needed to keep their marriage alive.

AUTHOR'S REFLECTIONS

I have certainly learned over the years that "all marriages are not made in heaven!" This is especially true for the couples who come to our therapy offices. Working with the material entrusted to the therapist from the real-life experiences of the couple prepares us to enter on a journey with them that may succeed or fail. Helping couples to uncover their pain and resolve their issues, which can enable them to continue a life together, is a valued trust and can be very rewarding. It reflects our knowledge, skills, experiences, abilities to delve deeply into another human being's life, and our goals of providing resolution. Therefore, it behooves us to gather all the knowledge, experience, and wisdom available to us to treat those who trust us enough to say "We need your help!"

REFERENCES

Guerin, P.J., Fay, L.F., Burden, S.L., & Kautto, J.G. (1987). *The evaluation and treatment of marital conflict.* New York: Basic Books.

McGoldrick, M., Pearce, J. K., & Giordano, J. (Eds.) (1982). *Ethnicity and family therapy.* New York: The Guilford Press.

Napier, A.Y. (1988). *The fragile bond.* New York: Harper and Row.

Nichols, W.C. (1988). *Marital therapy: An integrated approach.* New York: The Guilford Press.

Nichols, W.C. & Everett, C.A. (1986). *Systemic family therapy: An integrative approach.* New York: The Guilford Press.

Pittman, F.P. (1989). *Private lies, infidelity, and the betrayal of intimacy.* New York: W.W. Norton & Co.

Stuart, R.B. (1980). *Helping couples change: A social learning approach to marital therapy.* New York: The Guilford Press.

Chapter 5

Four Predivorce Marital Typologies That Aid Clinical Assessment

Derek Ball
William Hiebert

Tribute to William C. Nichols

Bill Nichols and I have followed each other around the publishing world for the past twenty years. When Bill was the founding editor of the Journal of Marital and Family Therapy, *I was the founding editor of the* Family Therapy News *(AAMFT). When I retired from* Family Therapy News, *Bill succeeded me as its second editor. Some years later, Bill was the editor of the* International Connection, *the newsletter of the International Family Therapy Association (IFTA). When he became president of IFTA, I succeeded him as its editor. We both served together as editors of the Geist and Russell MFT series.*

In addition to our publishing connections, Bill and I were involved in many AAMFT committees and later served on the IFTA board together. All of these mutual involvements led to many conversations regarding the field. During these years, I have always respected Bill's organized vision of whatever venture we were involved in. I appreciated his clarity of where we needed to be headed, and I welcomed his ideas of how to get there. The field of MFT and the professional organizations of AAMFT and IFTA are in better shape today due to Bill's enormous and energetic input. We would all be the poorer for it if Bill had not given so much of himself to these professional causes!—WH

THE CRITICAL ISSUE

A couple's understanding of their relationship as they move toward divorce may affect their motivation to work in therapy. It is common for individuals to talk about divorce: their own, their friend's, their neighbor's, those of the rich and famous, and those of anyone else they find interesting. This chapter is concerned with this phenomenon, which Catherine Kohler Riessman (1990) has defined simply as "divorce talk." More specifically, it will address the conversations of individuals at a particular moment in the divorce process—when divorce is being considered alongside the possibility of the couple working to save the relationship. In other words, as therapists, we want to be concerned about the nature of these conversations before the partners know what the outcome is going to be, i.e., whether they will decide to divorce.

This chapter will explore the narrative accounts provided by marital partners in couple therapy sessions. We will look at couples who have recently entered therapy at a time when the therapist is attempting to learn who they are, what their marriage looks like, and what their future prospects as a couple might be. Four case studies will be used to illustrate a typology that the authors have constructed out of their experiences as couple therapists. These typologies are not intended to serve as a predictor of the potential for "saving" a troubled marriage. Rather, they are created as portraits of common problems and possibilities inherent in many of the couples seeking therapy. As such, typologies are tools that a therapist can employ to depict how the couples frame their interactions and situations. For our purposes here, we are interested in identifying the typologies to inform our selection of clinical interventions.

THE DIVORCE PROCESS

Waller (1967 [1938]), in one of the earliest studies published on divorce, suggested:

> It rarely happens that people wake up one morning, find that they want to get divorced, and proceed to consult a lawyer the same day. Such a decision is usually reached after long deliberation, if not debate, in which one or the other of the mates takes the aggressive role. (p. 14)

In most cases, divorce is a process that takes time, with couples moving from intimacy to social separation and ultimately to living apart. It is not a singular event or decision.

A number of models have been developed to explain the process of uncoupling in divorce. Wiseman (1975) viewed divorce as a grief process, and applied Elisabeth Kübler-Ross's stages of grief to marital dissolution. Kessler (1975) identified seven stages in her understanding of the divorce process. Guttman (1993) proposed a psychosocial model entailing four stages: deciding, separating, struggling, and winning. This model viewed the divorce process as circular rather than linear, progressing from one stage to the next, as well as having the potential to move from one stage back to an earlier one.

The divorce process begins when one of the partners first considers the prospect of ending the relationship. One can assume that a large number of married individuals think about divorce, whether it be for a brief moment, sporadically, frequently, or persistently. Some may think about divorce privately and never act upon their thoughts. Others may talk more openly about divorce and finally confront the spouse about her or his unhappiness. The spouse's statement might be taken by the partner as a threat, a challenge, a confession, an apology, or a sad realization.

Some spouses often initiate divorce talk with someone other than the spouse. An individual might first broach the topic to a close friend or relative, a co-worker, a pastor, or someone else who the person trusts and in whom she or he is willing to confide. This may simply be an outlet that substitutes for talking with the spouse directly before one is ready. Or, this may serve as a "dry run" experiment before the bigger step of actually discussing divorce with the spouse. We will examine couples who have chosen to pursue the route of marital therapy. It would be interesting to know the proportion of couples who discuss divorce and then choose to begin therapy. Of those that do take this step, the decision to find a therapist requires not only a recognition of the level of problems in the marriage, but an acceptance of the idea that therapy could help.

FOUR TYPOLOGIES

Four types of couples considering divorce, who all entered therapy, will be discussed. Each type focuses on the issue of change insofar as it impacts their marriage. However, each couple also defines change differently. The shared assumption of both parties in each of these types is that their relationship problems have led them to a crossroads and the status quo is no longer viable. The ways in which these couples defined their concerns affected how they saw their relationship and how hard they were willing to work toward changing and improving their marriages.

The four typologies to be discussed are:

1. Couples who are unclear about what needs to change: "Something needs to change."
2. Couples who place the responsibility for change on the spouses: "She/he needs to change."
3. Couples who see their relationship as beyond change: "It is too late to change."
4. Couples who share the responsibility for change: "We need to change."

Each of these types has its unique characteristics regarding behavior, the definition of divorce, the structure of the relationship, and the role of children. When viewed together, these characteristics point very clearly toward the likelihood of change for each couple. The value of recognizing these typologies is that each requires a different response from the therapist based upon their unique characteristics.

To identify these types comparatively, we will make use of Olsen's (1993) "circumplex model" which has two dimensions that form a grid on which any couple or family can be located. The first dimension of the model is the structural dimension that assesses the organizational and hierarchical structure present in the marriage. On this dimension a relationship can be overly structured such that it is rigid, it can lack adequate structure and thus be chaotic, or it can be structured between these two poles. The second dimension of this assesses the relative connection in a relationship. This assesses the emotional closeness present in a relationship. Thus, a relationship can be overly connected (i.e., enmeshed or having no personal boundaries), it can be under connected (i.e., disengaged or having no emotional connection between the spouses), or it can function between these two poles.

We will also identify these couples based on the dominant narrative which they portray during the use of the Structured Initial Interview (SII) (Hiebert, Gillespie, & Stahmann, 1993). The SII is an assessment and intervention model which elicits the courtship and marital narrative during a chronological exploration of the marriage from the onset of the relationship to the point of therapy. The SII allows the therapist to view the particular marital "dance" that each couple has evolved during the course of their relationship. With the SII, the therapist is able to identify the structural and connectional dimensions of the relationship, and also locate where the dance falls within the Olson model. These clinical data can identify potentially long term difficulties and estrangements in marital relationships.

We have found two variants of the "something needs to change" type (1)—one type is passive and the other type tends to be aggressive. We are not presenting an example of the latter because this type rarely seeks therapy. However, it is represented by a chaotically enmeshed couple that often threatens change during crisis situations but does not have the motivation to pursue change once the crisis has subsided.

"Something needs to change."

The first type of couple is distressed but have no clear concept as to why they are distressed. This is the type of couple that tends to be passive regarding their marriage. During the SII, they identified as something that happened *to* them rather than something created by them. Also, no crisis or clear issue of immediate concern was identified by the couple at any point during the review of their timeline, unlike some of the other couple types. The SII can be framed for the couple as an opportunity to clarify relationship patterns and problems that have been unidentified or that have gone unspoken. However, in this type, as their narrative unfolds, their relationship appears to deteriorate before their eyes and yet they cannot find a way to articulate why that was happening.

This pattern of slow deterioration, articulated by one or both partners, in this type is illustrated by Mark and Jennifer who were college sweethearts. They met in their junior year, dated each other exclusively, became engaged, and got married following their graduation because it was "the next step." During the SII, Mark and Jennifer were quizzed about historical issues such as how they had decided to make their relationship exclusive, how they decided to become engaged, and how they recalled their relationship's strengths and weaknesses. This couple, as is typical with this type, could not clearly articulate much conscious decision making in any of these relational hallmarks. Rather than having made conscious decisions, the couple seemed to be following traditional blueprints and extended family expectations. When they came in for therapy they had been married for seven years and had a two-year-old son. Neither partner reported any clear issues of distress, but they had mutually consented to therapy because Mark had told Jennifer that he was considering divorce.

Hopper (1993) stressed that the vocabularies that describe one's motives for pursuing divorce take shape over time and, at the beginning of the process, divorce talk is full of ambiguity and confusion. This is clearly evident in this typology and in this case. Mark is beginning to develop an account of the marriage that stresses his lack of fulfillment, but he is not quite prepared to cast blame on his spouse.

For this couple, given that the problems were so vague and undefined, Mark saw divorce as the easiest option. Their relationship story is filled with helplessness and confusion. The only thing Mark understood was that he felt unhappy. Therefore, he concluded that he should look elsewhere for a partner who would have the power to keep him constantly engaged and invigorated. Jennifer was baffled, hurt, and angered by the very fact that Mark would consider leaving her. She had a difficult time considering that she needed to change in any way for the relationship. Similarly, she saw their relationship as something that should not need to change as time went on. The fact that they were experiencing problems was utterly confusing to both partners.

During three therapy sessions this couple showed initial improvement in their ability to articulate feelings and understand their patterns as the narrative unfolded. As therapy explored the decision making around the attraction issues in the relationship, the couple began to see some of the factors that drew them together, and characterized their courtship and early marital interactions. However, they were only starting to address changes when they dropped out of therapy. When contacted by the therapist, they reported that things were "fine" and that they would no longer need therapy. The relief of a few symptoms had led to a common response—passivity.

According to the typologies of Olsen's (1993) circumplex model, this couple would be categorized as "chaotically disengaged." In this type the marriage lacks internal organization and hierarchy (the structural dimension of the model) and is also disconnected emotionally (the connective dimension of the model) (Olsen, 1993). Their relationship can be viewed as a feather in the wind, blown to and fro by influences beyond their control. This type tends to be more reactive than the other types due to the fact that they have no inherent structure that gives their relationship predictability. And, similarly to Mark and Jennifer, they have little staying power and tend to drop out of therapy when their feelings improve. Although the SII can provide couples such as these temporary structure, many do not stay in therapy long enough to gain the necessary insights about themselves and their relationship that would allow them to create permanent and positive changes.

Children in families of this couple type tend to be as confused as their parents. The decision to divorce is seen as a random event that can create a difficult transition and adjustment to the divorce. In the negotiation process, the children may be involved, but this is rarely in a direct fashion. Typically, these parents may make a decision to stay together "for the sake of the kids." Thus, the children's roles in the family can have a tremendous impact on whether or not the parents stay together, even though remaining together may not create happiness.

"She/he needs to change."

The second type of couple that we have observed involves partners who place the responsibility for change on the spouse. This is the most combative type of the four typologies. During the SII this relationship is marked by severe and frequent conflict with one spouse frequently mentioning divorce as a means of persuading and/or threatening the other spouse into a change of behavior. Emotionally, this type manifests a high level of dependency, especially with regard to each partner's self-identity. Each partner depends on the other person for constant approval. In addition, they cannot tolerate the partner thinking differently from them. Because of this dependence on the other's agreement and approval, a differing opinion is experienced as frightening and threatening. In this couple's narrative differences are a threat that must be eliminated at all costs. The crisis for the couple is obvious, as is the solution: the spouse needs to change. The therapist is brought into the picture to change the spouse. The assumption by the partner is that if the spouse changes all will be right with the world.

Jeff and Michelle are a couple who had been engaged in divorce talk for some time. Each blamed the other for their marital problems. Jeff's account focused on Michelle's argumentative challenges as the reason for withholding information from her. Michelle blamed her aggressiveness on Jeff's secretiveness and used that to justify her threat of divorce.

In their first therapy session both saw the problem as being rooted in the other spouse's behaviors. Neither of the partners seemed willing to look at their contributions to the problem. Michelle typically resorted to threatening divorce even though what she wanted was openness. Her persistent threats caused Jeff to distance himself from her further. This couple was locked in their respective positions. It was only when they were able to understand the other's position that they were able to achieve change.

In ten sessions of marital therapy this couple was able to achieve a common ground and begin to work toward a concrete and pragmatic solution. They renegotiated their roles regarding their finances and established a routine in which they held a weekly meeting where they discussed prioritizing and organizing bill payments. This accomplished a significant change, and they were able to apply this to other areas of their lives.

This couple would be categorized as "rigidly enmeshed," according to Olsen's model (1993). In this type the marriage has too much internal organization and hierarchy (the structural dimension of the model) and it is also overly connected emotionally (the connective dimension of the model) (Olsen, 1993). Their identities are fused together such that any differences are threats to their sense of personal well-being. Such couples practice a relationship style that is fraught with "guilt trips," manipulation, and resentment.

The prognosis for therapy for this type is mixed. If they were able to relinquish their positions of blaming each other and learn to collaborate together, they might achieve constructive change. However, if one or both partners maintain a blaming stance and insist on being "right" rather than "understanding" the other person, they are very likely to divorce. The contentiousness of the marriage will then carry over to the divorce process, making it more adversarial, lengthy, and expensive.

Children in families with this type are the most likely to become enmeshed into the parents' conflicts and problems. Depending on their ages, children either blame themselves (younger children) for their parent's divorce or blame one of the parents (older children and adolescents). Many of these children feel manipulated by one or both of the parents. The children in these families are the most likely of all four types to be involved in the negotiation of divorce. While this may be unhealthy for the children, they are simply following the family rule of enmeshment set forth and reinforced by their parents. This role may cause the children to suffer due to the loss of attachment with one parent or by being pulled into too much exposure to the parents' personal conflict.

"It's too late to change."

This type involves a couple who is enmeshed in a relationship in which one of the spouses sees the marriage as being beyond the hope of change. In such a situation the other partner is usually the one to initiate marital therapy. However, on occasion the hopeless partner may seek therapy as a means of finding validation for their assessment of the hopelessness of the relationship. These marriages may have long histories of emotional, physical, and/or sexual abuse. The SII for this type of couple will find issues of addictions, serial affairs, and/or neglect. As the hurt for one or both partners has unfolded in the marital dance, emotional "scars" develop and the relationship becomes increasingly rigid and inflexible.

When asked by the therapist to describe their feelings of intimacy during each year of their marriage, this couple often reports declining levels of intimacy. Eventually the wounds become so deep and intractable that one of the partners loses hope for the future for the relationship.

Chris and Miriam are a couple who appeared for therapy after twenty-three years of marriage. They had two children who were twenty-two and seventeen years respectively. The seventeen-year-old was graduating from high school soon. Miriam, a housewife, reported that she felt alone and constantly put down by Chris. He was a very successful realtor.

Marital therapy with this couple involved trying to redefine the problem and to look for new ways to help them relate. However, it was apparent at the beginning of therapy that Miriam was immovable in her desire for a divorce. As the marital narrative evolved, it was clear that Miriam had made the transition from thinking about divorce, to speaking about divorce, to finally creating an emotional divorce in the relationship some years ago.

Miriam's account of the relationship problems focused on Chris' history of verbal abuse and emotional withdrawal. This served as her justification for initiating and persisting in divorce talk. For his part, Chris showed little interest in sharing his hurt or any other vulnerable feelings. This seemed to confirm Miriam's decision to leave. Indeed, in assuming the role of noninitiator, Chris' narrative entailed the image of husband as the economic provider, and nothing more. During the SII, it became clear that Chris had performed the duties expected of him, even though he acknowledged that he did so without feelings. While it struck him as absurd that Miriam wanted a divorce, he clearly indicated that earlier he, too, had concluded they were living as if they were divorced.

Chris and Miriam were divorced seven months later. For these two individuals, divorce seemed to be their only option. Their story about their relationship was filled with hopelessness and negativity. They were focused solely on their own hurt and disappointment. This type of couple could be described as rigidly disengaged in Olsen's model (1993). Their positions are extremely inflexible and there is very little closeness or intimacy reported by either partner. This rigid disengagement creates a poor prognosis for change in marital therapy. Typically, therapy is used as a place to "drop off" the spouse that is being left or it has been used as a safe place to make the final announcement of the decision to divorce.

For children in families with this type, life also feels helpless. Given that at least one parent is intractable and moving toward divorce, the children are left out of the process. They have very little emotional leverage in the negotiations of the decision to divorce. Since the problems for their parents may have been present for several years, there may be two common responses by the children. First, they may feel relieved. Adult children of divorce have reported to us that they saw their parents' decision to divorce as an end to the negative cycle they had observed and in which they lived. Thus, in these families divorce may be seen by the children as a healthy step. Second, the children may feel powerless. Younger children tend to see the decision to divorce in this couple type as a sudden move, even though it may have been a very long process for the parent. This is because they have been witnessed the conflicts and problems in the marriage but had not been privy to discussions about the prospect of separation and divorce. Given the immovable position for the divorce by one parent, the children may feel helpless in a decision that impacts them greatly.

"We need to change."

The final couple type is composed of two partners who are distressed but are willing to take accountability for their part in the relationship issues. This couple tends to have higher self-esteem and to be more actively engaged in their marriage. In their narrative, problems are defined as something to which both parties have contributed and, therefore, something to which both parties can and must participate in changing. Although these problems are still very distressing, divorce is mentioned only as an option or as a "final straw," it is not used as a threat or a bargaining chip.

> Mike and Cheryl have been married for seven years and have one child, age two. They were considering having another child before Mike changed jobs. One of the consequences of his new job was that he had experienced greater employment-related stresses because he had been forced to work longer hours. These changes had contributed to an increase in the level of conflict in their marriage. Cheryl was also concerned that Mike may have been having an affair with a co-worker.

Mike and Cheryl were similar in that both expressed unhappiness with their current state of affairs. Both partners were willing to discuss their mutual sense of feeling disconnected in recent months. Each were careful in constructing their respective descriptions, employing a shared rhetorical strategy that was intended to avoid blaming the partner, while looking for a mutually agreeable way to deal with the problems.

After seven marital therapy sessions which focused on Mike's "work first" orientation, he realized that he needed to reevaluate his priorities and set appropriate boundaries at work. Cheryl realized that she had not articulated her needs in the relationship clearly. She often dismissed her complaints as frivolous compared to Mike's job demands. When they both made changes, they saw a significant improvement in their level of marital satisfaction.

Cheryl was prepared to see divorce as an option, especially if the problem could not have been resolved. Although their relationship story was filled with hurt, it also reflected a willingness to accept responsibility and to exhibit caring for each partner. They were able to see the other's perspective, with some prompting, and, were able to express empathy. This created the precondition for them to proceed to work toward a solution that was satisfying to both of them.

This couple could best be described as balanced in Olsen's model (1993). This type is the healthiest and is located on the grid in the middle of each dimension rather than at any of the extremes. On the structural dimension, the healthy relationship is one that balances relational organization with personal freedom. On the connection dimension, the healthy relationship is one that balances relational closeness with separateness. This demonstrates independent thinking and at the same time a connection between partners that motivates them to negotiate conflict constructively. Their relationship is stable and balanced, while also having the capacity to change and adapt as life requires. This couple type is likely to experience the greatest benefit from therapy. They are able to take the challenges presented in therapy and have sufficient strength to practice their newly learned skills outside of the therapist's office.

Children in families of this type tend to be the healthiest of the four types. The decision to divorce, should it occur, would be seen as a loss just as in any of the other couple types. However, the difference here is that parents who decide to divorce with these skills will also apply those healthy skills to their postdivorce parenting relationship. They are the most likely to minimize conflict regarding the children and to realize that each parent continues to have a unique relationship with the children after the divorce.

In the negotiation process, the children are rarely involved. This is not to say that they are kept in the dark about parental decisions but that they do not become participants in the process. Typically, the parents are motivated to work things out "for the sake of the kids" as opposed to staying together. Children in families of this type will find that if their parents consider divorce their best interests will be considered without them having to be involved in the negotiation process.

AUTHORS' REFLECTIONS

As the preceding section indicates, we have observed that couples considering divorce who seek therapy tend to fall into four distinct types. Each type displays a varying degree of success and failure in either preserving a marriage or terminating it. Although there is no guarantee that these couples who enter therapy will stay together, the ones who are willing to identify their problems with each other are more likely to be able to work through their issues in a healthy manner. The narratives that each of these couples tell about their relationship and the prospect of divorce impact their ability to deal with marital distress in different ways. Being able to define their issues clearly and in a shared manner gives the couple the greatest flexibility and motivation to continue working on their problems to a satisfactory conclusion.

The role of the therapist is to look at this process from a different perspective before a divorce has occurred. The therapeutic process offers a distinctive setting for divorce talk, one in which the partners have opted to share their vocabularies of motive with a trained professional. The four typologies that we presented indicated that some couples entering therapy have relatively little insight into their situation, while others bring a fairly clear set of ideas about what their problems are and what needs to change.

For a therapist to proceed, it is necessary to do interpretive work based on the talk that the clients present. While couples experiencing marital problems often understand their situation as unique, the fact that a typology can be constructed suggests that there are certain commonalities that can be identified. Indeed, from the perspective of a therapist, making such interpretive assessments is essential both to predict the likelihood of therapeutic success and to guide decisions about how to proceed (Crane, Soderquist, & Frank, 1995; Hampson, Prince, & Beavers, 1999).

The primary task of the therapist is to assist the couple to achieve greater clarity in their own interpretive work, which involves not only making sense of one's own divorce talk, but that of their partner as well. It is only when couples come together to do so that they can proceed to talk about strategies for change. These couples will have the potential to construct a new narrative, one that looks to a future that is different from the narrative of the past and present.

REFERENCES

Crane, D. R., Soderquist, J. N., & Frank, R. L. (1995). Predicting divorce at marital therapy intake: A preliminary model. *American Journal of Family Therapy 23*, 227-236.

Guttman, J. (1993). *Divorce in psychosocial perspective: Theory and research.* Hillsdale, NJ: Lawrence Erlbaum Associates.

Hampson, R. B., Prince, C. C., & Beavers, W. R. (1999). Marital therapy: Qualities of couples who fare better or worse in treatment. *Journal of Marital and Family Therapy 25*, 411-424.

Hiebert, W. J., Gillespie, J., & Stahmann, R. (1993). *Dynamic assessment in couple therapy.* New York: Lexington Books.

Hopper, J. (1993). The rhetoric of motives in divorce. *Journal of Marriage and the Family 55*, 801-813.

Kessler, S. (1975). *The American way of divorce: Prescription for change.* Chicago, IL: Nelson-Hall.

Olsen, D. (1993). Circumplex model of marital and family systems. In F. Walsh (Ed.), *Normal Family Process* (pp. 104-137). New York: The Guilford Press.

Riessman, C. K. (1990). *Divorce talk: Women and men make sense of personal relationships.* New Brunswick, NJ: Rutgers University Press.

Waller, W. (1967 [1938]). *The old love and the new: Divorce and readjustment.* Carbondale, IL: Southern Illinois University Press.

Wiseman, R. S. (1975). Crisis theory and the process of divorce. *Social Casework 56*, 205-212.

Chapter 6

Disclosing Gay or Lesbian Orientation Within Marriage: A Systems Perspective

Jerry J. Bigner

Tribute to William C. Nichols

I first became acquainted with Bill Nichols while I was in the second year of my doctoral program at Florida State University. On something of a dare from another student, I submitted a revised term paper that I had prepared for a family studies class to Bill as editor of Family Coordinator (the predecessor of Family Relations). I don't know if he knew this was my first foray into academic publishing but he was very kind, very helpful, and made this first experience with editors one of the best. Our paths crossed many years later when he invited me to contribute a chapter for his edited text on family therapy. That experience also was very pleasurable. Over the years, Bill has made his mark not only on the field of marriage and family therapy but on many of us who have grown personally and professionally as a result of our contacts with him. He is truly a giant as a human being and as a mentor.

Disclosure of gay or lesbian orientation within marriage is a family event affecting all members to some degree. This article discusses how each aspect of a family system (the disclosing spouse, the spouse, and their children) reacts to the disclosure event as well as copes with the divorce of the adults. A family systems theory approach is combined with the ABC-X model of family crisis management to illustrate how this crisis is resolved often with the help of a competent therapist.

As clinicians, we know that systems theory succinctly targets the interrelatedness of all family members. This is observed in a variety of ways in family functioning but especially when one member experiences some type of major change. Any major stressor can produce critical effects on the person directly but these also ripple throughout a family system and manifests themselves in a number of ways.

There are many major stressors that can be expected as well as unanticipated ones over the life span of a family. Part of my work has focused on the dynamics that occur when a spouse discloses her or his (sometimes newly discovered) true gay or lesbian orientation. This often follows many years of heterosexual marriage and having children. For the majority of these individuals, divorce is inevitable. Coming out—disclosure of one's sexual orientation—is always a family affair when it occurs within the context of a heterosexual marriage (Buxton, 1994, 2004).

THE GORDIAN KNOT
OF SEXUAL ORIENTATION DISCLOSURE
IN MARRIAGE

> Throughout my life, I have grappled with my own identity, who I am . . . By virtue of my traditions, . . . I worked hard to ensure that I was accepted as part of the traditional family of America . . . I married my first wife . . . we have a wonderful, extradordinary daughter . . . I then had the blessing of marrying Dina . . . together we have the most beautiful daughter . . . Yet . . . At a point in every person's life, one has to look deeply into the mirror of one's soul and decide one's unique truth in the world, not as we may want to see it or hope to see it, but as it is. . . And so my truth is that I am a gay American. (CNN.com, 2004)

These words, spoken in feelings mixed with pain, sorrow, and—paradoxically—relief, are from James McGreevey, the former Governor of New Jersey who publicly came out after being threatened with exposure for having an extramarital affair with a male government official. These words poignantly portray what millions of other married and formerly married gay men and women have felt and experienced in somewhat similar situations. Many were forced from their closet of denial to confront their true sexual orientation at a difficult juncture in life when other developmental landmarks were being experienced as well (Bigner, 1996, 2004).

A family crisis emerges, often unexpectedly, with this pronouncement of homosexual or bisexual orientation, regardless if spoken by a husband or a wife. The interrelatedness concept from family systems theory comes to life as everyone in the family is affected in varying degrees and ways by the revelation. The reactions of each part of a family system will first be examined here within the context of disclosure in marriage followed by an examination of the system's reaction as a whole. We will then briefly examine therapeutic issues in working with clients affected by this circumstance.

THE DISCLOSING SPOUSE

Disclosure is always a momentous experience (Eichberg, 1990). The process that brings someone to this place is long and arduous, especially when one has been in the closet or has attempted to hide or deny this aspect of their self over a long period of time. The developmental path taken by gay and lesbian individuals who married and became parents is different, obviously, than for those who have been able to face and accept their sexual orientation in their earlier years (Bigner, 2004). Hypothetically, it is possible that disclosing spouses are perhaps more sensitized to the feelings and attitudes termed heterosexism (the notion that heterosexuality is superior and preferable to homosexuality) and homophobia (an irrational avoidance of homosexuals and homosexuality) than others. They perhaps have denied their same-sex feelings and orientation more strongly and deeply because of numerous reasons. For example, puberty is the time when most adolescents explore a variety of sexual feelings and experiences, homosexual as well as heterosexual in nature. Many who discover that their homosexual feelings are stronger than those that are heterosexual, or discover an almost complete lack of heterosexual feelings, learn to disguise these in order to avoid detection and stigmatization as being gay or lesbian. Only later, perhaps after leaving their families of origin in early adulthood, do they allow these feelings to emerge and evolve into the coming out process that leads to the development of their gay or lesbian orientation as a healthy, appropriate aspect of their personality. These individuals experience an identity-shaping process that is based on and incorporates their sexual orientation as normal and acceptable just as do those who develop and accept their heterosexual orientation. However, those that experience difficulty in allowing this aspect of their personality to develop and emerge may enter into a state of identity development known as *identity moratorium* (Seifert & Hoffnung, 2004) wherein acceptance of this integral aspect of their personality is indefinitely placed on hold. Some of these individuals hope deeply that their same-sex feelings and attractions will never emerge because of fears of rejection by family, friends, and community. Others sometimes experience intense pressures from their families of origin to deny this aspect. They may have received implicit and even explicit messages that a homosexual family member is unacceptable and that this carries dire consequences. Others believe that they will not be able to attain social status, career goals, or personal happiness by coming out as gay or lesbian. And so the charade begins. There is divorce of the true self from reality and a false self becomes adopted instead. The proverbial (homosexual) square peg tries to fit into the (heterosexual) round hole made by society that defines acceptance, tolerance, and even love.

There is the misunderstanding that many individuals in this situation deliberately enter heterosexual relationships as a means of escaping their reality as being gay or lesbian (Bigner, 2000). This may be true for some who enter heterosexual relationships hoping to be healed of their undesired same-sex feelings. A fairly small group reports (often while in therapy) that they were totally unaware of what was missing from their lives until falling in love with a same-sex best friend shocked them into acknowledging that the missing piece in their life was being true to a different, perhaps up until then unknown, sexual orientation.

However, clinical experience again strongly suggests that many of these individuals, regardless of why they entered into heterosexual marriages, truly love their spouses and care deeply for and love their children. Fear of hurting these individuals as well as their family of origin has often maintained their closeted existence for many years. Many feel trapped in their situation, and it is not unusual for emotional depression to develop along with a number of other unhealthy, inappropriate, and ineffective means for coping with what seems to be a problem with no workable, viable solution.

This state of affairs has its limits, however. What often works as the trigger mechanism to initiate bedrock changes for these individuals is the midlife transition event/experience that occurs typically when many enter their fortieth decade. This may affect men more than women in bringing about life-changing experiences. Some individuals come to the realization that they cannot continue to have a life based on lies, deception, and lack of integrity to their self. Being unhappy, and deeply so, they come to realize that it is wrong on all grounds to be a gay or lesbian person trying not to be so. Others, such as Governor McGreevey of New Jersey, have to be threatened or figuratively hauled and dragged out of their denial because of their false belief that a closeted existence provides security. Their spouses may discover their clandestine sexual activities and interests or they may be arrested for such activities and even experience attempted blackmailing.

Regardless of how or why disclosure takes place, voluntarily or otherwise, the person leaves their closeted existence and begins the divorce process of shedding a false heterosexual identity and acquiring a true homosexual identity. Space does not allow for a complete description of the path that is usually taken by both men and women as they struggle to form a new personal identity at midlife; this may be studied elsewhere (Bigner, 1996; D'Augelli & Patterson, 1995). What becomes a liberating experience for these individuals becomes in turn a personal crisis for spouses and for their family system. What becomes crystal clear for many is that this new existence and reality cannot take place within the context of a heterosexual marriage. Therefore, most individuals eventually divorce from their heterosexual marriage in order to truly come into their own as a complete and whole person. Many will seek the assistance of therapists to disclose their sexuality to their spouse, prepare for divorce, disclose to children, and develop their new personal identity and lifestyle.

Only in hindsight do many disclosing individuals understand and allow a grieving process to take place over the many losses that are incurred as a price for attaining or regaining personal integrity. These often become obvious only through introspection experienced in therapy as the person recognizes multiple losses. These include relationships involving spouses, children, and family of origin, as a false sense of security and a false identity that were comfortable and familiar though undesired, among others.

THE SPOUSE TO WHOM DISCLOSURE IS MADE

There has been considerably less research performed and published about the experiences of spouses of disclosing individuals. Much of what is known comes from anecdotal material and clinical observation (Buxton, 1994, 2004, in press) that describe the reactions of spouses to the disclosure and what ensues thereafter. While space limits a complete discussion of these experiences, therapists working with mixed-orientation couples will be impressed with the incongruence between these two parties. The disclosing individual often is at a very different place psychologically and emotionally in dealing with the coming out issues, because he or she has had the opportunity to work and deal with these for some time. The spouse to whom disclosure is made is likely to be experiencing shock in digesting the revelation and all that it implies. In the initial phase of dealing with the news, it is not unusual for spouses to experience a wide range of reactions and feelings, often felt intensely. These can involve confusion, emotional numbness, anger, fear, dread, sadness, and even hatred. The ripple effects of initial disclosure from a spouse typically elicit many questions from spouses about their own personal sexuality and sexual orientation, confusion about not truly knowing their spouses, feelings of rejection as well as hostility, fears of personal safety regarding sexually transmitted diseases such as AIDS, fears for the welfare of children because of impending divorce, and sadness and grief with the prospects of lost dreams, lost love, and lost relationships.

Issues involving trust may be the most difficult to cope with and master, a situation not unlike what is found in heterosexual marriages when an extramarital affair takes place and becomes a reality in the relationship. A loss of trust occurs not only in the disclosing partner but also in one's own sense of judgment. A low sense of self-worth often results, setting the stage for depression. The perception of being deceived may never be overcome by some spouses. This prevents future intimate involvements or may make these difficult at best. Many spouses feel helpless in not knowing how to compete with someone who is the same sex as their spouse in an intimate relationship.

Eventually, the seeds planted by a disclosing spouse can develop into a secret shamefully held by spouses and other family members. The confinement of their closet becomes a reality for many who do not know with whom to share this information about their disclosing partner or are fearful of doing so. Some, being unused to acting deceptively themselves, are extremely uncomfortable in withholding this information. Now the deceived must act as the deceiver—the shoe ill-fitting the individual and confusing the situation even more.

The healing process for spouses can take years to be complete, if at all. Buxton (1994, 2004, in press) describes this process as being like a transfiguration because the spouses (who by now are typically ex-spouses) have restructured their lives, their attitudes, and their lifestyles as well. This is described in more detail in a later section that describes the reactions of the entire family system to disclosure.

CHILDREN OF DISCLOSING INDIVIDUALS

Again, there are little data describing the reactions and adjustments of children to the disclosure by a parent of their homosexual orientation. Both gay fathers and lesbian mothers find this to be perhaps the most difficult aspect of their new identity development process since loss of children's love and acceptance may be at stake.

What is known is that the age of children at disclosure can be a critical element in their reactions to this information (Bigner, 1996, 2004). The basic issue in discussing and advising about disclosure issues with children is whether they have experienced puberty and whether they are old enough to understand the situation. In general, older preschool-age children and school-age children can be expected to react more favorably to disclosure than adolescents. Teenagers tend to find this news disturbing and shameful because of their own developing sexuality and exposure to homophobic attitudes by peers.

One research finding stands out clearly regarding the importance of disclosure to children: The parent-child relationship appears to be strengthened following disclosure since children understand that their parent is being truthful and authentic rather than attempting to continue a charade of being someone who they are not (Bozett, 1987; Dunne, 1987). The disclosing parent models honesty in the relationship by setting a positive example that is impressed into children's memories. This can last a lifetime.

FAMILY SYSTEM REACTIONS

Perhaps the best model that depicts the reactions of the entire family system to disclosure is the ABC-X family crisis management model described by Hansen and Hill (1964) and updated by Laszloffy (2002) using family systems theory constructs (see Figure 6.1). In this model, three factors—(1) the stressor event (disclosure) + (2) a family system's strategies for coping with severe stress (healthy or unhealthy) + (3) the interpretations of the stressor event (meanings associated with homosexuality)—produce a family crisis (X) (Bigner, 2002). Homeostasis of the system is severely impaired by the disclosure. A disorganization phase is experienced as a result as the entire system attempts to bring order to family functioning.

As the spouse and other family members attempt to make sense of this whole chaotic disarray into which their world has evolved, they may place everything on hold regarding the future. A separation often is instituted to help make sense of the situation, and what it means for now and in the long run. Children may not be told of the parental difficulties at this time but they frequently are aware that something is offbase.

Buxton (2004, in press) states that it may take spouses up to three years or more to begin their healing process following disclosure. A point is reached when confusion, disorganization, and lack of certainty about how to act and what to do are no longer effective nor feasible. For many, divorce becomes part of the healing process that allows closure, time for introspection, and gaining a new perspective. These frequently are facilitated by working with a competent therapist who is familiar with coming out issues and how these affect individuals as well as the an entire family system. Clinical observation suggests that those spouses as well as those family systems that seek assistance from reliable outside sources often make the most successful and healthy adjustments to these significant personal and family changes. Education about homosexuality can be critical in this process. Old ideas, misconceptions, and stereotypes may be dismantled by firsthand experiences through support groups such as PFLAG (Parents, Friends, and Families of Lesbians and Gays). In effect, spouses must implement new values and belief systems that guide their future (Buxton, 2004, in press).

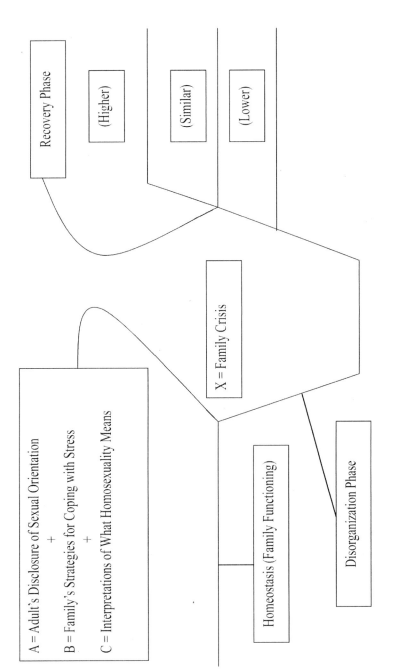

A = Adult's Disclosure of Sexual Orientation
+
B = Family's Strategies for Coping with Stress
+
C = Interpretations of What Homosexuality Means

X = Family Crisis

Recovery Phase

(Higher)

(Similar)

(Lower)

Homeostasis (Family Functioning)

Disorganization Phase

FIGURE 6.1. The ABC-X model is adapted to illustrate how disclosure affects family functioning.

RECOVERY

As the family system recovers, the disclosing spouse is embarking on a path leading to a new personal identity as a gay or lesbian parent. This process often parallels the identity development process that begins in adolescence and is completed in early adulthood by those individuals who are not sidetracked by internalized homophobia into marriage. For the disclosing spouse, this process is off-time developmentally since it usually takes place at midlife. This individual is likely to experience the excessive stresses of working through the usual mid-life transition challenges simultaneously with coming out (developing a new personal identity) and dealing with the ramifications of divorce as well as all that this entails. Most disclosing men and women want someone special in their lives and often seek to duplicate or at least approximate what they wanted but found lacking in their previous heterosexual relationship. The trials and tribulations involved in all this has been outlined elsewhere (Bigner, 1996, 2000). Needless to say, the proverbial monkey wrench is thrown into the workings of a family system as both adults attempt to establish new lives and new personal directions.

Children, upon disclosure, often react positively or at least in a tolerable manner about the information. Again, this may depend on their ages at the time of parental disclosure. Many determine that this news should be kept secret from other children. Some learn about prejudice and bigotry by disclosing to others who turn out to be untrustworthy. Bozett (1987) identified a process used by the children he studied following parental disclosure to maintain privacy rather than secrecy about this information. Terming this *boundary control,* he described how children managed the parents' sexual orientation information, and thereby made this into a more healthy way of protecting themselves from ridicule and from those whom they could not trust with the information. Researchers have not yet provided data on the long-term aspects and consequences of having a gay or lesbian parent for children. However, extant literature has repeatedly confirmed, using different methodologies and different ages of children in samples, that sexual orientation of a parent is irrelevant or nondetrimental to children's welfare in every area studied (Bigner, 2002; Buxton, 2000; Patterson, 1992; Stacey & Biblarz, 2001).

The divorce process is inevitable for most couples and their children. It is unclear presently whether the greatest adjustments required of all family members are those related to the disclosure or to the divorce. It may be impossible to separate the effects of these on a family system and its members since both are likely to be experienced at the same time. The stress of having to attend to two major family crises simultaneously can take its toll on the health and well-being as well as emotional and mental attitudes of all family members. On a more positive note, it appears that most families involved in this dilemma eventually reach some level of resolution. The transitions that occur to resolve the stress of both crises most likely take place as the adults reach solutions. These may involve redefining parenting roles, developing new patterns and rules that govern roles and relationships, and establishing a binuclear family system that involves children. No set period of time can be expected for this resolution to be reached in all families since each system is different.

THERAPEUTIC IMPLICATIONS

One of the first things to be considered in therapy with this situation is whether the therapist is competently trained and skilled in working with this particular type of case (Bigner, 1996, 2004; Buxton, 1994, 2004, in press). Although the importance of similarity of sexual orientation between therapist and client is uncertain, there is a distinct possibility that such similarity can facilitate successful work with individuals as well as families who are attempting to cope with disclosure issues. However, heterosexual therapists can develop informed empathy by seeking GLB-oriented and affirmative supervision and training (Clark, 1987; Long & Lindsey, 2004; Wetchler, 2004). Because gay fathers and lesbian mothers experience a different developmental path in acquiring their identity and new lifestyle (Bigner, 1996), therapists working with clients on these issues are likely to need additional supervisory experiences. It is critical for all therapists, regardless of their sexual orientation, to become aware of and learn how to confront their own feelings of homophobia, heterosexism, and guilt that can impede effective work with these clients. Furthermore, many heterosexual therapists need additional education and work in learning about gay and lesbian culture, sexuality, and

family structures and functioning. Wetchler (2004) also advises heterosexual therapists to use those times when they themselves were an
outsider (e.g., being teased by other children; being in a foreign country; being refused service; being rejected socially) as a way to understand the particularly unique situation of sexual minority clients.

Therapists who are asked to work with individuals, couples, and
families who seek assistance with issues related to disclosure are
likely to feel overwhelmed at first with the enormity of the presenting
problem. This is, indeed, a Gordian knot in therapy. In evaluating or
assessing the situation, it is common to recommend individual work
with both adults separately, work with both in couple therapy, and
work with the entire family system as well. Depending on who seeks
assistance first, it is likely that issues relating to the continuation of a
marriage will need to resolved first. Some therapists prefer not to
work with clients in individual therapy while also working with them
simultaneously in couple therapy. Others feel that working simultaneously in both contexts is advantageous to the process of reaching
closure about the marriage issues.

For all practical purposes, the therapeutic approaches used in
reaching closure in this situation are similar to what is used to assist
couples regarding divorce for other reasons. Child custody issues are
perhaps the most contentious of those that will arise for some couples
due to the highly emotional reactions and feelings that are brought
into therapy relating to homosexuality and parenting by a nondis-
closing spouse. It is at this juncture that legal positions may supercede therapeutic solutions to this thorny dilemma. Sometimes involving a court-appointed advocate for children helps to keep everyone
focused on what is truly important here, namely the best interests of
the children.

Individual therapy is another matter and calls for different therapeutic goals for each adult. In general, while there is little research to
document the therapy experiences of gay fathers and lesbian mothers
(Bigner, 1996; Smetana & Bigner, in press), therapists may expect
the therapeutic needs of each to involve

1. dealing with depressive symptoms;
2. assisting with disclosure to self and the spouse (in some cases)
   as well as children;

3. addressing internalized homophobia and heterosexist attitudes and feelings;
4. developing a positive identity as a gay man or lesbian woman;
5. encouraging opportunities to learn the gay and lesbian culture and lifestyle;
6. developing a social network in the GLB communities;
7. Addressing couples issues as intimate relationships develop with other same-sex individuals; and
8. addressing gay or lesbian stepfamily formation and functioning.

These issues have been addressed in detail in other sources (Bigner, 2004; Bradford, 2004; Buxton, 2004, in press; Greenan & Tunnel, 2003, 2004; Smetana & Bigner, 2005). The therapeutic work with spouses is much different than with what is called for in working with the disclosing individual. Again, space does not permit a complete discussion of these particular issues, but the reader is directed to the other discussions in meeting the needs of spouses (Buxton, 2004, in press).

Family therapy issues can parallel what is taking place in individual and couples work prior to or following divorce in these circumstances. Children's issues often dominate the focus of therapy as well as the concerns of spouses about parenting, lifestyle, and identity changes. Frequently, spouses and ex-spouses do not commence family therapy until the disclosing individual becomes involved in their first serious intimate relationship with someone else of the same sex. This often brings major concerns that may not have been addressed previously between the two, especially when it appears that the disclosing individual is forming a binuclear family structure that will include the person's children from the previous relationship. Therapists often must help clients negotiate the influence of homophobic and heterosexist notions and feelings that arise once again, sometimes in a context similar to what was observed as reaction to the initial disclosure experience.

Gay and lesbian stepfamily issues are not dramatically different from those observed among heterosexual stepfamilies (Baptiste, 1987; Benkov, 1994; Bigner, 1996, 2004). For example, therapists may be asked to help these families with problems expressing affection between stepparent and stepchildren, or assisting children having difficulty accepting their parent's new same-sex partner. Issues relating to rules that may conflict within both binuclear families are not uncommon. Therefore, including all adult parties in negotiations may be appropriate. As difficult as such interactions may be, therapists can offer a safe environment in which to settle differences and conflicts.

AUTHOR'S REFLECTIONS

Coming out at midlife within the context of marriage and parenthood creates a difficult dilemma that affects the entire intergenerational network of family systems. Often taking years to resolve, the outcomes are not always predictable. More important, this particular family crisis could be lessened or at best prevented with broad changes in existing societal attitudes about homosexuality. These homophobic and heterosexist attitudes promote the highly negative conclusions that insidiously lead people to hide in the closet and convince them to portray themselves to be someone who they clearly are not. These attitudes wrap individuals into an envelope of false selfhood in an attempt to be imagined as acceptable, appropriate, and healthy human beings. By trying to pass as heterosexual and entering into relationships in which there may be commitment and love but lacking in authenticity, their integrity is sacrificed with the price of choosing to live a lie. The ramifications that come from the emotional wounds experienced by close family members when the cloak of a false self is removed via disclosure could be spared—most likely if we did not live in a society that promotes homophobia and heterosexism.

Given a society that is free or freer of these attitudes, gay and lesbian individuals might be permitted to pursue the creation of family systems in which resolutions are reached far ahead of the time before children are produced and in which roles, boundaries, and rules regulating behavior are well defined. Such families already exist, although rarely noticed or heard about, and have been labeled *hetero-gay* (Segal-Engelchen, Erera, & Cwikel, in press). This family structure resembles that of a binuclear family in two key aspects. First, in hetero-gay families, as in many postdivorce binuclear families, both the gay or lesbian parent and the heterosexual parent share parental responsibilities although they do not share a residence. Second, the children live with only one of the parents, usually the mother. In contrast to binuclear families, the parental partnership in hetero-gay families is not based on a previously established intimate relationship. While this is an emerging family structure rarely visible in society today, it may offer a better solution for the desire for parenthood and sense of family (that many gay men and lesbian women share with heterosexuals) than the route that results from denial and the adoption of the pretense of heterosexuality observed today and in the past.

REFERENCES

Baptiste, D. A., Jr. (1987). The gay and lesbian stepparent family. In F. W. Bozett (Ed.), *Gay and lesbian parents* (pp. 112-137). New York: Praeger.

Benkov, L. (1994). *Reinventing the family: The emerging story of lesbian and gay parents.* New York: Crown Publishers.

Bigner, J. J. (1996). Working with gay fathers: Developmental, postdivorce parenting, and therapeutic issues. In R-J. Green & J. Laird (Eds.), *Lesbians and gays in couples and families: A handbook for therapists* (pp. 370-403). San Francisco: Josey-Bass.

Bigner, J. J. (2000). Gay and lesbian families. In W. C. Nichols, M. A. Pace-Nichols, D. S. Becvar, & A. Y. Napier (Eds.), *Handbook of family therapy: Dynamics and therapeutic interventions* (pp. 279-298). New York: John Wiley.

Bigner, J. J. (2002). *Parent-child relations: An introduction to parenting* (6th ed.). Upper Saddle River, NJ: Prentice Hall.

Bigner, J. J. (2004). Working with gay and lesbian parents. *Journal of Couple and Relationship Therapy, 3*(2/3), 85-93.

Bozett, F. W. (1987). Children of gay fathers. In F. W. Bozett (Ed.), *Gay and lesbian parents* (pp. 39-57). New York: Praeger.

Bradford, M. (2004). Bisexual issues in same-sex couple therapy. *Journal of Couple and Relationship Therapy, 3*(2/3), 43-52.

Buxton, A. P. (1994). *The other side of the closet: The coming-out crisis for straight spouses and families.* New York: John Wiley & Sons.

Buxton, A. P. (2000). The best interest of children of lesbian and gay parents. In R. Galatzer-Levy & L. Kraus, (Eds.), *The scientific basis for custody decisions* (pp. 319-346). New York: John Wiley & Sons.

Buxton, A. P. (2004). Paths and pitfalls: How heterosexual spouses cope when their husbands or wives come out. *Journal of Couple and Relationship Therapy, 3*(2/3), 95-109.

Buxton, A. P. (in press). A family matter: When a spouse comes out as gay, lesbian, or bisexual. *Journal of GLBT Family Studies.*

Clark, D. (1987). *Loving someone gay* (rev. ed.). Berkeley, CA: Celestial Arts.

CNN.com (2004). McGreevey: "I am a gay American:" Transcript of news conference comments. Retrieved August 13, 2004, from http://www.cnn.com/2004/ALLPOLITICS/08/12mcgreevey.trancript/inex.html.

D'Augelli, A. R., & Patterson, C. J. (Eds.). (1995). *Lesbian, gay, and bisexual identities over the lifespan: Psychological perspectives.* New York: Oxford University Press.

Dunne, E. J. (1987). Helping gay fathers come out to their children. *Journal of Homosexuality, 14,* 213-222.

Eichberg, R. (1990). *Coming out: An act of love.* New York: Viking Penguin.

Greenan, D. E., & Tunnell, G. (2003). *Couple therapy with gay men.* New York: Guilford Press.

Greenan, D., & Tunnel, G. (2004). Clinical issues with gay male couples. *Journal of Couple and Relationship Therapy, 3*(2/3), 13-26.

Hansen, D. A., & Hill, R. (1964). Families under stress. In H. Christensen (Ed.), *Handbook of marriage and the family.* Chicago, IL: Rand-McNally.

Laszloffy, T. A. (2002). Rethinking family development theory: Teaching with the systemic family development (SFD) model. *Family Relations, 51,* 206-214.

Long, J. K., & Lindsey, E. (2004). The sexual orientation matrix for supervision: A tool for training therapists to work with same-sex couples. *Journal of Couple and Relationship Therapy, 3*(2/3), 123-135.

Patterson, C. J. (1992). Children of lesbian and gay parents. *Child Development, 63,* 1025-1042.

Segal-Engelchen, D., Erera, P. I., & Cwikel, J. (in press). The hetero-gay family: An emergent family configuration. *Journal of GLBT Family Studies.*

Seiffert, K., & Hoffnung, R. J. (2004). *Child and adolescent development* (5th ed.). Boston, MA: Houghton-Mifflin.

Smetana, D. J., & Bigner, J. J. (2005). Therapeutic experiences of lesbian couples: An exploratory qualitative analysis. *Journal of Couple and Relationship Therapy.*

Stacey, J., & Biblarz, T. J. (2001). (How) does the sexual orientation of parents matter? *American Sociological Review, 66,* 159-183.

Wetchler, J. L. (2004). A heterosexual therapist's journey toward working with same-sex couples. *Journal of Couple and Relationship Therapy, 3*(2/3), 137-145.

Chapter 7

Issues of Separation and Divorce in Families Affected by Domestic Violence

Michele Harway

Tribute to William C. Nichols

I have never met Bill Nichols. However, I have had a perfectly delightful phone and e-mail relationship with Bill over the past five to six years. Bill first contacted me a number of years ago about writing a chapter on working with families that were experiencing domestic violence. He had heard about me from a mutual colleague. I was really flattered to be asked since I certainly knew of Bill and his reputation! Working with him was easy. He was one of those editors who was grateful for authors' contributions and flattering about the quality of their work. His comments about needed changes were gently presented and I respected him for his tact as well as his intellectual acumen.

A few years later, when I was putting together an edited volume on couples therapy, I asked Bill to write a chapter. His behavior as an editor was exactly paralleled by his behavior as an author. He was the first one to turn in a chapter. It was impeccably written and I think makes a wonderful contribution to the book. The bottom line is that Bill is a gentleman and an incredibly gifted and warm one at that.

Margot* sought therapy because she was having difficulty getting out of bed each day to take the children to school. She acknowledged a rocky marriage with Tim, her husband of eight years, but also indicated that she loved Tim very much. While there were some things she would like to change in him, she indicated that she had no interest in leaving the relationship. Upon

---

* The female pronoun is used throughout to represent victims of battering and the male pronoun to represent the abuser although not all abusers are male, nor victims female.

When Marriages Fail
© 2006 by The Haworth Press, Inc. All rights reserved.
doi:10.1300/5562_07

further inquiry, it was clear that Margot's depression was at least a function of being in a long-term abusive relationship with several episodes of danger-ous violence. The inexperienced and/or uninformed therapist might assume that one of the goals of therapy would be to help Margot prepare to leave the relationship. However, like most battered women entering psychotherapy, Margot's goal was to get help in ending the violence but not to end the rela-tionship. Any investment on the therapist's part to encourage her to leave Tim would almost certainly result in her terminating therapy.

Issues of divorce and separation need to be considered from a dif-ferent perspective when working with couples affected by domestic violence. It is not that divorce is not common among those couples. In fact, there is some evidence that, in North America, a substantial per-centage of abusive marriages end in divorce. Bowlus and Seitz (2002) reported that in Canada, women "who experienced high severity abuse in a first marriage have a divorce rate of 75 percent" (p. 8). Lo-gan, Walker, Horvath, and Leukefeld (2003) conducting a search of court records of a random sample of divorcing couples in an urban Kentucky county found 20 percent of cases mentioning spousal vio-lence.

Certainly there is a relationship between being involved in an abu-sive relationship and making a decision to divorce. However, the goals of the therapy and the demeanor of the therapist in dealing with these issues must be considered separately.

THE APPROPRIATENESS OF SYSTEMS APPROACHES IN DOMESTIC VIOLENCE CASES

One of the dilemmas faced by the systems-trained clinician is that treatment of couples who are experiencing severe domestic violence must not be allowed to proceed in a couples modality. While there is some disagreement among experts about this issue (see for example Geffner, Barrett, and Rossman, 1995), the general consensus among leaders in the field is that it is inappropriate to work in a conjoint mo-dality with couples experiencing domestic violence. The most salient reason for this is that by working systemically, even the most careful therapist may subtly communicate that both partners are co-responsi-ble for the violence. Because there is strong evidence that domestic violence is solely a disorder of the abuser, attributing co-responsibil-ity to the victim contributes to furthering the cycle of violence.

On the one hand, abusers chronically attribute causality of their abusive behaviors and for the unfortunate things that happen to them to others. Co-responsibility for the victim would therefore be interpreted by the abuser as confirmation of their basic belief that the victim is in fact wholly responsible for the violence. In addition, since victims have the tendency to blame themselves, attribution of co-responsibility could contribute to the victims' belief system that the violence is indeed their fault.

There is evidence that conjoint work is simply not effective in stopping abusive behavior. Jacobson, Gottman, Waltz, Rushe, Babcock and Holtzworth-Munroe (1994) demonstrated in a laboratory setting that an individual's abusive behaviors were unrelated to the behaviors of his partner, whether they be conflict-engaging, conflict-lessening, or simply conflict-avoidant. Thus, focusing on the relational issues cannot be effective in stopping abusive behavior. There is also some concern that focusing on real relational issues in a couple for which violence continues to exist may exacerbate the danger to the victim.

Thus, the intervention that every first-year family therapy student is entreated *not* to do, is actually the treatment of choice when couples who are violent present for conjoint therapy, i.e., separating the couple for treatment purposes. Referral to a treatment group for individuals with issues of abuse is the most appropriate treatment for the abuser. Working individually with the victim is also recommended. (See Harway & Hansen, 2004, for an elaboration of assessment and treatment issues in working with this population.)

For the therapist working with the victim, developing and rehearsing a safety plan is a typical early focus of therapy. Working on issues of empowerment usually is a major focus of the middle stage of therapy. Here the therapist is challenged to follow the client as she often alternates between a wish to leave the relationship and a desire to remain in the relationship but to keep it violence-free. For the therapist to encourage her to separate from or divorce the batterer is ineffective and may result in her leaving therapy.

Moreover, leaving an abusive relationship has been shown repeatedly to increase the danger to the victim. For example, Wilson and Daly (1993) reported that when compared to couples who stayed together, separation resulted in a six-fold increase in homicide risk to the victim. The National Crime Victimization Survey indicated that separated women were three times more likely to be assaulted than divorced women, and this proportion increased to twenty-five times more likely to be assaulted than married women (Bachman & Saltzman, 1995). The National Violence Against Women Survey (Tjaden & Thoennes, 2000) also showed that sexual assault was more likely to occur following separation/divorce.

WORKING WITH THE ABUSE SURVIVOR IN THERAPY

We met Margot at the beginning of the chapter. Recall that Margot's clinical symptoms could be directly related to her being involved in a violent relationship but that her goals upon entering therapy were unrelated to issues of divorce and/or separation. Margot came for weekly psychotherapy. She described many violent episodes with her husband over several months of therapy. After developing a safety plan (see Harway, 2000) which included deciding upon issues such as where to go to avoid the worst of the next violent episode, what to take with her, and what precautions to take, we rehearsed the plan with multiple variations. These included (1) how to get out of the house if she was in the bedroom and Tim was in the living room; if she was in the yard and Tim was in the garage; or if she was in the kitchen and Tim was in the living room, and (2) how to make sure that the children were with her.

In therapy we also rehearsed how to let Tim know that she was taking a "time out" and that she would return when the violence was over. This was so as not to contribute to his abandonment issues which often triggered his violent episodes and which could make the current episode more serious. Margot successfully weathered several violent episodes in a six-month period. While the episodes did not seem to be getting more violent, she was getting increasingly concerned because Tim now seemed to be targeting the children as well. As the therapist, I had to call Child Protective Services on two occasions to report the violence, but the agency quickly closed their investigations.

One day Margot entered our therapy session announcing that this time she had had enough and wanted to pursue a divorce. Tim's behavior had taken a turn for the worse and he had threatened to kill her and the children. While he had made such comments before, this time she believed that he was serious. She had mentioned divorce before but this was the first time that she seemed likely to follow through with it. Unlike most battered women who vacillate back and forth about wanting to leave their abuser, Margot seemed determined. Also, unlike many others, she knew that she had to carefully develop a plan to end the relationship without further endangering herself or the children. She was aware of the statistics of increased danger to women who left their abusive spouses and did not want to suffer a similar fate.

From that point on, we spent some time in each therapy session contributing to the development of her plan. Margot had a close friend from high school (Janet) who lived in a remote part of West Virginia. Using money that Margot had been carefully hiding from Tim over a period of several years, Janet purchased a small house for Margot and the children, but she kept the house in her own name. Janet also began to scout for a used car, a company that would hire Margot sight unseen, and a school for the children. Because Margot's parents had died some years earlier and she had been an only child, there was no extended family to help with developing this plan.

Margot and I rehearsed her departure and discussed the pluses and minuses of pursuing it, including possible legal repercussions for her. Because I was concerned about the transition, I found several competent psychotherapists to whom I was able to refer Margot. Margot was also able to save a small amount of money that she could use during the transitional period. When all of the elements were in place, Margot said that was ready. In order to protect me, she did not tell me ahead of time that she and the children were going. She did call me when she had reached her destination to let me know that she and the children were safe. She also called me two years later to tell me that she had obtained a divorce, full custody of the children, and that Tim was still unaware of her location.

Margot has been luckier than most. She has not had to confront the largely unsupportive nature of the legal system and she has been able to recreate a life for herself.

Consider now the case of Suzanne. Like Margot, Suzanne has young children, is involved in a violent relationship, and after two years of agonizing about how she can change herself to make the violence stop, she realizes that her husband Peter's violence is unlikely to remit unless he gets some help. She has begged him to consult a therapist and/or to go to AA. She has left him on three occasions and each time he briefly sought help. He even enrolled in a group for abusive men. However, each time she returned home, he quickly went back to his old ways. Recently she reported that they had

had a particularly ugly fight and that the children had been terrified. Her daughter Renee, age eight, had witnessed the fight. This time, when I called CPS, they decided to act. As more information emerges about the long-term impact on children exposed to violence, many child abuse authorities are taking action when contacted about situations involving partner violence. Suzanne and Peter were required to attend a parenting class and Peter was sent to an anger management group. Suzanne continued in therapy with me during this time.

When his fifty-two weeks of mandated group were up, Peter emerged more abusive and controlling than ever, except this time, he knew how to behave so as to be just under the radar of interested authorities. Often, when interventions focus solely on controlling anger, participants emerge with the underlying pathology virtually intact but more efficient at behaving in ways that, on the surface at least, have social approbation. Now, Peter demanded that Suzanne cease her therapy with me contending that I was one of those therapists who were intent on destroying good marriages. Suzanne, wanting to placate him, agreed to seek out a different therapist.

A year later, Suzanne contacted me in tears. She had once again left Peter, had discontinued her work with the other therapist and now wanted to start therapy with me again. She told me that this time, she was intent on seeking a divorce. However, she was concerned that Peter was suicidal and afraid that he would follow through on this threat if she pursued the divorce. Because of her concern for Peter's safety, she once again returned to him. After three months of unremitting abuse, she consulted an attorney, rented an apartment and filed for divorce. As she pursues this process, she is shocked to discover that she must share custody of the children with Peter. This will mean constant contact with him as they continue to make joint decisions about the children. Moreover, she has found that it will be difficult to collect any of the assets the two of them have generated over the course of their marriage as Peter has successfully hidden anything of value and shows instead a mountain of unpaid bills. She feels that the legal system has failed her and that instead of attaining the peace she had so fervently hoped for, she will be legally required to continue a relationship with Peter. Early evidence has already shown that this relationship will continue to be an abusive one and that she will need to continue to subject herself to it if she wishes her children to maintain a relationship with their father and if she intends to behave according to the law. Needless to say, it is a terrible dilemma and she rails against the injustice of it whenever I see her. Meanwhile, the situation is such that rather than focusing on her own growth and healing, she remains emotionally entangled in the relationship with Peter.

Another case hedging around issues of abuse and separation/divorce was that of Maribella. She was a late middle-age woman who had been separated sixteen years from her abusive husband John. He was a government employee and had excellent health benefits. Since Maribella had a variety of chronic illnesses, which would preclude her from obtaining her own insurance, the couple had remained married so that Maribella could remain on John's insurance. They share a grown son, Theo, who had subsequently married and was the father of three children. Both grandparents adored the grandchildren and spent as much time as they could with them.

The family situation was complicated because Maribella refused to see her son and grandchildren when John was visiting, and John would not go there when Maribella visited. The holidays were particularly difficult for everyone. In therapy, Maribella still demonstrated the scars of sixteen years of extreme verbal and psychological abuse. The fact that she has been separated for such a long time had taken away little of the pain. In therapy we focused on rebuilding her self-esteem. However, progress on issues of empowerment and progress was slow.

Unlike physical abuse, the impact of psychological abuse is difficult to see but often is more deeply felt. Perhaps this is because, since there is no physical evidence of abuse, it is easier for the victim to continue taking responsibility for it. There is some evidence that victims of psychological and emotional abuse have a more difficult time in recovery. In Maribella's case, her recovery was complicated by the fact that she remained legally married to John and dependent on him for her physical well-being (through the health insurance).

AUTHOR'S REFLECTIONS ON THE POSTURE OF THE THERAPIST

Therapy with couples affected by domestic violence is unlike any other kind of clinical work. The neutral stance of the therapist is often challenged by the need to take an advocacy position to protect the client. Traditional training, which focuses on providing appropriate therapeutic boundaries and limiting therapeutic involvement to the four walls of the therapy room is often challenged by the realities of working with victims of violence. These clients, like Margot, may put therapists in uncomfortable positions in order to keep themselves and their children safe. When Margot began to speak about disappearing into "the hills of West Virginia" and taking her children with her, as a therapist, I struggled with my responsibilities vis-à-vis the legal system. Would her plan be considered kidnapping? In some jurisdictions, battered women have been arrested for doing just that. And yet the reality of Margot's life and that of her children suggested that it was extremely dangerous for them to stay in the situation in which they were living. Margot was aware of my ambivalence regarding her intended actions and it was for that reason that she remained vague about her intentions to follow through and did not advise me of the timing of her departure.

When battered women that I am working with call me, it is often with the request that I not return a call to their home (they do not want their partners to know they are seeing me). Some women have left me the phone number of a friend. They often call me from the friend's location and ask me to return calls only to that number. Some of these women have had to use third-party intermediaries to set up appointment times. Likewise, trusted friends have had to act as intermediaries in a number of situations. Were I to keep the strict therapeutic boundaries with which I was trained and which I employ with most of my (nonabused) clients, I would be doing these clients a disservice. I have had to learn a whole new way of being therapeutic with abused clients, a role that is more proactive and that takes more of an advocacy stance. I also have to keep in mind that a key part of my role is the duty to protect my client—to the best of my ability. I have managed to do ethically and legally responsible work throughout this process, but sleep has not always come easily.

On the plus side, seeing an abused woman "wake up from a long sleep" and find her own voice again is very rewarding. It is even more exciting when her partner is willing to seek his own treatment and the relationship which emerges is a satisfying one for both parties. This does not happen often enough for my taste, but then I have always been an idealist!

REFERENCES

Bachman, R., & Saltzman, L.E. (1995). *Violence against women: Estimates from the redesigned survey.* (Bureau of Justice Statistics Special Report NJC 154348).Washington, DC: U.S. Department of Justice.

Bowlus, A.J., & Seitz, S.N. (2002). Domestic violence, employment and divorce. Working Paper No. 1007, Department of Economics, Queen's University, Kingston, Ontario, Canada. (Forthcoming, International Economic Review.)

Geffner, R., Barrett, M.J., & Rossman, B.R. (1995). Domestic violence and sexual abuse: Multiple systems perspectives. In R.H. Mikesell, D.D. Lusterman, & S.H. McDaniel (Eds.), *Integrating family therapy: Handbook of family psychology and systems theory* (pp. 501-517). Washington, DC: APA Books.

Harway, M. (2000). Families experiencing violence. In W.C. Nichols, M.A. Pace-Nichols, D.S. Becvar, & A.Y. Napier (Eds.), *Handbook of family development and intervention.* New York: John Wiley & Sons.

Harway, M., & Hansen, M. (2004). *Spouse abuse: Assessing and treating battered women, batterers, and their children,* 2nd ed. Sarasota, FL: Professional Resource Press.

Jacobson, N.S., Gottman, J.M., Waltz, J., Rushe, R., Babcock, J., & Holtzworth-Munroe, A. (1994). Affect, verbal content, and psychophysiology in the argument of couples with a violent husband. *Journal of Consulting and Clinical Psychology, 62,* 982-988.

Logan, T.K., Walker, R., Horvath, L.H., & Leukefeld, C. (2003). Divorce, custody, and spousal violence: A random sample of circuit court docket records. *Journal of Family Violence, 18*(5), 269-279.

Tjaden, P., & Thoennes, N. (2000, February). Prevalence and consequences of male-to-female and female-to-male intimate partner violence as measured by the National Violence Against Women survey. *Violence Against Women, 6*(2), 142-161.

Wilson, M. & Daly, M. (1993, Spring) Spousal homicide risk and estrangement. *Violence and Victims, 8*(1), pp. 3-16.

Chapter 8

Children's Voices in the Midst of Parental Breakup: A Qualitative Study of Trauma in "Ordinary" Families

Wencke J. Seltzer

Tribute to William C. Nichols

It is with great pleasure I contribute to this book in honor of Bill Nichols. I remember the first time we met at the IFTA congresses in Israel more than a dozen years ago. I saw you as a Giant, a tall, distinguished man, with white hair, and a kind, but distinct and determined face. I knew the two of us would be working together for many years as officers on the executive board of IFTA! I was delighted, but your mighty being also instilled a sense of apprehension in me. Would I be able to handle this great, powerful, insightful, orderly and professionally competent man? We shared and alternated roles as editors of the International Connection *newsletter and presidents of IFTA.*

As a team, we accomplished several world family therapy congresses! I appreciated your help. Later, when you became president, I knew IFTA was in good hands. You saved it many times from potential lethal injury. At the IFTA congress in Oslo, we had the opportunity to visit with you and Mary Anne at my summer cabin by the Oslo fjord. We loved being there with the two of you, serving you fresh fish from the fjord! Bill, you are a giant HUMAN BEING. Thank you!

Some of the work reported here has been conducted by a multidisciplinary team at a Family Guidance Clinic in Norway. The team included the following family therapists: Geir Vik, social worker; Per Midtstigen, psychologist; Aagot Stigen Sørhagen, pedagogue; Torbjørg Rønning, nurse; and Kari Lien, head of office affairs. External participants included: Michael R. Seltzer, PhD, cultural anthropologist; and Wencke J. Seltzer, PhD, clinical psychologist. Aspects of this work were presented at The Nordic Congress on Family Therapy, Iceland, August, 2002. This chapter is based partially on the material from this study and conceptualized by the author.

This study focuses on children's experiences while their parents are in the process of divorce. Although this may be seen as an "out of the ordinary family event," separation and divorce occur with great frequency in today's Western societies. Many children report this experience as a time of crises and trauma. Even though family disruption and reorganization occur commonly, the statistics representing such events do not speak to the broader psychological and emotional consequences that such separations place upon the family system— the children as well as their parents.

Follow-up studies of children who have experienced parental separations have been reported by Jacobson (1978), Rosenthal (1979), Wallerstein and Lewis (1998), and Hetherington and Kelly (2002). Hingst (1981) addressed the child's own views on divorce. Although therapists, teachers, and other helpers know from their work with children that the actual separation may be experienced as devastating to the child, it appears that more systematic studies of these situations are called for and would benefit the helping fields.

Our team looked at divorcing parents, as well as other family constellations, which presented themselves to a clinical setting in Norway. The focus was on what the children had to say about their experiences of their families' breakup. Only children who were residing in the divorcing families were included in the study. We focused on their feelings, thoughts, social interactions, and the contextual and structural issues of the families at the time of the separation. To the knowledge of the team, these children did not have any prior psychological or psychiatric histories, school issues, social or peer problems, or other mental health issues. Our clinical impressions of the children were that, prior to their parents' marital separations, they appeared to have functioned well physically, intellectually, emotionally, cognitively, and socially.

THE CLINICAL SETTING

Family Guidance Clinics in Norway offer clinical services primarily to adults, and they do not, as a rule, include children in the therapy. Children commonly receive clinical services in separate Child and Adolescent Guidance Clinics. A review of the annual reports for a number of Child and Adolescent Guidance Clinics for the year 2000 indicated approximately eighty percent of referrals of children identified specific problems associated with parental separation and divorce. These children often reported serious feelings of sadness at the time of their parents' separations and many appeared to have suffered a loss of executive functions of their parents. It appeared that the parents were so burdened with their relational breakdown that they were emotionally unavailable as responders to their children's needs for care and support. It also appeared that the children had not been able to share their fears and feelings of abandonment with adults in their lives during this period of family disruption and that many of these emotional issues may remain unresolved for these children for years.

Methodological Premises Involved in the Study

Although the initial referral of all of the families in the study concerned the adults, our team included the children in the interviews as a result of their parents' requests for help. The children were seen either alone or with their family. The data for the study were based on the narratives of the children themselves—their expressions through drawings and words. The interviews were videotaped, transcribed, and categorized following qualitative ethnographic research methods.

An additional aspect of our study involved the presence of a clinical team observing behind a one-way mirror. These team members functioned as discussants and observers for the therapists, prior to, during, and after the talks with the children. The team was helpful in offering reflections on "internal" and "external" perspectives. For example, if a child expressed feelings of social shame (common in small communities)—a feeling that they were the only ones in the world experiencing a family breakup—the therapists in the interview would watch closely the subjective words of the child, making sure that her or his concerns were heard, while the team reflected on the child's experience of this in the community. The team may observe that the child actually shared similar feelings with other "normal" families and children who had separated. At times an observing team member might be invited into the interview to share reflections. This team member might function to normalize the child's feelings by making common what may have been felt as shameful (Seltzer, 1985a,b).

The goal of this study was to focus on the exploration of meaning as it *evolves* in the therapy process. A particular challenge for this type of study, particularly in working with children, was to search for *meaning attribution* as it was experienced by the child. Confidentiality, according to ethical and legal statutes were followed closely.

FAMILY DYNAMICS DURING SEPARATION AND DIVORCE: A CHILD'S FEELINGS OF HELPLESSNESS

Many parents, while expressing concern for their children during this family crisis, also reported feelings of helpless in knowing what to do. These experiences for both children and parents can be exacerbated by what we observed as a pattern of *emotional infection.* This concept described the underlying conflict that we observed in the deterioration of the parental relationship as it spread throughout the family system. It tended to inhibit the children's abilities to cope and also provided a powerful model depicting how conflict was to be resolved by adults in their relationships.

In this study we wanted to hear what the children had to say and focus on their *feelings* that may often go unexpressed. Many family systems have internal themes that are sometimes mythical (Seltzer, 1989), or as I have referred to them elsewhere, "silent stories" (Seltzer, 1994, 2003, 2004). We observed these around issues of infidelity in which children were aware of this on the part of one of their parents, apparently before the other parent was informed. These children experienced a sort of double bind in which their feelings of anger and despair left them feeling guilty and as participants in the betrayal.

In my practice I have encountered many such "impossible" silenced stories. Some such issues have had content that was only partially "conscious" to the child, thus making it difficult to grasp and verbalize at a cognitive level in therapy. In these cases, nonverbal approaches, such as drawing and telling imaginary stories were helpful (Seltzer, 1985b, 2003, 2004).

Many of the couples seen at this preseparation stage tried to avoid the expression of hurtful feelings toward their partners, often by withdrawing emotionally and limiting communication. The couples reported experiencing sadness, remorse, and grief. It appeared that this stage of emotional separation occurred before the actual physical separation. Thus, these children may have been exposed to a silenced and "toxic" emotional climate in their families for lengthy periods (perhaps years) prior to their parents' actual separation. We know little about how the children sense or process these early experiences, but in therapy we see that this emotional child/parent accessibility makes a difference.

Also in this stage the divorcing couple is struggling to deal with practical issues such as moving, where and with whom the children shall live, where they will go to school, finances, finding jobs, and proper housing. This period of relative preoccupation by parents in the midst of the crisis may appear to be confusing for the children. They may not know what to expect and they may feel unsettled about issues that directly impact their daily lives.

Often the parents' disclosure of their plan to divorce is received by the children as a shock. Ducibella (1995a,b) and Westberg, Nelson, and Piercy (2002) reported on various problematic issues concerning parents disclosure of divorce to their children. Often the children may feel deceived that their parents had not been "truthful" with them earlier. For some children, their insecurity and fear may become encapsulated and silenced within them.

In my practice I have seen these issues masked by depression and low self-esteem in older children and young adults. I have observed an exaggerated fear by these children of becoming attached and trusting others in relationships (Seltzer, 2004). A twenty-three-year-old female told me that she ended the relationship with her boyfriend because she was "afraid he might leave me." I asked if he had indicated that he might do so and she said: "No, but we are getting really close, and I know I would not be able to live through a breakup." In this case we spent the next few sessions working through the her traumatic experience of her own parents' divorce. Weitoft, Hjern, Haglund, and Rosén (2003) reported, from a Swedish study, how practical, economic, and psychological problems follow children living with a single parent subsequent to parental divorce.

THE APPLICATION OF TRAUMA THEORY TO CHILDREN'S EXPERIENCES OF THEIR PARENTS' DIVORCE

In my experience I have found that the research and clinical literature on trauma, crises, and catastrophes offers a helpful theoretical model (see Esser, 2002; Mohr, 2002; Weaver, 2002; Zubenko & Capozzoli, 2002) for understanding children of divorce. As I have discussed, these children experienced trauma, a loss of mastery, and, consequently, helplessness in these family crises. Traumatic theory describes symptoms of fear, anxiety, emotional/cognitive incompatibility (a term I will elaborate on later in this paper), increased arousal, reexperience of previous emotional issues, irritability, poor concentration and insomnia, fear of separation and loss, school problems, somatic reactions, and depersonalization and partial loss of memory. We know that many of these symptoms are present in children during the time of their parents' divorce. Of course these are in a different context than conditions external to the family, e.g., war, natural disasters, fires, floods, and accidents. Of course, the context is even more dramatic when the trauma is seen as "self-inflicted," i.e., coming from *within* the family. While parents would protect their children from external disasters, the marital breakup disrupts the family normal protective mechanisms.

Cognitive and Emotional Incompatibility As Part of Family-Inflicted Trauma

In the child's experience of divorce the most highly esteemed adults—their parents—have instigated disaster upon the family system. This awareness may be difficult for the child to "digest," both cognitively and emotionally. It is difficult for a child to integrate her or his emotional love and admiration for parents in the midst of cognitive recognition and experience of parental conflict and animosity.

The term *cognitive dissonance* was introduced in Leon Festinger's studies on the role of "group belonging" (Festinger, 1950). These studies identified inconsistencies between one's beliefs (perceptions) and one's experiences (overt behaviors). Festinger demonstrated that perceptions of dissonance generally end with the moderation of both perceptual and behavioral components, and sometimes with a change of attitudes. In working with children of divorcing parents we often encounter psychological mechanisms similar to those reported by Festinger. However, we have observed in clinical situations that the children's experiences of *emotional/cognitive* incompatibility differ from Festinger's *perceptual/behavioral inconsistency*. I have conceptualized this situation, in which components do not give way to cognitive or emotional factors, with the term *emotional/cognitive incompatibility*. Such incompatibility may leave the subject in a state of either temporary or long lasting psychological arrest and immobility, i.e., he or she unable to move forward or backward.

When this "incompatibility" occurs in a child whose parents are divorcing, the child may be experiencing betrayal of the family, whether it be through violence, infidelity, wanting to be free from responsibility, preferring another family instead of the one to which the child belongs, or threatening suicide. These situations may reflect the following dynamics:

1. The child may develop confusion, meaning that neither the child's emotions, nor her or his cognitions (perceptions, thinking), are able to explain the situation. Although the child's "ideal" image of the parent may be held on to, it can no longer be viewed as compatible with what is actually happening within the parental relationship and the family.

2. For certain children the observed traumatic event may be so noxious (i.e., violent) that she or he is unable to grasp and incorporate it in one's cognitive experience. The child may then experience a splitting of cognition and emotion, alternating in adherence to one *or* the other. Some children may alternate between the perspectives of the mother and those of the father. I have observed in court cases reports describing the child as unreliable because she or he reported one perspective when with one parent and another view while with the other parent. The two are simply not compatible for the child.

3. Young children may not be able to recognize that the emotions and thoughts/perceptions are really two aspects of one parent. This may cause the child to develop depersonalization and/or deteriorated memory.

4. For the child, this cognitive/emotional incompatibility involves a splitting of the communication between emotion (the limbic system) and cognition (the prefrontal cortex), with the result that the child, at a later stage, may need help reintegrating associative activity between these functions.

5. This splitting may lead to a partial or total dissociation for the child such that some components that are present at the time of the event may be partially erased from her or his conscious memory.

6. This dissociation becomes a protective mechanism that "shakes off" unacceptable and threatening feelings. In the brain, the amygdala (in the limbic system) serves as a gatekeeper and will not allow similar threats to reach the child. At that point, painful events may be stored and protected in a state of dissociated amnesia. If this state occurs, specific therapeutic interventions are necessary to restore the individual's full memory.

Many children who experience trauma associated with divorce may carry deeply buried, yet "silent" and subclinical depressions (sadness), for years within themselves. Clinicians often find such "silent depression" in therapy with children who have been left by one parent, or who have observed family violence or other forms of domestic abuse. A team member observed a child who had "discovered" the infidelity of one of her parents. As this parent also expressed suicidal wishes in the presence of the children (possibly as a way to gain sympathy from the children), one of the team members observed: "From this day on, these children will never again believe in Santa Claus." In these situations, we see clear conflicts of interests between the parental and child subsystems—the children are wishing that the family will stay together while the parents are wanting to separate.

Family Structural Power Issues

As therapists, when we work with a family system, we need to recognize that we are dealing with two family structures that are ruled by differential judicial conditions simultaneously. In the divorce process the power is held clearly by adults with the children feeling helpless. A child is born into her or his biological family with an immediate and permanently defined role and status—it is a life-long membership. The child's parents, on the on hand, are linked by voluntary choice to be in a relationship with a legal blessing that allows them to continue or terminate that relationship.

FINDINGS OF THE STUDY:
THE CHILDREN'S VOICES

Issues Regarding the Change of Schools and Friends

The following are excerpts from a dialogue between two sisters whose parents have just divorced, Karen twelve, and Maren fourteen, two therapists, and a clinical/research team behind the mirror.

MAREN: They are in gangs, you know [referring to children in their new school] . . . and they have secrets. [Both girls looked very sad, and there is a notable pause.]

T1: So this is an unfamiliar situation for you to be in?

MAREN: Yeah, but *we* did that in the old school too, . . . we are in a way not inside the gang, we were in our old school [barely audible voice, Karen nods, confirming her sister's statement].

T1: So, the new school seems to be a little bit like the old one? [Both girls nod; heads bend down.]

T2: So, do you get to be in some of the gangs then? Are you picked out by someone there to take part? Or, can you choose yourselves, who you want to join?

MAREN: No, I am just there, in a way inside, but not *really*. But in class they have talked about that it is *not allowed* to lock someone out, so, if we go to a gang [group], and they say we cannot be in with them, that is *not* allowed in the school.

Commentary: In this vignette we see how the children are struggling with issues of belonging in the new school situation. The issue of being "taken in" and included by the other children is experienced by the sisters as a strain, a real challenge. In the last sentence, we see how the teacher has exerted authority and issued a rule that no one shall be excluded, may help them feel a little more secure. We can sense the stress the children experience here in the midst of being uprooted from their former school, friends, and family. In the following exchange the sisters talk about wanting to commute and go back to their old school. As discussed previously, the children had little power and were moved to the new school against their will.

T1: If you were to choose at this point, how would that be for you?

KAREN: I would choose both schools.

T1: Both?

KAREN: Yeah [drawing a deep breath, changing her sitting position]. But, I'd rather be back in MY school. For, you see, I could get some new friends there [the old school]. But, it's very difficult to think that I am not there anymore . . . all *my* friends [tears].

T1: Yeah, I can see that [other therapist nods in a confirming way]. So have you lost contact with your friends at the old school? Or were you thinking you have to cut the contact?

KAREN: No, I'll never cut them out. I call them sometimes.

T1: Yes?

T2: Do you meet them sometimes too?

KAREN: Yeah . . . when I go for music training. And I am playing today, in a contest [with her old group].

T2: So, now you have *more* friends, some new and some of the old ones?

Both girls nod and look somewhat surprised, looking at each other.

Commentary: In this dialogue we see the ambivalence regarding their sense of belonging with peers and how the conversation moves from all negative, toward alternative considerations. They are beginning a process of reorientation in which the issue of losing contact with "old" friends changes and they are able to see that they may continue to be with old friends too. This discussion about school and peer issues continued, and in the process, the acknowledgment of the pain and uncertainty they felt were viewed by the therapists as perfectly legitimate and natural. The girls eventually talked a great deal about emotional issues as well, related to feelings of losses that were inflicted on them despite their wishes to keep their family together.

Issues of Fitting in with Mother and Father in Separate Households

The girls have indicated that it is difficult to talk about their feelings related to the family dissolution with their parents. It was easier for them to begin by talking about more external problems, such as the change of schools.

T1: We were wondering what it might be that keeps you from talking about those things that make you feel sad [in the family]?

KAREN: It's like there are things we cannot talk about, . . . because . . . because . . . they might turn sour [tearful].

T1: So that might be a hindrance? [Karen nods in agreement] . . . Or they might feel sad and that there might be things they want to keep to themselves?

MAREN: Yes. Mom usually asks us if we are angry about something. She doesn't understand all the time, but. . . .

T1: Does she get an answer from you then?

MAREN: Not all of it.

Commentary: As these interviews proceed, the children learned that the father has a relationship with another woman, and that this is still a subject not openly talked about in the family. We feel that the girls are protecting their parents, and perhaps themselves, from facing this issue. Maren seems to feel she has to protect her younger sister. In other conversations the children tell us about their secretly having listened to their parents quarrels at home, even though the parents tried to protect them from their anger. They also identified their feelings of betrayal. We have encountered many such situations in therapy in which children knew about issues or secrets but were seen by the adults as ignorant of them. These are the "silent stories" I mentioned earlier. Finally, the girls talked about losing touch with their father, who they described as "working late, and who needs to rest when we are visiting at his house."

The Children Express Their Own Feelings

T2: So, how do you yourselves feel, and what do you do with your feelings?

MAREN: We listen to music, [she has tears in her eyes] and then some tears fall, and I try to stop. [She continues to tell us about the text in the music, where the singer tells a story about loss of anchorage.]

KAREN: I am angry! I scream to my MOM. Don't you understand that, I scream [raises her voice]. I AM ANGRY!

T2: So, when you say this to your mother, she wants to know why?

KAREN: Yeah, it's like they think [meaning "pretend"] there is some problem between me and my friends, but it isn't. It's *them*! [her parents].

T2: Can you say that to them?

KAREN: Yeah, but she, Mom, she understands [us], but it is just very hard! [Both girls have tears rolling down their faces again, implicitly referring to the "silent theme."]

T1: So, what do you do when you feel this way?

K: I am very angry, and I want to destroy things! Want to tear paper apart, and destroy it! Like if I am angry at MOM! Make the paper crumble into nothing!

T2: So you tear it and curl it together!

KAREN: Um-uh. I throw it around, all over!

T2: And?

KAREN: Then I scream out loud! Tear apart and scream and scream! Loud!

T2 TO MAREN: Do you join in too [somewhat humourous tone]?

MAREN: Yeah [small glimpse of a smile].

KAREN: She [Mom] is angry inside, but she cannot show it! [Maren nods to confirm.]

Commentary: In this dialogue we hear about Karen's experience of incompatibility between emotion and cognition. She expresses confusion about what is happening. One minute she is *angry* (emotion) at her mother, the next minute she *knows* (cognition) that the mother really understands them, because: "Mom really understands us, because she feels like us herself"(implicitly referring to the silent theme having to do with infidelity). At another point, it appears they feel the mother should *show* her feelings; perhaps that would confirm their own feelings as well? As they talk about how their mother understands them, but cannot show it or talk about it, this cognitively derived distinction between anger (emotion) and speaking (cognitive function), may actually help them sort things out.

The therapists (T1 and T2) talk together, in front of the girls, mentioning how "normal" it is for persons to feel really angry and sad when they are in the middle of such a situation. The girls seemed to listen very carefully to this parallel conversation between the therapists.

KAREN: Mama has said that too, that it is normal!
The therapists nod in agreement.

Commentary: As the girls continue, it occurs to the team that their angry feelings are somewhat overwhelming [and confusing], and that they may wonder what is really "normal." It seemed important in this situation to call their feelings "natural." Gradually the girls seem to feel more comfortable with their mother's position (her choice of not pulling the girls into her own dilemma). They seem to be identified with her while at the same time feeling sad that their contact with their father may be less than satisfactory. Maren feels somewhat responsible for the well-being of the father and tries to be of support to him by spending more time with him, even though he sleeps when she is there.

T1: But, even though this [feelings of anger] is not unusual, it is still sad?

KAREN: Yeah, I go out. And walk, and wish I were not here.

T1: So, sometimes you feel you were not here?

KAREN: Yes. I walk and feel really angry.

Pause [Both girls tearful].

KAREN: I want everything to be like it was, my old school, my friends and everything! And I am angry at both Mom and Dad. I don't want them to separate.

T2: That is how you feel?

KAREN: Yeah, because it's like they just walk out in different directions, while Maren and I are left behind, standing back, while they walk straight on, away from everything, and decide because they are adult, and we? We are *just children!*

T1: So, you are left behind, you mean?

KAREN: Yes! It's like we are left in another *land,* while Mama and Papa, they walk off in different directions, and we are left at the corner, and *just stand there!*

Commentary: Here we feel the girls are talking about the liminal situation they feel left in, i.e., neither here nor there. They express clearly their vulnerability in this "in-between" stage. The statement about wishing she were not here may represent suicidal thoughts.

They express feelings of being estranged, and again they feel help-less. Do they go Mama's way . . . Papa's way?. . . . No way?

KAREN: It is like we are not a regular family anymore. We are parted up, Mama one part, Papa another part, and us children a third part. [Karen makes a mathematical computation here, and ends up with the conclusion that the parents should not decide, because if they could have voted according to democratic principles, the children should have had as much to say in this situation as the adults! Con-clusion: The situation is not FAIR!]

Commentary: Our thinking is that these children are at a develop-mental stage in which morals and fairness are very important issues.

Children Drawing and Telling Their Stories

KAREN: It's like we divided into parts.

Here the therapists asked the girls to draw pictures of how they felt. (Because of confidentiality, I have chosen not to reprint the children's drawings.) Their pictures were dramatic, showing loneliness and how their close milieu was ruptured. One symbolic picture was of a big, sturdy tree being sawed down, and children crying. Another picture was of the children hanging by their fingertips from the edge of a bridge, barely able to hold on, over a fierce stream of water. Up from the water came a shark, ready to swallow them. Their parents were also on the bridge, both standing there, helpless, and watching the dangerous situation for their children. The children explained that their parents were not able to do anything to protect them from the dangerous situation. Some of their other drawings included sad sto-ries of their senses of loss about leaving their pets when they moved. As the children continued to draw pictures the process seemed to help them reorient themselves and take a more active part in their new life situations. Gradually they were able to reflect on what had happened to their parents, in more realistic terms, and spoke openly about previously "silenced" issues.

An Example of a Preverbal Child's Response to Parental Conflict

In interviewing a family with three children, the youngest boy, Ola, had just learned to walk (approximately thirteen months old). He was still preverbal, but he was very attuned to sentiments in the family. After several interviews we asked the baby's brothers how he was doing. They were proud to report that he had just began to walk, but he had started a peculiar behavior.

BROTHER: He has started banging his head in the wall, on the floor, and on the table. He has blue marks on his face because of the head banging.

THERAPIST: Is he doing it on his own, or is he falling into things [by chance]?

BROTHER: No, he does it by will, and sometimes he screams and bangs his head simultaneously!

The brothers reported that their mother was really worried about him and that they had bought him a bicycle helmet to protect him from injuring himself. We asked the siblings what meaning they thought that this behavior had and they said that he did it because he was angry at his parents for quarreling. He wanted to stop them!

The little boy had come to several interviews with his parents but we had never seen this peculiar behavior before. Our impression of the child had been that he was a robust, healthy, and strong little boy. During the next session, with the entire family, the parents began to speak in a tense tone to one another, which led to a quarrel with both raising their voices. The little boy got up on his feet, "toddled" over to the wall and banged his head, very hard, against the wall several times. Both parents stopped arguing, and his mother put him on her lap. She talked softly to him, stroked his head, and he quieted down. The parents understood that he did this as a reaction to their quarrel, and to get their attention.

We have seen many situations in which children, not yet verbal, found desperate ways to express their anxiety as the adult executive level of the family became dysfunctional. We do not know how this experience was stored within the mind of the baby, and if and how it may influence the child's psychological functioning in later life. However, this case illustration speaks as evidence that even preverbal children react to parental discord (through a "reading" of sentiments in the family) with anxiety and fear. Although the head banging could be explained by theories of classical conditioning, I feel the experiential aspects of this baby's behavior, occurring in an emotionally toxic context, can offer another explanation.

AUTHOR'S REFLECTIONS ON HELPING CHILDREN EXPRESS THEIR FEELINGS IN THE THERAPY SETTING

Based on our work in the study and my own clinical experience, here are some suggestions for therapists that help children express their feelings about these family crises.

1. Let the child take her or his time in therapy. Remember, in the initial sessions, it is more of a project for the child to adjust to simply being in the room with the therapist.
2. When the child begins to speak, it is more important that the therapist listen and be attentive than focusing on the words.
3. The therapist should be truthful and straight forward with the child. Do not avoid themes that are unpleasant if the child wants to talk about them. Do not try to rid the child of sad feelings or give the impression that you can bring the parents back together.
4. Accept the child's formulations as they are presented. Never try to "improve" the child's choice of words or correct the child's way of speaking.
5. Remember, you cannot erase the trauma. Let the child know you understand. If you do not understand, ask for concrete examples. These might help you and the child share an understanding.
6. Never try to challenge a child's words or statements, they may be a novel way of leading to reoriented pathways.
7. Do not be demanding. Respect a child's lack of utterance. Talk back and forth with your co-therapist in front of the child about her or his experiences. In this way the child can be a listener or a commentator.

8. Always find something in your office to do that the child perceives as fun. Even if the child feels sad, the therapy session does not been to have an absence of humor.
9. If the child appears tired, shorten the session. This is a matter of being attentive to the child. Some children may be exhausted, others may sleep poorly.
10. Keep all of your language simple. Try to adjust your way of speaking to meet the child's developmental stage.
11. Never miss a chance to encourage the child and to let her or him know you think she or he is clever and capable of mastering her or his life. Let the child know you like her or him.
12. If you do not connect with a child, let another therapist take your place.
13. Always speak about the child's parents with respect. Never let anyone tempt you to be judgmental or critical of her or him, or anyone else in the child's family.
14. Never try to pinpoint who the child looks like, which one of the parents the child behaves like, etc. This can be devastating.
15. Make clear what you think is right and/or wrong, if asked.
16. Maintain a generous attitude toward the child. Give the child something, if you can, like a puppet, share an apple, bring her/him a set of crayons. Work together drawing houses (Seltzer, 1994, 2004).

REFERENCES

Ducibella, J.S. (1995a). *An investigation into the effects of how children are informed of their parents' divorce process decisions.* Unpublished doctoral dissertation, Florida State University, Tallahassee.

Ducibella, J.S. (1995b). Consideration of the impact of how children are informed of their parents' divorce decision: A review of the literature. *Journal of Divorce and Remarriage, 24* (3-4), 121-141.

Esser, J.A. (2002). Post traumatic stress disorder and reaction. In W.N. Zubenko & J. Capozzoli (Ed.), *Children and disasters* (pp. 85-100). New York: Oxford University Press.

Festinger, L. (1950). Laboratory experiments: The role of group belongingness. In J. G. Miller (Ed.), *Experiments in social process.* New York: McGraw Hill.

Hetherington, E.M., & Kelly J. (2002). *Divorce reconsidered.* London: W.W. Norton & Company.

Hingst, A.G. (1981). Children and divorce: The child's view. *Journal of Clinical Child Psychology, 3,* 161-164.

Jacobson, D.S. (1978). The impact of marital separation/divorce on children: III. Parent-child communication and child adjustment, and regression analysis of findings from overall study. *Journal of Divorce, 2*(2), 175-194.

Mohr, W.K. (2002). Understanding children in crisis: The developmental ecological framework. In W.N. Zubenko & J. Capozzoli (Eds.), *Children and disasters* (pp. 126-144). New York: Oxford University Press.

Rosenthal, P.A. (1979). Sudden disappearance of one parent with separation and divorce: The grief and treatment of preschool children. *Journal of Divorce, 3*(1), 43-54.

Seltzer, W.J. (1985a). Conversion disorder in childhood and adolescence: A familial/cultural approach, Part I. *Family Systems Medicine, 3*, 261-280.

Seltzer, W.J. (1985b). Conversion disorder in childhood and adolescence: Therapeutic issues. Part II. *Family Systems Medicine, 3*, 397-416.

Seltzer, W.J. (1989). Myths of destruction: A cultural approach to families in therapy. *Journal of Psychotherapy and the Family, 4*, 17-34.

Seltzer, W J. (1994). Peter Petersen's Saga (using a drawing and telling method in working with a silenced story regarding the disappearance of the boy's father). Presented at a world family therapy (IFTA) congress in Hungary. Published in the *Hungarian Family Therapy Journal*, Csakad, Gyermek, Ifusag, Budapest.

Seltzer, W.J. (2003). *Familiehemmeligheter: Tause fortellinger fra terapirommet (Family secrets: Silent stories from the therapy room)*. Oslo, Norway: Gyldendal.

Seltzer, W.J. (2004). Norwegian families from a psychocultural perspective: A challenge to therapeutic theory and practice. In J.L. Roopnarine & U. Gielen (Eds.), *Families in global perspective* (pp. 259-277). New York: Allyn & Bacon.

Thomas, C.E., Booth-Butterfield, M., & Booth-Butterfield, S. (1995). Preceptions of deception, divorce disclosures, and communication satisfaction with parents. *Western Journal of Communications, 59* (Summer), 228-245.

Wallerstein, J.S., & Lewis, J. (1998). The long-term impact of divorce on children: A first report from a 25 year study. *Family and Conciliation Courts Review, 35*(3), 368-383.

Weaver, J.D. (2002). Disaster mental health: Trauma relief, concepts, and theory. In W.N. Zubenko & J. Capozzoli (Eds.), *Children and disasters* (pp. 34-71). New York: Oxford University Press.

Weitoft, G.R., Hjern, A, Haglund B., & Rosén, M. (2003). Mortality, severe morbidity, and injury in children living with single parents in Sweden: A population-based study. *The Lancet, 361* (January 25), 44-59.

Westberg, H., Nelson, T.S., & Piercy, K.W. (2002). Disclosure of divorce plans to children: What the children have to say. *Contemporary Family Therapy 24*(4), 68-82.

Zubenko, W.N., & Capozzoli J. (2002). *Children and disasters*. New York: Oxford University Press.

Chapter 9

The Influence of Divorce on Children: A Special Focus on Iceland

Toby Sigrun Herman

Tribute to William C. Nichols

It is hard to find words that truly capture my respect and admiration for Bill Nichols. Through my professional career and my work for the International Family Therapy Association (IFTA)—as an IFTA member, board member, recording secretary and president elect—I have worked with a number of capable people, yet all fade in comparison to Bill. He is enormously bright, fair, forthright, and respectful to one and to all. Through the years Bill is the person that I have enjoyed working with the most and have learned from the most. He has always been willing to provide help, advice, collaboration, and encouragement and has never, ever asked for anything in return. Working with him independently and on teams has been an enriching experience. I have come to respect him enormously and I consider it a true privilege and an honor to have had the opportunity to work with him.

Much research concludes that divorce has negative consequences for the children. My experience in the school system in Iceland as a family and educational counselor supports this conclusion. Children and youths have increased emotional difficulty while the parents are going through the process of divorce and in the first years after it occurs. At this time the children must adapt to the new family circumstance while learning to live in a new environment without the physical presence of both parents. The children's difficulties are reflected in a decline in interest in school-related matters as well as the capacity to study.

When Marriages Fail
© 2006 by The Haworth Press, Inc. All rights reserved.
doi:10.1300/5562_09

Jóhannsson (1992) studied primary school children who had been referred to the department of psychology in Reykjavik due to difficulty in school during the school year 1989-1990. He discovered that 56 percent did not live with both their biological parents and 38 percent had been raised in a one-parent household. It is due to statistics like this and my own experience with these children that I am focusing on the influence of divorce on children and youths and two interventions that may be especially helpful in reducing the negative effects of divorce on them, namely divorce mediation and joint custody.

DIVORCE STATISTICS IN ICELAND

The timing of our concern could not be more important. Since the 1970s divorce in Iceland has increased significantly, just as it has in the United States. There also has been a progressive increase in marital separations. The increase in disrupted relationships across the past four decades can be seen in Table 9.1.

It is estimated that, in Iceland and in the United States, more than one-third of all children that are born in any given year will live primarily with one parent before they reach eighteen years of age and that a significant proportion of them will experience a remarriage of that parent. Not only divorce, but also membership in stepfamilies can be difficult for children and youths (Coffman & Roark, 1988; Heaven, 2001; Júlíusdóttir, 2001; Kristjánsson, 2003).

TABLE 9.1. Divorce and separation in Iceland by decades.

Year	Divorce	Divorce and Separation
1970	246	843
1980	441	1077
1990	479	1142
2000	545	1225

Source: Statistics Iceland, 2003.

INFLUENCE OF DIVORCE ON CHILDREN
AND YOUTHS

An unhappy marital relationship is always difficult for children. They do not understand the reasons for the unhappiness, arguments or silences of their parents. Research that has been done on the well-being of children show that divorce can be better for them than a long-term, hateful relationship between the parents (e.g., Booth & Amato, 2001). However, because research methods have been so varied it is difficult to compare research studies on the effects of divorce on children and to draw sweeping conclusions from them. Nevertheless, with care, significant information can be deduced (Grych & Fincham, 1992; Heaven, 2001; Þorgilsson & Smári, 1992).

For example, many studies have asked whether children of divorced parents have a more difficult time adjusting than children who live with both parents. These studies have focused primarily on the following:

- Outward problems such as aggression, hyperactivity, and truancy
- Internalizing symptoms such as anxiety, social isolation, and depression
- Interaction with peers
- Problems in school and learning
- The need for psychological help

The most common reaction of children of divorce seems to be internalizing symptoms, i.e., anxiety and depression along with sorrow and despair over what will become of them. Such children have a difficult time concentrating in school as well in play. They often fear that they will be rejected by the parent that they do not live with as well as losing the parent that they do live with.

Children who live in such environments show serious psychological symptoms (Grych & Fincham, 1992; Þorgilsson & Smári, 1992). Since most children do not think of their parents divorcing as a likely possibility, the decision often strikes them wth lightning force and they do not understand why their family is being forced to split up. Most children are fiercely loyal to both parents and want them to stay together (Nagy & Spark, 1984; Satir, 1985). The reactions of the children are often most intense at first, when their parents are blinded by their own emotions and their strength diminished. Often parents at that time can offer little support to their children. The long-term effects of divorce on children are more difficult to infer because so many factors intervene, yet the main conclusions of research are that children of divorced parents do in fact usually have more difficulties then other children (Grych & Fincham, 1992; Heaven, 2001; Þorgilsson & Smári, 1992).

REACTIONS OF CHILDREN, VARY WITH AGE

The effects of divorce appear to be less if the child is young when the parents divorce, and still young when the parents enter a new marriage. Young children forget this as they forget many other things and seem to have an easier time bonding to a stepparent and adapting to membership in a stepfamily (Grych & Fincham, 1992; Heaven, 2001; Kristjánsson, 2003). Nevertheless, young children can have a variety of misconceptions about the reasons for the divorce and they may blame themselves in some way for its occurrence.

School-age children are more likely to become anxious and experience grief so intense that they show psychological and physical symptoms. They can also bond intensely with the parent that they live with and stand with them on any and all issues. Much older children can protect themselves from the pressures better. They are often preoccupied with social activities outside of school and can direct their frustration and release pent up emotion and pressures there (Grych & Fincham, 1992; Heaven, 2001; Júlíusdóttir & Sigurðardottir, 2000; Kristjánsson, 2003; Þorgilsson & Smári,1992). However, with these older children one question is whether difficulties appear later on. For example, many of these children later complain of physical symptoms such as headaches and stomach problems that are indicative of pent-up emotion.

For teenagers and youths, the divorce of their parents often adds another stress factor during a time when other pressures abound. There may be gender differences. Teenage boys, especially those with attention-deficit hyperactivity disorder (ADHD), deal less effectively with the additional stress that comes with their parents divorcing. Consequently, stuck in anger and bitterness, they are more likely to get into trouble after divorce (Heaven, 2001; Kristjánsson, 2003).

Also, with males, a direct relationship exists between a limited relationship with the father and low performance in school, and this leads to low self-esteem, depression, and anger.

Girls tend to keep their pain inside rather than expressing it overtly. Their relationship with their fathers during the teenage years is extremely important. If contact with the father is minimal then girls tend to become sexually active early or avoid sexual contact later in life (Kristjánsson, 2003; Heaven, 2001).

Teenagers that seem to best deal with the stress of divorce are the ones that have managed to stay outside the conflict between the parents from the beginning and those whom the parents have allowed to remain outside it (Þorgilsson & Smári, 1992). Nevertheless, their memories of divorce remain painful and negative, and they themselves are more likely to divorce when they grow up than are children from intact marriages (Kristjánsson, 2003.)

CLINICAL INTERVENTIONS

Therapy or intervention refers to the process by which we try to work with problems in order to reduce the negative effects and prevent problems later. Divorce is almost always painful, but the deeper the prior emotional connection the more painful the divorce. Divorce can be likened to death or the loss of a loved one (Nichols & Everett, 1986; Nichols, 1988; Nichols, 1996). Although the love has diminished, the effort invested in the relationship leaves something behind. It can also be difficult to live with anger and lost hope while seeing the estranged spouse/parent living with another partner and other children. However, the bereaved family members often receive little if any support from the environment or from the family and friends of the one who has left. The bereaved are likely to hide this pain from their closest friends and family and especially so if they themselves have acquired a new family with a new stepparent.

Grych and Fincham (1992) discuss three types of intervention that are common in the United States in matters of divorce, namely therapy for the children, therapy for the parents, and systemic environmental intervention.

Treatment for children is often in groups (four to ten children) and within the school day. The children share their experiences and the group can give support to the individual and normalize the divorce or normalize the experience of divorce. The child may have an easier time expressing his or her feeling about the experience with peers than with grown ups. The school is most often a venue for this kind of therapy and thus it is possible to reach more children, especially children from the lower socioeconomic strata. The group work can be educational as well as therapeutic. Despite the popularity of this type of therapy there is still not enough research to confirm its effectiveness. School counselors are in a key position to offer this type of therapy in Iceland and to research its effectiveness in this country.

Therapy with parents is of two types. In one the focus is on the parental role, i.e., helping the parents deal with the children's behavior, maintaining a positive relationship with the children, and helping the parents create a spirit of cooperation. The other type of therapy is aimed at trying to help the parents adjust to the divorce. The focus is then on the personal problems of the parents more than on the parental roles. The therapy is usually group therapy and offered by churches, health centers, and schools. Little is known about the effectiveness of this kind of treatment. Apparently, it helps mothers adjust personally after a divorce, but may not improve their parental skills.

Systemic environmental interventions appreciate that stability in the nearest environment of children and youth is more important than the type of family in which they grow up. Most important is that these children experience stability and feel safe and that their parents are satisfied with their own lives and cooperate in the specifics that concern the welfare of their children (Grych & Fincham, 1992; Heaven, 2001; Júlíusdóttir & Sigurðardóttir, 2000; Kristjánsson, 2003; Þorgilsson & Smári, 1992). Environmental interventions nurture such a climate. Two such interventions are mediation and joint custody arrangements.

MEDIATION AND JOINT CUSTODY

Many changes have been made in the legal system in Iceland and in other Western countries in the past decade due to the demand for increased well-being of children. For example, in Iceland fathers now have the right to take time off from work and stay with their newborn child just as the mothers do. Fathers that stay home with their newborn children strengthen the bond between themselves and their children. In the past, Icelandic mothers have had the primary role in parenting and Icelandic children have spent more time alone and have been less "pampered" than children in other Western countries (Kristjánsson, 2003). Now that both parents take responsibility for caring for their children and their home, both parents are able to perform better at home and in the work place and to enjoy their lives. Some hope that fathers staying home with their newborn children will reduce the divorce rate. The most significant advantage to both parents being home with their newborn is that their children enjoy a stronger bonding with and closeness to both parents.

Mediation

Mediation refers to the process whereby the couple meets with a mediator who helps them make decisions with regard to the divorce. Mediation is now available to parents who choose to divorce, but it is not a legal requirement here in Iceland. However, it is likely that in the future couples will be required to seek meditation before divorcing as is the case, for example, in Norway and in some parts of the United States.

The goal of mediation is cooperation between the parents and it is the parents who control the process (Júlíusdóttir & Sigurðardottir, 2000). Mediation is not therapy. Its purpose is not to resolve conflict or emotional issues but to reach a fair and just agreement between those involved in the divorce. The policy in the United States is that mediation be increasingly used instead of couples going directly through the litigation process (Grych & Fincham, 1992). Not much is known of the psychological effects of mediation, but it is thought to increase the feeling that the agreement reached is just, which in turn would have an effect on the behavior of the parents after the divorce. Since men on the average are happier after going through mediation, perhaps they are more likely to maintain a stronger relationship with their children after a divorce. Mediation seems to help the parents to not see themselves as losers or winners as is common with litigation.

Research has shown that mediation is highly successful in resolving conflict after divorce (Júlíusdóttir & Sigurðardottir, 2000). Mediation has been proven to lower the rates of court cases after divorce and to increase the satisfaction of the parties involved in terms of the divorce itself.

Joint Custody

In 1992 the children's law was changed in Iceland so that parents were given the right to seek joint physical and/or legal custody. After that there was a significant rise in joint legal custody. In 1992, sixty-five couples had joint custody of their children. Today more than a third of divorced parents have joint custody (see Table 9.2).

Júlíusdóttir and Sigurðardóttir (2000) performed a study on joint custody in Iceland and the well-being of children after divorce. The results showed that most of the children lived with their mothers (it was rare that they had two homes)—joint legal but not physical custody—but the grandparents from both the mothers' and fathers' side remained active in the lives of the children. One of the most significant conclusions was that the parents looked to each other for support if something happened to their children or if they needed something. With joint legal custody there is more continuity in the relationship of the child with both parents and both families. The results of the study also suggested that

- joint custody reduces conflict and the formation of alliances.
- the health of the parents that share custody is mostly good and better than in parents who do not share custody. This difference is more significant in fathers.
- certain ailments were significantly less in parents with joint custody, for example, depression, headaches, and anxiety.

Joint parental responsibility and an increase in equal time with the children are becoming more accepted. The results of this re-

TABLE 9.2. Joint custody in Iceland.

Year	Custody		
	Mother	Father	Joint
1971-1975	2268	151	0
1981-1985	2222	254	0
1991-1995	2210	190	396
1996-2000	1593	98	1119

Source: Statistics Iceland, 2003.

search showed that joint custody, even if just legal and not physical, can give parents an increased possibility of creating a positive growing environment for their children after divorce. The results suggested that parents with joint custody are more satisfied than parents who have sole custody, and can do more to ensure the welfare of a child than can only one parent. These parents are more likely to be role models in this aspect as well as in other aspects of their children's lives, and this is expected to have a resonating effect into the next generation.

AUTHOR'S REFLECTIONS

In the Western world more emphasis is now placed on emotion within a relationship than on social status or money as in years past. Women go to school and prepare themselves for actively participating in and having a place in the workplace and perhaps postpone having children. Therefore, marriage and family do not build to the same extent on joint chores and invested interest as before. Now they build first and foremost on emotional relationships (Júlíusdóttir, 2001). Because of these changes over the past decades, there is an increase in the demands on the core family unit. This is supposed to protect the children while giving each member of the family equal opportunity to grow and increase his and her self-respect (Satir, 1985). One might deduce that marriage does not have as much significance as before but we who work with divorce know that it does—and especially when a deep emotional relationship is terminated. Sickness, death of a previous spouse, or a marital split, can summon incapacitating sorrow, guilt, and unresolved emotional trauma.

Therefore, if a divorce is imminent it is imperative that parents work together, side by side, on all issues that concern their children after a divorce. This includes those things involving child custody, social ties within and outside of the extended family, financial issues, and decisions with regard to the children's schooling, among others. Therefore, the relationship between them and how they manage to work through the divorce makes it important.

It is of course not viable to make divorce illegal but it is possible to mandate counseling. Moreover, in all cases in which counseling does not lead to resolution of the conflict it is possible to mediate. Most important there is a need to increase education on and before marriage and before a couple has children, emphasizing the responsibility that is involved in family life and in having and rearing children.

Divorce is not painful for all. There are cases when couples recognize and understand that the close emotional bond that they sought within the relationship is just not there and arrive jointly at an agreement. But examples of children not being affected by divorce are very few. Children's difficulty with a divorce can appear in a lack of interest in school, difficulties in attention and learning, and deficits in overall well-being. It is therefore important that the schools respond in some way. For example, they may offer preventive techniques such as education and group work with other children and youths who have experienced the divorce of their parents.

In closing, it is important to increase positive discussion on topics such as resilience (e.g., Cicchetti & Garmezy, 1993; Walsh, 1996) in order to ensure that the children do not feel they are stigmatized due to a divorce. Divorce is on the rise but the painful effects can be reduced. I conclude with a poem by my friend and colleague Gunnhildur Sigurjónsdóttir (1995).

FATHER

Tell me again
When you were little
And woke in the night
To the sound of your mother
Crying in bed
Beside you
I will kill myself
I will kill myself
And held the scissors to her bosom

Tell me
How scared you were
When you ran
Into the night
In search of your father

REFERENCES

Booth, A., & Amato, P. R. (2001). Parental pre-divorce relations and offspring post-divorce well-being. *Journal of Marriage and the Family, 63,* 197-212.

Cicchetti, D., & Garmezy, N. (1993). Prospects and promises in the study of resilience. *Development and Psychopathology, 5,* 497-502.

Coffman, C. G., & Roark A. E. (1988). Likely candidates for group counseling: Adolescents with divorced parents. *The School Counselor, 35,* 246-252.

Grych, J. H., & Fincham, F. D. (1992). Interventions for children of divorce: Toward greater integration of research and action. *Psychological Bulletin, 111,* 434-454.

Heaven, C. L. (2001). *The social psychology of adolesence* (2nd ed.). Basingstoke, UK: Palgrave.

Jóhannsson, B. (1992). Skilnaður og börn (Divorce and children). *Barnaheill, 1*(3), 22-26.

Júlíusdóttir, S. (2001). Fjölskyldur við aldahvörf. Náin tengsl og uppeldisskilyrði barna (Close relationships and conditions of raising children). *Articles on families and Icelandic children's upbringing conditions.* Reykjavík: University Press.

Júlíusdóttir, S., & Sigurðardóttir, N. K. (2000). *Áfram foreldrar. Rannsókn um sameiginlega forsjá barna við skilnað foreldra* (Onward Parents. Research on joint custody). Reykjavík: University Press.

Kristjánsson, B. (2003). Börn og barnafjölskyldur í skugga nútímavæðingar (Children and families with children in the shadow of modernisation) (pp. 63-81). *The scientific web.* Reykjavík: University of Iceland.

Nagy, I. B., & Spark, G. M. (1984). *Invisible loyalties.* New York: Brunner/ Mazel.

Nichols, W. C. (1988). *Marital therapy: An integrative approach.* New York: Guilford Press.

Nichols, W. C. (1996). *Treating people in families: An integrative framework.* New York: Guilford Press.

Nichols, W. C., & Everett, C. A. (1986). *Systemic family therapy: An integrative approach.* New York: Guilford Press.

Satir, V. (1985). *Conjoint family therapy* (3rd ed.). Palo Alto, CA: Science and Behavior Books, Inc.

Sigurjónsdóttir, G. (1995). *Sólin dansar í baðvatninu* (The sun dances in the bathwater). Reykjavík: Andblær.

Statistics Iceland, (2003). Retrieved from http://www.hagstofa.is/template40.asp? PageID=261.

Þorgilsson, H., & Smári, J. (Eds.) (1993). *Sálfræðibókin* (The book of psychology). Reykjavík: Mál og Menning.

Walsh, F. (1996). The concept of family resilience: Crisis and challenge. *Family Process, 35,* 261-281.

Chapter 10

Postdivorce Relatedness Between Parents, Their Divorced Sons, and Their Grandchildren: A Pilot Study

Florence W. Kaslow

Tribute to William C. Nichols

Bill Nichols is a superb scholar, clinician, teacher, author, editor, organizational leader, and innovative professional. Personally Bill is a devoted husband, father, and grandfather, and a valued friend. Together he is a Renaissance Man for All Seasons.

I first met Bill Nichols in 1975. He was finishing his term as founding editor of the Journal of Marriage and Family Counseling *(later to become JMFT). Having been selected as his successor, I visited him at Florida State University to receive some tutelage on being an editor. Over the years this acquaintanceship has grown into a deep and abiding friendship, and we consider each other to be trusted and respected colleagues. We have presented together, written chapters for each other's books, and have enjoyed many experiences, including fine and not-so-fine dinners together, in the United States and abroad. I coaxed Bill to become involved in the International Family Therapy Association (IFTA), and he was soon appointed editor of* The International Connection, *the IFTA newsletter. Bill did his usual superb job of editing, just as he had done for several journals, and continues to do for* Contemporary Family Therapy. *Because his organizational talents and know-how were quickly recognized in IFTA, he went on to become its president in the late 1990s, and served IFTA with the same kind of clarity and distinction that he had served AAMFT when he was its president and on its board.*

Much has been written about the financial, psychological, and social impact of divorce on women, especially those who are mothers (e.g., Treiman, 1985; Uhlenberg, Cooney, & Boyd, 1990). However,

doi:10.1300/5562_10

similar energy has not been paid to men. Moreover, there is a paucity of literature regarding what happens to the relationship between paternal grandparents and their grandchildren during and following the advent of their son's divorce. This article attempts to address this gap in the literature and in the field. Given that over 50 percent of children have parents who are divorced and that between 85 percent and 90 percent of mothers are legally designated as the primary residential parents (U.S. Bureau of Labor Statistics, 1992), the intent of this chapter is to explore what this does to the connection and bond between the children and their paternal grandparents. It is predicated on what we know from the divorce literature, clinical observation, and a small pilot study conducted with paternal grandparents with divorced or divorcing sons.

THE RELATIONSHIP OF THE PATERNAL GRANDPARENTS TO THE DIVORCED FAMILY

Finley (2004a) reports that contemporary divorce law and court practices are based on presumptions of gender inequality regarding parenting rights, and that there often is an absence of due process. Consequently, divorce (often) transforms the divorced family into a postdivorce matriarchy when it grants the major portion of physical custody to the mother and assigns her the primary tasks and responsibilities of the socioemotional role, and perhaps a portion of the instrumental role also. All too often this translates into her having (almost) absolute control over the life of the child. This postdivorce family structure has serious relationship implications for the children's fathers, the children themselves, and the paternal grandparents.

The husband's parents are often in a difficult position. They may be saddened by the divorce and frightened by its portents, but they also are disheartened by their son's emotional, financial, and logistic plight as he sets up a second household suitable for the children (Ricci, 1980). Frequently his parents will try to offer him words of comfort and encourage him to be optimistic about the future. They may try to help him defray his unexpected and unplanned-for financial burdens. However, while trying to help him deal with this unwanted event in his life's trajectory, they are simultaneously coping with their own grief about their son's losses and their own. Their own losses may include a daughter-in-law about whom they cared but who they now view in a different light, their hopes and dreams for the continuity of their family into the next generation of grandchildren who will perpetuate their family name and legacy and, most important, continued and unimpeded loving contact with their grandchildren. They may be worried about a range of events such as being invited to the children's birthday parties at their ex-daughter-in-law's home, calling them on the phone at her house, spending family vacations together, and being able to bestow loads of love on them in a spontaneous way.

Grandparenting constitutes an important part of the family life cycle, and the grandchild/grandparent relationships sometimes are undervalued as a key component of emotional well-being of senior adults and children. Yet often those in these two generations have a close, satisfying, mutually supportive and enhancing relationship (Kennedy & Kennedy, 1993). In fact, the terms *grandmother* and *grandfather* often evoke positive feelings and images (Ganong & Coleman, 2004). However, the nature and extent of this contact is threatened when there is a disruption or change in the middle (parent) generation brought about by their adult child's divorce or death (Rossi & Rossi, 1990). When this results in the disruption of the grandparent/grandchild relationship, many grandparents are vulnerable to prolonged grief reactions, resulting in emotional and/or physical health problems (Parkes, 1996; Owen, Fulton, & Markse, 1982). The role of grandparents becomes increasingly ambivalent postdivorce when they become "quasikin" to their former daughter-in-law (Bohannon, 1970).

It has been estimated that approximately 50 percent of noncustodial fathers in Canada, the United Kingdom, and the United States ultimately lose contact with their children (Kruk, 1995). This often means that, if the custodial mother is not willing to grant them access, the paternal grandparents' contact with their grandchildren is severed (Drew & Smith, 1999, 2002). Many states in the United States do not have grandparent's rights laws any longer, but have ceded full discretion regarding access to the custodial parent who becomes the gatekeeper. Therefore, grandparents whose ties are severed by a former daughter-in-law who never liked them, or who wants to punish her ex-husband by hurting his parents, or who does not want them to exercise any influence over the children, can be cut adrift with no recourse. They are literally at the mercy of their ex-daughter-in-law and they may be quite heartbroken by this radical family heart surgery (Kaslow & Schwartz, 1987). Their grandchildren, in turn, may be faced with yet another loss, but afraid to confront their mother. They may fear she will be displeased and angry at them if they do confront her or, worse yet, "divorce" or get rid of them for disagreeing with her, as she did their father. This alienation of affectional contact can and does contribute to grandparent hurt and disappointment, unfulfilled dreams of being reunited with the grandchild, and often, elevated levels of stress and stress disorders. Several studies conducted in Canada and England (Kruk, 1995; Drew & Smith, 1999) found that following the termination of contact with grandchildren, grandparents retrospectively reported symptoms of bereavement as well as deteriorating physical and emotional health.

PATERNAL GRANDPARENTS' REACTIONS TO SON'S DIVORCE AND POSSIBLE CHANGES IN RELATIONSHIP TO CHILDREN

In September 2004, the author sent a questionnaire to twenty-three paternal grandparents whose sons were divorced or in the process of divorcing. A network sampling method (Kunzel, 1994) was used and nineteen usable answers were received within six weeks of the questionnaires being mailed. This is a return rate of 83 percent. This sample is too small for the findings to be generalized beyond the study population. However, the data are interesting and suggest that this study will be replicated with much larger samples, and also with a control group of paternal grandparents whose sons are in intact marriages.

The Study Sample

Of the nineteen respondents, six were men and thirteen were women. In addition, one man declined, and one did not answer. Two women did not respond. In terms of socioeconomic status, five men rated themselves as falling in lower-upper strata (herein defined as $80,000 to $250,000), and one as upper-upper (over $250,000). Three women checked upper-middle ($30,000 to $80,000), five rated themselves as lower-upper, and two as upper-upper. Three women did not answer this query. Since thirteen of the seventeen subjects checked lower-upper and upper-upper (combined $80,000 to over $250,000), the majority of the study population were reasonably affluent. Twelve of the seventeen respondents were Jewish; five men and seven women. This reflects the sampling method. I solicited names of potential respondents from my colleagues and acquaintances and they largely are Jewish. Five females and one male were protestant and one female was Roman Catholic.

FINDINGS AND IMPLICATIONS

Length and Type of Marriage

Only one multiple divorce (an individual's third) was mentioned. The length of sons' marriages prior to divorce ranged from eight years (three) to twenty-seven years (two), with nine people reporting marriages of thirteen or less years, and ten parents indicating their sons were married between fifteen and twenty-seven years. Eight couples had lived together, and eleven had not. Those who had cohabited had also done so for two years or less, so it does not seem that inability to make a commitment was a factor in the ultimate demise of these marriages. No significant difference was found in decision to divorce between those who had and had not cohabited.

There was nothing remarkable regarding age of marriage, including no large intracouple age differences. These couples were neither extremely young at the time of their marriages, nor appreciably old. The sons' age of marriage ranged from eighteen years to thirty-six years, with the average being twenty-seven years of age. The women's ages ranged from eighteen to thirty years, with the median being twenty-six years. Only one respondent indicated that the couple had gotten married because the woman was pregnant.

Occupation

All but one divorced sons' occupations could be classified as a business or professional endeavor. None of the sons were in a particularly high-stress field, such as a police officer or a security guard, or at high risk of being pursued by other women, such as an entertainer or professional athlete. The daughters-in-law worked outside the home in a wide variety of fields ranging from clerical to professional. Only two ex-wives were unemployed outside the home. There was enough variety among the occupational areas of these divorcing women and men to suggest no major association between job field and proneness to divorce.

Number of Children

None of the couples were childless. Only one couple had one child. Fourteen of the nineteen couples had two children, and four had three children each. This might be taken to indicate that all had hoped to stay married and wanted to be part of their family of creation.

Substance Use and Infidelity

Often it is assumed that an affair or an addiction is a contributory factor to a partner seeking a divorce. Even though the paternal parents might not know for sure, everyone answered without equivocating. Seven indicated an affair was going on prior to the divorce. Two said it was the son who was involved, and five said it was the daughter-in-law. Only one mother indicated her son was a heavy drinker, used marijuana, and abused drugs seriously. This is the son whose mother was reporting on his third marriage. No daughters-in-law were thought to have these addictions. However, two parents indicated that their daughter-in-law gambled (too much). Thus, in this sample population, addictions were not in any way a pervasive problem. However, in seven of the nineteen couples someone was having an affair, and it was most often the woman. In the two cases in which it was the son, the mothers stated their perturbation over their sons' behavior.

The Parents' Opinions About Their Sons' Marriages

These parents of divorced sons were asked to indicate on a five-point scale whether they originally thought their sons' "original choice of wife was a good one." (A note of caution: It cannot be determined whether this is primarily a retrospective view, or actually represents how these parents felt when their son initially chose his wife.) Five said "yes," six indicated "somewhat," three said that they were neutral, four indicated "tending toward no," and four said "no."

Who Wanted and Pushed for Divorce, and How it Was Obtained

Fourteen respondents indicated it was the daughter-in-law who asked and pressed for the divorce, while only four sons requested and wanted it. (One answered "don't know.") This corresponds with the statement made earlier that more than 50 percent of divorces now are sought by women.

Reflecting recent trends, seven couples mediated, one sought a collaborative divorce (Nurse & Thompson, 2000), and one did a pro se filing. Five resorted to traditional litigated divorces. Two divorces were not yet final, two parents did not know what process was used, and one parent wrote "marriage counseling" (which was not listed as an option, and is not a divorce process). It is interesting to note that more than one-half of these couples, predominantly business and professional people, chose nonadversarial divorce processes.

The postdivorce acceptance and adjustment of the grandparent generation was still in its beginning phase. Out of the seventeen respondents, four of the divorces were still under way and nine of their sons' marriages had been legally terminated for only one year or less. Overall, the time since finalization ranged from two months to six years.

Shared Parenting Time

Responses to the question, "What percentage of the time does your son have the children?" were somewhat surprising and may reflect the fact that in contemporary North America many fathers are actively pursuing decrees that grant them equal time as well as joint custody. Three fathers had the children nine days and nights out of thirty. Six fathers had them twelve days; and three had them fifteen days. One father had his children twenty-one days, or 70 percent of the time. Two fathers had children over eighteen years of age, so custody was not an issue—the children could decide where they wanted to visit. One father answered "rarely," and three gave no response.

Relationship to Ex-Daughter-in-Law

These parents of divorced sons were asked if their ex-daughters-in-law called them and, if so, how often. "Yes," 3; "No," 11; "Occasionally or seldom (quarterly or monthly)," 5. Similarly, when asked if they themselves called their daughters-in-law and how often, the data were "No," 9; "Monthly," 3; "Rarely or occasionally," 6. Several respondents indicated that their former daughters-in-law kept them at arm's length.

Changes in Relationship to Son and Grandchildren

A final group of questions were open-ended. They called for answers in the form of comments.

How has the divorce changed your relationship with your son?

The written comments suggest diversity in amount and kind.

- Has improved greatly:
  — He is more open with us, sometimes confides in us
     and seeks guidance.   7
  — The tension is gone; freer to visit each other and be
     together.   4
  — Daughter-in-law did not encourage closeness.   2
- No change.   4
- Quite worried about him.   3
- Although he had been financially independent for a long
  time, divorce settlement, child support and alimony have
  left him in bad shape financially, and we have been helping
  him directly, and with the children's expenses.   3
- Lived with mother or both parents for a few months
  following the separation and divorce.   3
- Urged him to maintain a civil relationship with ex-wife
  for sake of children.   2
- Less contact with him than formerly, as he has a girlfriend.   1
- Always a problem child, and still is as a grown up. Now
  on 4th marriage. "Do not trust him and do not care
  to be close to him."   1

*What changes have occurred in your relationship
with your grandchild/grandchildren?*

Again there is diversity in amount and kind of interaction.

- Spend more quality time with them—including day trips
  and weekends; try harder to have frequent contact. 6
- Ex-daughter-in-law made getting together difficult,
  restricted it; now more spontaneous and do not have
  to watch what we say. 5
- No change:
  — Never saw often, out of state. 2
  — Mom still encourages contact. 2
  — Already in college and have remained close. 2
- Worry about them more and try to reassure them
  that we are there for them. 2
- Less often:
  — But grandson more solicitous and closer. 1
  — Grandson wants to be with friends more when together. 1

*What were your feelings upon learning a divorce would occur,
during the divorce, and afterward?*

The main feelings were:

- Sadness and sorrow—upset at seeing son hurt,
  disappointed, disillusioned, discouraged, ended
  fantasy of happy family and its continuity for son and us. 9
- Surprised at extent of ex-daughter-in-law's viciousness,
  nastiness, hostility, deceitfulness, and attempts to keep
  making his life miserable. 7
- Glad son now happier—free of her lying and better
  off without her. 6
- Concern and dismay for children—worried about
  current and future impact of divorce on them and poor
  image of marriage. 6
- Shocked or stunned—did not know son's marriage
  was in trouble. 3
- Very supportive of son and try to help. 3
- Discouraged and angry—son's third divorce. 2
- Never liked her, was not close to her—no great loss. 2
- Anxious as to how they will handle unresolved problems. 2
- Wanted to persuade them to save marriage. 2
- Felt relieved, as saw marriage as rocky. 1

- Not surprised.   1
- Hope divorce will improve son's self-confidence
  (which she shattered).   1
- Feels "used" by son—has become estranged
  from supportive mother since he has a new girlfriend.   1
- Has grown closer to her ex-daughter-in-law.   1

The overriding sentiments obviously were sorrow and sadness over the divorce and their son's unhappiness and disillusionment; surprise at ex-daughter-in-law's nastiness and deceitfulness; and concern for son's and grandchildren's present and future well-being.

What gains and losses did you perceive to have accompanied the divorce?

This questions taps into some of the same issues discussed earlier. The similarity of responses underscores the consistency expressed regarding what they experienced. The *losses*, in descending order, were:

- Fracturing of family continuity and us all having
  a complete family.   4
- Not having holidays all together as a total family,
  and not seeing grandchildren on some holidays
  (including loss of most contact with ex-in-law family).   4
- Son's financial well-being and stability.   3
- Less chance to contribute guidance and love
  to grandchildren's lives.   2
- Loss of most interaction with ex-daughter-in-law,
  to whom they were attached.   2
- Seeing pain of son and grandchildren.   2
- Miss being with son and daughter-in-law as a couple.   1
- Continuous struggle—she's very disturbed and curtails
  access to grandchildren.   1

Conversely, the *gains* were:

- Greater closeness to son.   7
- See grandchildren more, and closer to them—no
  strings attached about visits when they are with father only.   6
- None.   2

Can the children contact the grandparents directly,
or do they need parental approval?

"Yes" responses included:

• Children over ten years of age (including young adults).	11
• Primarily from father's home.	7
• Mother does not interfere.	1
• Does so by e-mail.	1

In this study population, ongoing telephone contact did not seem to be a problem. Many of the children reportedly had and used their cell phones.

What changes have you (grandparents) made
in financial arrangements?

The responses indicated both short- and long-term arrangements.

- In annual gift giving:
  — One person said a clear "no"; two qualified that the daughter-in-law had only been a recipient of gifts for anniversaries and birthdays, and this had been discontinued. Three indicated there would be no further gifts to her.
- In the will:

— Yes; in favor of son and grandchildren.	9
— Have not changed. (This response was primarily given by those with the lowest incomes.)	4
— Yes; more to ex-daughter-in-law. (These parents were angry at their sons.)	1
— Yes; put irresponsible son's money in trust.	1
— Not yet; too soon.	1

The parental concerns over their son's financial plight concur with Finley's statement (Finley, 2004b) that noncustodial fathers (like custodial mothers) need legal and financial advice on (1) "how to stay out of debtor's prison" in the advent of job loss, or decline in income, perhaps because he has gotten called up for military service; (2) how to "get child support and alimony payments reduced before running into arrears"; and (3) how to "get child support and alimony payments set at a level that he can pay from current income and not have to spend down whatever is left from the divorce or go into debt." The divorced son's parents' worries may be justified. For the two sons whose ex-wives did not work outside the home, the income that formerly covered one household now had to cover two. Moreover, the distribution of assets, payment of child and spousal support, plus the son's need to take care of himself and his children when they are with him can be a costly package that can place an ex-husband in a dire financial situation for many years. Our study data indicate that caring parents and grandparents apparently pitched in to help financially and emotionally, to the extent that they could, for as long as they deemed necessary.

How willing are you to no longer celebrate family events together?

This phenomenon is often found to be important in perpetuating family legacies and traditions (Imber-Black, Roberts, & Whiting, 1988). Indeed fifteen of the nineteen respondents (80 percent) were unwilling to let go of family rituals. One abstained and three said that they were willing, but because it was necessary to avoid conflict with a difficult ex-daughter-in-law. Similarly, seventeen (89 percent) of these parents of divorced sons were unwilling to let go of celebrations and special events. Divorce, followed by a discontinuation of celebrating holidays and special events together was a happenstance these grandparent responders clearly did not want to have occur. Their son's children, and thus their grandchildren, were a vital part of their lives and occupied a prominent place in their family's genogram (McGoldrick & Gerson, 1985; Kaslow, 1995). Without the children's active presence, they experienced an enormous void.

Additional Comments

The final section asked whether the respondents had any additional comments to make. Most comments repeated what had been said earlier. However, a few were different, and will be mentioned here. Fears were expressed that because the children were quite young and the mother had primary custody and tended to be very controlling, she would sway them against their father or put the children "in the middle." Two added that they hoped the couple would reconcile. The majority of those who provided additional comments stressed that they hoped their son and ex-daughter-in-law would put the children's needs first and not use them as foils, and that ultimately "something positive" (left nebulous) would result from the divorce for the children and their son. One mother said that she thought her role was to be available, but neither intrusive nor judgmental.

CLINICAL IMPLICATIONS

It has become clear from the literature, from clinical observation, and from the pilot study, that the divorce of a son may contribute to a changing relationship of the parents to that son, often in the direction of becoming closer. These parents are frequently worried about the emotional and financial impact of the marital dissolution on their son and his children. They may exhibit concern over the well-being of their grandchildren and attempt to stay actively involved in their lives, seeing them as frequently as possible and celebrating special events and holidays with them. The vast majority may feel sad about the divorce and regret that it was the choice of one (or both) partner. Multiple losses were felt, and a few gains perceived.

Other works have discussed the emotional and physical health of grandparents in the event of loss of contact with grandchildren. (See, for example, Kruk, 1995.)

It is also recognized that grandparents' emotional well-being benefits from involvement with their grandchildren (Kivnick, 1982), and reveal that when this relationship is disrupted, harmful consequences to their emotional and physical health are apt to occur. Often these grandparents remain in a state of bereavement because of their inability to reunite with their grandchildren (Owen, Fulton, & Markse, 1982), and this grief may continue throughout their lives.

AUTHOR'S REFLECTIONS

Clinicians should understand the influence of the divorce process—from its inception through all of the stages of this heart-wrenching, major life transition—on the children, the divorcing couple, *and* the grandparents (Kaslow & Schwartz, 1987). They should be conversant with the literature of divorce and the fact that divorce is never completely over if children are involved. Contact continues around visitation, children's health, vacations, schooling, and much more. Contact continues even when the children are grown. There are holidays, college graduations, weddings, and the birth of grandchildren.

Knowledgeable and wise therapists will attempt to have each party to a divorce tell his or her own story and, in so doing, help them make sense out of what has occurred, reinterpret the process in a more positive light, and cope with the situation much better. Much attention may have to be given to how they might change their interactions so as to improve relationships in the postdivorce family and thereby minimize losses and maximize gains within the evolving new family structure.

It is hoped the pilot study conducted as part of the data gathering for this article will be replicated using larger and more diverse samples, so that more data on grandparents' relationships with grandchildren following a son's divorce will be available and become generalizable. A growing body of data will enable us to assist postdivorce extended families function optimally.

REFERENCES

Bohannon, P. (1970). Divorce chains, households of remarriage, and multiple divorces. In P. Bohannon (Ed.), *Divorce and after* (pp. 347-362). New York: Doubleday.

Drew, L. M., & Smith, P. K. (1999). The impact of parental separation/divorce on grandparent-grandchild relationships. *International Journal of Aging and Human Development, 48,* 191-215.

Drew, L. M., & Smith, P. K. (2002). Implications for grandparents when they lose contact with their grandchildren: Divorce, family feud, and geographical separation. *Journal of Mental Health and Aging, 8,* 95-120.

Finley, G. E. (2004a). Divorce inequalities. *National Council of Family Relations Report: Special Issue on Inequalities and Families, 49* (3), 9-10.

Finley, G. E. (2004b). Divorced fathers need investment advice, too. *Wall Street Journal,* November 3, p. 15A.

Ganong, L. H., & Coleman, M. (2004). *Stepfamily relationships: Development, dynamics and interventions.* New York: Kluwer Academic/Plenum Publishers.

Imber-Black, E., Roberts, J., & Whiting, R. (1988). *Rituals in families and family therapy.* New York: Norton.

Kaslow, F. W. (1995). *Projective genogramming.* Sarasota, FL: Professional Resource Press.

Kaslow, F. W., & Schwartz, L. L. (1987). *Dynamics of divorce: A life cycle perspective*. New York: Brunner/Mazel.

Kennedy, G. E., & Kennedy, C. E. (1993). Grandparents: A special resource for children. *Journal of Divorce and Remarriage, 19,* 45-68.

Kivnick, H. Q. (1982). Grandparenthood: An overview of meaning and mental health. *The Gerontologist, 22,* 59-66.

Kruk, E. (1995). Grandparent-grandchild contact loss: Findings from a study of A Grandparents Rights' members. *Canadian Journal on Aging, 14,* 737-754.

Kunzel, A. J. (1994). Sampling in qualitative inquiry. In B. F. Crabtree & W. L. Miller (Eds.), *Doing qualitative research* (pp. 31-44). Newburg Park, CA: Sage.

McGoldrick, M., & Gerson, R. (1985). *Genograms in family assessment*. New York: Norton.

Nurse, A. R., & Thompson, P. (2000). Collaborative divorce: A human, interdisciplinary approach. *Innovations in Clinical Practice: A SourceBook, 18,* 169-184.

Owen, G., Fulton, R., & Markse, E. (1982). Death at a distance: A study of family survivors. *Omega, 23,* 25-35.

Parkes, C. M. (1996). *Bereavement: Studies of grief in adult life* (3rd ed.). London: Routledge.

Ricci, I. (1980). *Mom's house, dad's house: Making shared custody work*. New York: Macmillan.

Rossi, A. S., & Rossi, P. H. (1990). *Of human bonding: Parent-child relations across the life course*. New York: Aldine de Gruyter.

Treiman, D. (1985). The work histories of women and men: What we know and what we need to find out. In A. Rossi (Ed.), *Gender and the life course* (pp. 213-231). Hawthorne, NY: Aldine.

Uhlenberg, P., Cooney, T., & Boyd, R. (1990). Divorce for women after mid-life. *Journal of Gerontology, 45,* S3-S11.

U.S. Bureau of Labor Statistics (1992). *The American women: A status report 1990-1991*. Washington, DC: U.S. Department of Commerce.

PART III:
SYSTEMIC FAMILY INTERVENTIONS

Specific and practical systemic treatment interventions are discussed in this section. The issues considered and illustrated with case examples represent both similarities and crucial differences when diverse families—the young, the aging, the GLBT—separate, divorce, and remarry. They include partner violence, protecting children, and nurturing distraught spouses caught unawares of affairs or the divorce.

Chapter 11

Family Therapy with a Lesbian "Stepparent" Couple Experiencing Partner Abuse: A Case Report

David A. Baptiste

Tribute to William C. Nichols

I first became acquainted with Bill Nichols in October 1974 at the joint AAMFT/NCFR conference in St. Louis, Missouri. I was a graduate student and I remember that it was Wallace Denton, then an MFT professor at Purdue University, who introduced us. I remember Bill then as the consummate professional who seemed to know everyone in sight.

I was reintroduced to Bill by Kenneth Hardy, Bill's former student at Florida State University, about three years post-graduate. Since these meetings Bill has had a significant impact on me as a professional and as a person. Bill was never my formal teacher, but over the years he has taught me much, and guided and nurtured me both as a person and a professional in the AAMFT and NCFR. During Bill's tenure as president of each respective organization, he was influential in opening doors for minority members. In doing so, his role allowed me access to the sanctum sanctorum of those organizations and provided me opportunities to serve the organizations in several roles. My thirty-plus years of knowing and working with Bill have been characterized by mutual respect, sage guidance, friendship, and collegiality. Today when others assert, "You are just like Bill Nichols," I consider that the highest compliment anyone can pay me.

Since the early 1970s concern has been growing about the increase in domestic abuse/violence in heterosexual relationships—marital and nonmarital. This increased awareness and concern paralleled a concurrent increase in the reported incidents of domestic violence after many years of minimizing and/or denying its exis-

When Marriages Fail
doi:10.1300/5562_11

tence in intimate heterosexual relationships, in particular marital relationships (Poorman, 2001). The societal awakening emphasized and presented domestic violence exclusively as a male-to-female problem (Hammond, 1989). As a result, attention was focused primarily on heterosexual relationships, marital and nonmarital, and tended to ignore the existence and occurrence of domestic violence in both committed and casual homosexual relationships (Ristock, 1997). This was true especially among couples raising children in a "stepfamily-like" relationship.

LESBIAN DOMESTIC VIOLENCE AND PARTNER ABUSE: AN OVERVIEW

Lesbian domestic violence, battering, and partner abuse (which are often used interchangeably) is defined as any pattern of violent or coercive behaviors employed by one partner within a lesbian relationship to control the thoughts, beliefs, or conduct of the other partner. These violent/abusive behaviors can be physical, verbal, emotional, psychological, sexual, and economic. They are intended to intimidate, coerce, and dominate the abused partner, and to demonstrate and establish the abusing partner's power and control over the abused partner.

Prior to 1983 and publication of the Lesbian Taskforce of the National Coalition Against Domestic Violence's report (see Hart, 1986; Lobel, 1986), domestic violence within lesbian relationships had been mostly denied or altogether ignored by both heterosexuals and homosexuals (Balsam, 2001). This was surprisingly true of lesbian activists within the women's movement who were at the forefront of advocating for a cessation of violence against women. The lesbian activists believed that a public discussion of lesbian battering would reinforce homophobia, whereas heterosexual activists feared that such a discussion would negatively affect funding and even damage the battered women's public image. Benowitz (1986) further suggested that the lesbian community was invested in the belief of utopian lesbian relationships. Consequently, a focus on domestic violence in such relationships would have cast an unintended negative reflection on lesbians in particular, and the homosexual community in general.

Hammond (1989) suggested that lesbians in the women's movement may have denied and/or ignored lesbian battering because acceptance of woman-to-woman violence ran counter to the feminist explanation that domestic violence against women, in general, was primarily male-on-female. It was assumed that these resulted from society's support of patriarchy and gender inequality in male-female relationships. Regardless of the cause, the American public's awareness of domestic violence in lesbian relationships developed very gradually because of a societal reservation born of disbelief that women can be violent toward other women. Conventional wisdom, even among lesbian abuse victims, held that lesbian relationships were egalitarian, loving, passionate, but never violent (Morrow & Hawxhurst, 1989).

Today it is generally accepted that domestic violence does occur within lesbian relationships to a greater extent than previously thought (McLaughlin & Rozee, 2001) and in much the same ways as it occurs against women in heterosexual relationships. These patterns involve almost identical patterns of controlling behaviors that are manifested as physical, sexual, and emotional abuse (Morrow and Hawxhurst, 1989), and they are equally as serious with regard to the resulting trauma (Hammond, 1989). It is also similar in that it can be recurrent, and tends to escalate and become more lethal over time (Poorman, 2001). In this regard, Hammond (1989) has asserted that violence in lesbian relationships has been so severe that abuse survivors experienced post-traumatic stress disorder and in some cases lesbian batterers have killed their partners. However, in contrast to heterosexual women whose reports of domestic violence are legitimized and institutionally supported by society, lesbians experience a lack of social approval, legal and institutional support, and absence of appropriate role models for ways to deal with violence in their relationships. As a consequence, the experiences of lesbians in violent intimate relationships are uniquely different from that of heterosexual women since lesbian victims are stigmatized twice because of their victimization and their sexual orientation.

Some of the differences experienced by lesbians are

- unavailability of lesbian-friendly resources/services to help abused partners deal with or escape the violence, and to help abusing partners to learn nonviolent ways to express anger;

- insufficient numbers of mental health professionals experienced with lesbian issues and lesbian battering; and
- difficulty receiving appropriate help from law enforcement agencies—police and courts—because of explicit homophobia, and heterosexism.

Poorman (2001) reported that battered lesbians who sought help from community agencies and services, such as law enforcement, courts, women's shelters, and safe houses, experienced difficulty in accessing those services primarily because of rampant homophobia and heterosexism. Many reported that when they received help it was highly ineffective. Wise and Bowman (1997) reported that many mental health providers "perceived" male batterers of heterosexual women to have been more violent than lesbian-on-lesbian batterers. This view would tend to minimize the lesbian battering experiences as understood by therapists, and may lead to the male batterer being charged with assault rather than the lesbian batterer.

CHARACTERISTICS OF LESBIAN "STEPFAMILIES"

The term "lesbian stepfamily" describes a cohabitive living arrangement involving two lesbian adults and children, either biological, i.e., from previous marital or nonmarital heterosexual relationships, or adopted, or conceived through artificial insemination. The relationship is characterized by mutual commitment, sharing property, and sexual intimacies similar to that found among cohabiting heterosexual couples with children (Baptiste, 1987b).

All families parented by gay/lesbian couples are by virtue of their structure stepfamilies, and since the 1980s the United States has witnessed an increase in the number of lesbians who are becoming parents through either insemination or adoption (Baptiste, 1987b). However, the greatest numbers of lesbian families are headed by lesbian mothers, with children from previous heterosexual relationships (marital and nonmarital). As a result, there has been a concurrent increase in the number lesbians, divorced and never-married single parents, living in committed "stepfamily-like" relationships, with a same-sex partner and child(ren) from either one or both partners' previous heterosexual relationships (Baptiste, 1982, 1987a,b, 1995).

Lesbian "stepfamilies" share some similarities with heterosexual stepfamilies. For example, prior to joining as a family either one or both partners may have ended a heterosexual relationship through divorce, and one or both partners may be custodial parents. Similar to heterosexual female-headed stepfamilies, lesbian "stepfamilies" may be living economically at or below poverty level. In addition, much like heterosexual stepfamilies, partners in lesbian "stepfamilies" often confront affectional issues such as rejection of the nonparent partner by the parental partner's children. "Stepchildren" conflicts are also common to all stepfamilies, heterosexual and homosexual (Baptiste, 1987a,b).

However, despite these similarities lesbian stepfamilies' dynamics and concerns are different enough to set them apart as a unique subset of stepfamilies. Because of society's homophobia, prejudices, and general lack of receptivity to homosexuals, as well as the societal proscription against homosexuals as parents, lesbian "stepfamilies" are even more marginalized than heterosexual stepfamilies (Baptiste, 1987a).

Characteristics of Lesbian "Stepfamilies"
Experiencing Partner Abuse

Violence within single intimate/committed lesbian relationships, and nonparenting committed lesbian couples continued to be the focus and emphasis of the lesbian community's concerns. Despite the 1983 Lesbian Taskforce report that acknowledged the existence of domestic violence within lesbian relationships, domestic violence continued to be ignored in relationships that involved lesbian couples with children, living in committed "stepfamily-like" relationships. It would seem that the heterosexual public continue to believe that homosexuality and parenthood are mutually exclusive, and thus there is a continuing disapproval of homosexuals, especially gay men, as parents (Baptiste, 1987b). Interestingly, a significant portion of the gay/lesbian community, which is essentially a childless one, also share a similar belief and often disparage gay men and lesbians who are parents (Baptiste, 1987a).

Lesbians "stepfamilies" in which partner abuse is present often share some similarities with abused women in heterosexual stepfamilies because of the presence of children. They also share with abused heterosexual women the lack of societal recognition as a legitimate family form (Cherlin, 1978). Many lesbians "stepparent" partners—both batterers and victims—tend to be isolated from other meaningful relationships and emotional supports. This isolation often results from the machinations of the abusing partner or from the abused partner's avoidance of relationship conflicts that might disrupt the family, especially the children. This is especially true if the couple is estranged or closeted from their families. The relative isolation is also a means to avoid unwanted attention to the family because of the societal proscription against lesbian mothers living in a lesbian relationship and parenting their biological children. Although this situation is slowly changing, many courts have decreed lesbian motherhood to be unacceptable and have terminated the parental rights of lesbian mothers living in a same-sex relationship while parenting biological children from previous heterosexual relationships (Baptiste, 1987a).

When these partners are distrustful and isolated from other relationships, which can serve as buffers and provide support, the resulting stress often manifests as violence. In this regard, Coleman (1990) has reported that lesbians who learned in their families of orientation that violence was an acceptable means to redress loss of power are more likely to resort to violence because it becomes the most readily accessible coping strategy with which to deal with relationship loss, real or imaginary. Lesbian "stepparenting" partners who experienced early domestic violence, especially the abusing partner, also experienced high levels of insecure attachment. This contributed to high levels of emotional dependency of the abusing partner on the abused partner. Renzetti (1988) has identified insecure attachment as an important variable in predicting violence in intimate lesbian relationships.

Although not mentioned in the lesbian domestic violence literature, the author's clinical experiences with abusing lesbian "stepfamilies" have shown that domestic violence tends to be more prevalent in "stepparenting" couples *in which the abusing partner is at least ten or more years older than the abused partner.* Often these relationships take on a parent-child quality with the older partner (often the batterer) in the parental role. Frequently, the younger partner initially welcomes the "parentlike" attention given to her and her children. However, over time, as the younger partner begins to mature and/or object to the control exerted upon her, the relationship begins to experience difficulties which frequently are perceived as a loss by the older partner. At that juncture the fear of loss of the relationship, when coupled with the older partner's lack of trust, serves to increase that partner's insecurity about attachment to the younger partner. This in turn increases the older partner's dependency needs which often manifest as a greater effort to control the younger partner. Invariably, the younger partner continues to resist the older partner's controls and the older partner resorts to violence, initially verbal abuse that often escalates to physical violence. Similarly, in lesbian "stepparenting" families in which one partner perceives the other partner to be more privileged because of education, income, social-class, or race, the partner feeling less privileged often may use violence against the "privileged" partner to "cut her down a peg" in order to demonstrate her power and control in the relationship.

TREATING PARTNER ABUSE IN LESBIAN "STEPFAMILIES"

Many lesbians who experience partner abuse in their relationships have sought therapy from a variety of mental health providers, including marital and family therapists. While much of the professional literature addresses treatment issues for lesbian relationship abuse, in general, it remains silent about the treatment of lesbian domestic violence within "stepfamilies." While there are some anecdotal reports that abused lesbians' experiences with mental health providers have been negative, those reports are not corroborated by empirical studies (Poorman, 2001).

Similar to heterosexual stepparents, many lesbian "stepparents" seek treatment because of "stepparent"-"stepchild" conflicts. In the author's clinical experience, most lesbian "stepfamily" couples who experience domestic violence and seek treatment present the violence as a direct or oblique development of a "stepparent-stepchild" conflict that worsened and engulfed the adults. Invariably, as therapy progresses, the therapist soon discovers that the couple's own relationship difficulties are the major contributors to the violence.

Current therapeutic approaches are varied and based on existing approaches widely used with heterosexual couples experiencing domestic violence. Such approaches range from psychoanalytic to anger management and may include the following range of methods: individual/intrapsychic, individual group for the abuser only, conjoint-couple, combinations of couple/individual, family therapy including children, addiction models based on the twelve steps of Alcoholics Anonymous, feminist approaches, and combinations of the above.

It should be noted that none of the various clinical approaches have been found to be superior in treating lesbian batterers. The conventional wisdom of the feminist and lesbian communities cautions against using many of these approaches to treat abusing lesbian couples because of the potential harm to the abused partner (Morrow & Hawxhurst, 1989). From the perspective of the lesbian community, conjoint/couple therapy is counterproductive to the treatment effects because of the power dynamics in the relationship and may even result in further harm to the victim. The National Coalition Against Domestic Violence (NCADV) and Schechter (1987) have recommended against seeing the batterer and the victim as a couple. According to the NCADV, the systemic model of couples' therapy contributes to victim blaming, i.e., victims share responsibility for the abuse and encourage batterers to deny personal responsibility for the abuse. Schechter contended that a systems approach frequently escalates the abuse because batterers use their partners' reports in therapy as grounds for further violence.

However, in contrast, Leeder (1988) proposed a three-part model, designed specifically to treat lesbian couples experiencing domestic violence: (1) treatment begins individually with the batterer, then (2) moves to the victim, and then (3) to the couple's relationship in which the therapy is focused on developing trust, improving communication, and addressing issues specific to anger and the abuse. She also suggested that on occasion victims and abusers may need to see different therapists. Victims are encouraged to seek safety and to set limits.

In my experience, treating lesbian, abusing, "stepparenting" couples requires that the therapist pay attention to the unique needs as a "stepfamily" lest treatment compound their problems rather than alleviate them. Accordingly, in my clinical practice with these couples, since a majority of them express a desire to remain together, I have found it most effective to use an integrative systemic approach that combines couple, individual and family interventions, as needed. In using this approach, some of the goals of therapy may be the same for batterers and victims, while others are specific to the needs of each partner (see Table 11.1).

A Case Report

This case report describes therapy with a lesbian "stepparent" couple experiencing partner abuse.

Presenting Problem

Ana (age twenty-nine) and Marta (age thirty-two) were a Mexican-American lesbian couple living as a "stepfamily" with Ana's biological children,

TABLE 11.1. Goals of therapy.

Goals	Batterers	Victims
Implement a safety plan for the victim		X
Help both partners build self-esteem	X	X
Help both partners to rebuild trust in each other and the relationship	X	X
Help the abusing partner to learn different ways deal to with conflict	X	
Help the victim to develop different ways to deal with the abuser		X
Address empowerment issues and power dynamics issues		X
Explore better ways to communicate with each other	X	X
Learn better ways to express needs, emotions, anger, sans violence	X	
Learn to identify individual, couple, personal family, and larger systems issues that may unwittingly contribute to the perpetuation of violence	X	X
Learn what triggers the abuser's violence and new ways to manage it	X	
Learn new ways to be more emotionally independent of partner	X	
Teach the abusing partner to accept responsibility for the abuse and its effects	X	

Marisa (age nine) and Jorge (age seven). Ana and Marta began therapy three years after coupling as a "stepfamily" and were self-referred. In the initial interview Ana reported that, approximately one year earlier, "out of the blue," Marta began to physically abuse her. However, despite Marta's many apologies and promises to stop, the abuse continued.

Both partners had grown up in the same rural town in a Southwestern state but, according to Marta, they came from "different worlds," separated by socioeconomics. They attended the same high school and overlapped in attendance. Ana was a sophomore and Marta a senior, but they were only minimally acquainted with each other. They met later and began a relationship as a family while employed in a local hospital. At the time Ana had been a nurse for three years and Marta was a nursing technician with aspirations of becoming a nurse.

Both partners emphasized that the children had not affected by their violence. Neither Ana nor Marta remembered experiencing any lesbian stirrings during high school. Marta remembered being "made fun of because my family was poor and I did not wear cool clothes."

Ana's Story

Ana is the second of three siblings in her family of origin. She was divorced from a prior heterosexual relationship. Her mother was a licensed practical nurse and her father a high school mathematics/science teacher. In high school she was a varsity cheerleader, all around "miss popularity," and she associated primarily with the academic crowd. She enrolled in a university's nursing program after graduation, but at the beginning of her sophomore year (nineteen years old), she became pregnant and married her boyfriend, a senior in electrical engineering. She reported that although her parents were "pissed that I got pregnant," they supported both the pregnancy and the marriage. She was able to continue in school.

Two years later a second child, a son, was born. However, she was experiencing difficulties in her marriage as her husband was using and abusing drugs heavily. Ana had also used marijuana frequently prior to her first pregnancy. All her efforts for her husband to stop using drugs fell on deaf ears. Six months following her graduation she filed for divorce.

She reported that she had her first lesbian sexual experience as a college freshman. She said, "It was homecoming, we all were wasted and this girl started to play around. We all took turns experimenting." That experience awoke in Ana feelings she never before had brought to consciousness. As a result, she "experimented" with several women while in college but never admitted to herself or her partners that she might be lesbian. She said, "We all knew that we were only experimenting because we all had boyfriends, we were not lesbians." Her experimentations continued while she dated her husband and continued into their marriage.

Marta's Story

Marta was the fifth of eight siblings whose mother worked at a local motel and whose father was a construction laborer. She never married and was a sophomore nursing student and worked part time. In high school Marta had been a talented softball player and popular with the majority of students. However, she stated that she had not been "very good with books." Upon graduation from high school she enlisted in the United States Marines and served for six years. While in the Marines, she acknowledged her lesbian feelings but remained closeted: "I came out to myself and kept quiet. I needed the job because I could not figure out what to do with my life." Despite her decision to keep her lifestyle a secret, she briefly became sexually involved with a woman.

Following her discharge, she returned briefly to her hometown. There she experienced considerable stress and conflict between her need, "to be true to myself as a lesbian and feeling shame for being a lesbian." While sorting out this personal dilemma, she experienced recurrent bouts of depression because there were no other lesbians with whom to interact and share her feelings. To the best of her knowledge no other woman in town was a lesbian. As a result, she frequently traveled several hundred miles to the nearest large city to meet other lesbians. Her world came crashing down when someone from her hometown saw her walking hand-in-hand with another woman and informed the town's people that "Marta is a lesbo." That information eventually reached her parents. Confronted by them, she admitted that she was indeed a lesbian.

Neither parent reacted well to the disclosure: "My mother cried, blamed herself for me being a lesbian and told me to talk to the priest. My father was not that easy. He screamed at me, really beat up on me, called me a whore, and asked me if I learned that in the Marines. He said I was not his daughter anymore." Devastated, Marta moved to San Diego and lived there for one year. When she returned to the Southwest, she took a job at the hospital where she met Ana.

Therapy Session 1

In this initial session, following introductions, each partner steadfastly declared her love and caring for the other and reaffirmed her commitment to remain in the relationship. Asked what each one wanted from therapy, Ana said, "I just want her to stop beating up on me. I don't hit my kids and I'm not her damn kid, so I don't want her to beat up on me anymore. I want her to stop! What she is doing is beginning to get to me and is beginning to creep into my work. It is getting so that sometimes I don't feel like going home and purposely work double shifts. Last week she asked me why I work so much overtime and I tell her. That's why we're here."

Marta was very contrite and unequivocally said she wanted to stop battering Ana, but felt unable to control her violent behaviors. She did not know why she was battering Ana. She said, "I don't know why I hit her. I don't want to. I always promise myself I'll stop then I find myself doing it again. God knows she and the kids are all I got." After some reflection she offered, "Sometimes some things she says to me just makes me see red. I just can't stand her mouth." Asked for an example, Marta fell silent.

I emphasized to Marta that, regardless of what Ana might have said to her, she was responsible for the violence and its consequences. Ana reflected, "A year ago when this started, she would ask me a question about school and expected the answer, and got mad and called me all sort of names if I didn't give it to her. Her favorite is 'prom queen' because of high school. She tells me that I think that I am better that her. When I tell her that is not true, she would pull my hair and slap the shit out of me. Since then it got worse. Now she doesn't need a reason, any excuse will do. She gets mad at any and everything and if I ask her a question she flies off the handle. Now she punches and slaps me since I cut my hair short and she can't pull it. Just last week she spit on me. Can you believe that? That is the worse thing you can do to anybody."

Despite both partners' report that the children were unaffected by Marta's battering of Ana, I asked whether either one or both of them had ever witnessed the battering, and how they reacted. According to Ana, the majority of Marta's abusive behaviors occurred in the privacy of their bedroom. However, on two occasions at the dinner table the children had witnessed abuse. Ana said, "The first time she threw a glass of water in my face because she was mad that we had takeout since I did not cook dinner after working a double shift. The next time only Marisa was there. That time she slapped me because I told her I was not going to help her with her class project. Each time I smooth it over with the kids. I tell them that she has a lot on her mind because of school and doesn't really mean to be mean to me. I tell them she's never mean to them. They accept that because they don't know we're lesbians. I tell them, like I tell people at work Marta is a friend from back home who lives with us to help with expenses. Most of the time when she is mad, even in the presence of the kids, she cusses me and calls me nasty names in Spanish. The kids don't speak Spanish so they don't know what she is saying."

When I looked toward Marta she concurred with Ana's accounts. Crying, she stated: "I hated myself for doing that. I could not face the kids for a week. I apologized to them and promised that I never would do that again. When it happened again in front of Marisa I felt like a dog. I let myself down. I don't want the kids learning that kind of thing. My father used to do that to us and I didn't like it."

Based on this data, I decided to request a meeting with the children without their mother or Marta. I promised not to disclose the couple's sexual orientation, but suggested that they might want to consider doing so. I also obtained Marta's promise to stop the violence while in therapy. I explored with Ana plans to leave the house should the abuse continue. However, since they were living in Ana's house the discussion focused on how to get Marta to leave. After some discussion, Marta volunteered to leave "if things get out of hand." I felt a need to establish some boundaries so I was insistent that I would not continue to work with them should the abuse continue.

Therapy Session 2

In this session I met with the two children as a sibling group and I began by asking about their relationship with their mother and Marta. Both reported satisfactory relationships with Ana and Marta. The son, Jorge, reported feeling very close to Marta stating that she played baseball with him and she was "nice." The daughter, Marisa, was not as enthusiastic but was positive about Marta. She enjoyed listening to her play the guitar stating, "She said she will teach me how to play."

I ask them if anything had occurred in the family that they would like to talk about. Initially they could not think of any thing to say. They indicated that they were eagerly awaiting their grandfather's (Papa) upcoming visit. However, Marisa commented that, "Every time Papa comes Marta leaves the house and cries. She and Papa don't talk." Jorge added, "When Papa leaves Marta always gets mad at Mom and yell at us." Apparently neither child had ever asked why Marta left the house and cried, or why she got mad whenever Papa visited. I asked if their grandmother talked with Marta when she visited and, in unison, they replied, "Abuela (grandmother) don't come to our house, we go with Papa to her house. We're going this Friday." Based on the children's reports, the adults' conflicts and violence did not appear to be having an immediate negative effect on them. However, the underlying family dynamics were being revealed. Accordingly, at this time I made the decision to focus on the couple's relationship. Should the children have demonstrated an emotional or safety response to the violence, I would have taken a different therapeutic direction to protect them.

Therapy Session 3

In this session I met with the couple and shared my reflections on the meeting with the children. I explicitly reported on the children's interesting statements about Marta and the grandfather's visits. Both Ana and Marta expressed surprise that the children had "picked-up on that." Ana initially dismissed the children's observation, saying, "That's my father's issue. It don't have anything to do with us." Marta sternly disagreed, "It has everything to do with us." Ana replied, "That is the way it is. I thought you were cool with it." Asked for an explanation, Ana said, "My parents are not crazy about me being a lesbian but they, really my dad, still comes to see the kids and me. But he says that he won't come in the house if Marta is there. So every time he comes she has to leave. My mother won't come to the house at all. Dad takes the kids to see her. My parents still believe Marta messed my head up and made me a lesbian. They don't like her because of knowing her family from back home."

Marta concurred that Ana's parents believe "We're not good enough. And when Ana goes along with her dad that I should leave the house, which I help pay for, that tells me how she thinks about me." Marta acknowledged that Ana's acceptance of her father's rule for his visits rekindled negative feelings for her of how she saw Ana growing up and in high school. While both were growing up they were "on different sides of the world" residentially, socioeconomically, and academically. Despite Marta's popularity as a talented softball player, she always felt "less than" compared to Ana and her friends and family.

Angrily, Ana accused Marta of picking on her parents because, "they still talk to me." At that juncture Marta began to cry uncontrollably and Ana attempted to console her, but she would not be consoled. Upon regaining her composure, Marta said, "See, that's what I mean about her mouth and how she puts me down. She knows how I miss my family, and to say that just now is mean." Unlike Ana,

Marta's relationship with her family was limited to one younger sister. Marta admitted telling Ana she "was cool" about leaving the house during the father's visit, but deep down she felt hurt. Leaving the house reminded her of growing up poor and being "looked down upon by whites and Hispanics alike." Subsequent to her coming-out, her father "disowned me and said he would kill me if I ever went back home."

Ana also had been under a ban not to return home since her parents also were ashamed that she was a lesbian. However, unlike Marta, Ana believed that she was "eighty-five percent back in grace with my family." Her parents helped her financially and she was allowed to attend her sister's wedding, of course, without Marta. In contrast, Marta still was cut off from her family. Marta freely admitted feeling jealous of Ana's limited relationship with her family. This differential relationship between their respective families of origin contributed to Marta's anger and the verbal and physical abuse. Ana apologized for not understanding how Marta's experiences growing up continued to haunt her. She certainly did not understand how her comments contributed to Marta's pain about growing up poor and feeling put down. However, Ana promised, "never to go there again." Again, I reminded Marta that she was responsible for her violent behaviors regardless of the many contributing factors to her anger.

Therapy Session 4

In this session Ana and Marta sat apart from each other for the first time. Ana's face was stern, Marta's was beaming. Marta said she was proud of herself. In the two weeks between sessions she had been angry with Ana on several occasions but never struck nor cussed her, although she still felt that Ana was putting her down. Instead, she said, "I got mad but I just write it down like you said. That was hard but I feel good!"

I commended her for following through with the directive. Ana also expressed her appreciation to Marta, "Thank you for listening to him. I don't want you hitting or cussing me like before. But tell him why you got mad." Marta had asked Ana "nicely" for help with schoolwork because of difficulty completing an assignment. Despite asking politely, Ana refused. She suggested that perhaps Marta should try physical education instead of nursing since she was experiencing so much difficulty with the course work. Marta took umbrage and concluded that Ana was putting her down because Ana did not believe Marta was smart enough to be a nurse. Ana said her comment was intended to help Marta to "get out of something that was drowning her." She accused Marta of attempting to make her pay for all the bad things that happened to her in high school. However, after becoming a couple, Marta had shared with Ana her dream of becoming a nurse and her fear of not being smart enough to do so.

Initially, Ana willingly assisted Marta with her academic assignments and Marta flourished academically. After a while, Ana felt that Marta was not taking responsibility for her education, "She was expecting too much from me." To remedy that, Ana increasingly made herself unavailable to assist Marta with her academic tasks. As a result, Marta begun to fail in school and came home feeling angry. When Ana encouraged Marta to be less dependent upon her and to study more, Marta became enraged and increased her verbal attacks on Ana, "She tells me that I think I'm better than her because I'm already a nurse." Marta acknowledged that her violence toward Ana was, in part, an expression of her frustration with school and, in part, disappointment in her expectations.

Based on her recollection of a discussion with Ana prior to enrolling in college, Marta had erroneously concluded that Ana was going to be her in-house tutor. She had expected Ana to "help me get through school." She also believed that Ana's withdrawal of her assistance was intended to humiliate her, given what Ana knew about her academic shortcomings. Accordingly, abusing Ana was her attempt to get Ana to honor the unspoken contract to get her through school. I commented to Marta that she appeared to still be fighting the "class war" of high school that relegated her to something "less than Ana." I wondered aloud if becoming a nurse was her way of achieving the status she was denied in high school. Marta said that she always saw Ana as "having it all," thus, becoming a nurse, would let her for herself and others know that "I was only poor, not dumb."

Therapy Session 5

At the conclusion of the prior session I decided to offer to meet with Marta individually. In this session I commented to her that her growing-up experiences, especially high school, must have been exceedingly painful. This was evident in her many negative references to that period of life and her tendency to view the positives and the negatives of her relationship with Ana through lenses colored by those experiences. I also commented that she seemed to be consumed by anger at herself, Ana, and the world of her growing up, and I wondered whether her anger may be contributing to her tendency to interpret as a "put down" almost everything Ana said to her. This could be seen as a way to justify her abuse of Ana.

Marta admitted that anger was central to her feelings within the relationship and fueled her violence toward Ana. She perceived Ana's behaviors toward her, particularly with regard school, as a continuation of the humiliation/put downs she had suffered growing up in their hometown. However, she was adamant that Ana did indeed "put her down every chance she got." Because of that belief, she felt her anger at Ana was justified. Since she was convinced that Ana purposefully was humiliating her, I asked what had attracted her to Ana, and what was keeping her in the relationship? She shared that since high school Ana represented everything she wanted to be. Ana lived in the "right place," had the "right friends" and enjoyed a popularity different from her own. Based on that perception, coupling with Ana was for Marta "the best thing that happened to me. Being with Ana is like me being her." According to Marta, Ana was popular on the job and Marta benefited from that popularity. "Everybody at work likes her. And since they know I'm her friend, I can tell they treat me different."

Marta said that she remained in the relationship because Ana represented her "best chance to get through nursing school," and because of her relationship with the children ("I help raise them"). I wondered aloud whether those were sufficient reasons to stay in a relationship in which she believed she purposefully was being humiliated. She was clear that she loved Ana for herself, but since good things seem to favor Ana, she often imagined being Ana. Becoming a nurse, for Marta, was part of being Ana. She reiterated her dependence on Ana, "Ana and the kids are my only family," and voiced her fear of losing them because of her abusive behaviors toward Ana.

Toward the end of this session, Marta resolved to stop abusing Ana. I discussed with her the serious need for her to develop an identity that was separate from Ana's, emphasizing the importance for her to accomplish her own goal (e.g., becoming a nurse) as Marta not her alter ego. Her attempts to be Ana had so far been both frustrating and anger producing. Should she continue along that path she would forever feel second class to or less than Ana.

I also stressed the importance of her redefining her image of Ana from high school and learning to live in the present with her partner. For example, I suggested that when Ana tells her, "No, do it yourself, it is important to hear someone who cares about you and is encouraging you to be independent rather than hearing old echoes from high school." Marta was briefly silent, then admitted that she did not know how not to be "poor Marta" from the other side of the tracks. I invited her to talk with Ana in the present rather than from the past, and gain new insights of how to be a different Marta. She promised to do so.

Therapy Session 6

In this session I saw Ana and Marta conjointly again and I asked for a progress report. Marta proudly declared that she had not physically assaulted Ana since they had entered therapy. She asked whether I thought she had done well. I commended her for managing her anger, which was a central goal of therapy. However, I also cautioned that she still had several personal and relationship issues to resolve. I asked Ana how safe she felt at that point in therapy and she acknowledged that Marta had not hit her since beginning therapy. However she said that Marta had cussed at her at least three times. While she was appreciative that Marta had stopped hitting her, she strongly objected to Marta "cussing at me for the slightest thing." I reminded the couple of the no violence contract for the duration of treatment and emphasized that verbal abuse was also considered violence.

Marta apologized for violating the contract and shared that she had been thinking about our conversation about her anger. She had come to realize that much of her anger resulted from loss, shame, and the conflicts they engendered. Her major conflict was her traditional Mexican-American beliefs/values that taught her that "God cursed lesbians," indeed all homosexuals, as her father had told her the night she disclosed her lifestyle. Bothered by those comments, she had earlier sought guidance from a priest. However, all she sensed that the priest shared her father's view of how God sees lesbians. Marta revealed that she often "felt crazy" in her attempts to reconcile being a Mexican American, a Catholic, and a lesbian. She had learned growing-up that Mexican Americans were never homosexuals and she never knew any Mexican-American lesbians or gay men. Her difficulty in reconciling the contradiction often gave way to anger, especially because Ana seemed not to be bothered by the contradiction. She wondered how Ana had reconciled being a Mexican American, a Catholic, and a lesbian.

Ana shared that her family was less traditional and she never believed any of "the bullshit from the church." She asserted that there must have been homosexuals in their hometown but no one knew them. The primary loss was her cutoff from her family because she is a lesbian. For the first time Marta shared with Ana both her envy and pain that she felt when she saw Ana interacting with her family, "I know that as long as I'm a lesbian that is not going to happen for me." Ana suggested that Marta might have to adopt or create a different family that accepts her for herself. When initially shunned by her family, Ana filled her void with her children, her job and Marta: "Holidays were the hardest, not able to go home, especially for the kids. But I made do."

It seemed that coping with the cutoff was easier for Marta when she and Ana both experienced being banned. They became a family and helped each other to cope. As Ana improved her relationship with her family, it only intensified Marta's pain about being cut off and accentuated the loss of her own family. I invited the couple to reach out to the gay/lesbian communities in the city and at the university. Doing so would require them to come out as lesbians, but would provide them a community and another "family" in which Marta could find additional supports as she coped with the cutoff from her family. They promised to do so.

Therapy Session 7

Because of vacations and scheduling difficulties, six weeks had passed since I had seen the couple. Ana informed me they were doing well and several changes had occurred in their lives since we last met. Marta had not once struck or cussed at her. They had discussed many of the concerns we addressed in therapy and came to an understanding "that what happened in high school was then and this is now. Neither of us could change it so there is no point getting angry." Most important, she was not trying to humiliate or put down Marta, purposefully or otherwise.

Also, Ana had informed her father that Marta no longer would leave when he visited because she was important to Ana's life. He accepted the change. Marta had quit her part-time job to focus on school and agreed to request a tutor. They had affiliated with a lesbian group in a neighboring city (forty-three miles away) and were happy that they did so. They had chosen this out-of-town group so as not to cause concerns for the children. Many group members were Mexican Americans and custodial mothers.

Marta was stoic about never reconciling with her family. She accepted that "Ana and the kids are my family" and stated her understanding the Ana was not "looking to put me down." She shared that many of the Mexican-American lesbians in the group were "in the same boat and making it." She was positive that, no matter how long it took, she would graduate as a nurse for herself, not just to prove something. I commended them for their progress and important decisions, discoveries, and viable changes they had made, both individually and as a couple.

Overall, their communication with each other had improved, they had supported and validated the importance of each other in their lives, and Marta, in particular, had moved from thinking of herself in the past to looking toward the future. I asked Marta if she worried about the "old Marta" coming out again. She was clear, "That's not going to happen. A lot of those women (in the group) tell me things just like I was thinking and doing. Now I know how stupid I was." Ana commented that she was 99.99 percent sure that the old Marta was gone, "You think we had problems? You should talk to some of those women. They need to come see you." Since the therapeutic goals had been achieved, we terminated with a planned follow-up in six months.

AUTHOR'S REFLECTIONS

Therapy was terminated after seven sessions that had spanned nearly six months. At the six-month follow-up, the couple was still together and violence-free, with the exception of the usual relationship spats. Ana was still employed at the hospital and maintained a limited relationship with her parents. Marta was still plodding along in school but had not reconciled with her family. She was still present and future oriented, and had not reverted to the old Marta. Because of school and work limitations, they met infrequently with their lesbian group but were still affiliated. Both Ana and Marta reflected on their therapy and what they had learned. Marta said she learned a great deal and would do it again. Ana said that she was thankful because it had helped Marta to stop hitting her.

REFERENCES

Balsam, K. (2001). Nowhere to hide: Lesbian battering, homophobia, and minority stress. *Women & Therapy, 23,* 25-37.

Baptiste, D.A. (1982). Issues and guidelines in the treatment of gay stepfamilies. In A. Gurman (Ed.), *Questions and answers in the practice of family therapy* (Vol. 2, pp. 225-229). New York: Brunner/Mazel.

Baptiste, D.A. (1987a). The gay and lesbian stepparent family. In F. Bozett (Ed.), *Gay and lesbian parents* (pp. 112-137). New York: Praeger.

Baptiste, D.A. (1987b). Psychotherapy with gay/lesbian couples and their children in "stepfamilies": A challenge for marriage and family therapists. *Journal of Homosexuality, 14,* 223-238.

Baptiste, D.A. (1995). Therapy with a lesbian stepfamily with an electively mute child: A case report. *Journal of Family Psychotherapy, 6*(1), 1-14.

Benowitz, M. (1986). How homophobia affects lesbians' response to violence in lesbian relationships. In K. Lobel (Ed.), *Naming the violence: Speaking out about lesbian battering* (pp. 198-201). Seattle: Seal Press.

Cherlin, A. (1978). Remarriage as an incomplete institution. *American Journal of Sociology, 84,* 643-650.

Coleman, V.E. (1990). Violence between lesbian couples: A between group comparison. Unpublished doctoral dissertation. University Microfilms International No. 9109022.

Hammond, N. (1989). Lesbian victims of relationship violence. *Women & Therapy, 8*(1/2), 89-105.

Hart, B. (1986). Lesbian battering: An examination. In K. Lobel (Ed.), *Naming the violence: Speaking out about lesbian battering* (pp. 173-189). Seattle: Seal Press.

Leeder, E. (1988). Enmeshed in pain: Counseling the lesbian battering couples. *Women & Therapy, 791,* 81-99.

Lobel, K. (1986). *Naming the violence: Speaking out about lesbian battering.* Seattle: Seal Press.

Mclaughlin, E., & Rozee, P. (2001). Knowledge about heterosexual versus lesbian battering among lesbians. *Women & Therapy, 23,* 39-58.

Morrow, S., & Hawxhurst, D. (1989). Lesbian partner abuse: Implications for therapists. *Journal of Counseling and Development, 68*, 58-62.

Poorman, P. (2001). Forging community links to address abuse in lesbian relationships. *Women & Therapy, 23*, 7-24.

Renzetti, C. (1988). Violence in lesbian relationships: Preliminary analysis of causal factors. *Journal of Interpersonal Violence, 3*, 381-399.

Ristock, J.L. (1997). The cultural politics of abuse in lesbian relationships: Challenges for community action. In V. Benokraitis (Ed.), *Subtle sexism: Current practices and prospects for change* (pp. 279-296). Thousand Oaks, CA: Sage.

Schechter, S. (1987). *Guidelines for mental health providers in domestic violence cases.* Washington, DC: National Coalition Against Domestic Violence.

Wise, A., & Bowman, S. (1997). Comparison of beginning counselor's responses to lesbian vs. heterosexual partner abuse. *Violence and Victims, 12*, 127-134.

Chapter 12

Protecting Children When Parents Are Divorcing: Clinical Issues Through Three Systemic Stages of Divorce

Sandra Volgy Everett

Tribute to William C. Nichols

When I first met Bill Nichols he was already an icon in family therapy, venerated both for his vast experience in the field as well as for the breadth of his knowledge and depth of his devotion to the practice of family therapy. I was intimidated by his rather daunting presence as well as by his reputation for perfectionism.

However, I have found through many years of knowing Bill, at conferences, at seminars, living in a tree house in the jungle of Brazil, and enjoying his company on vacation, that he is a warm, caring individual who is intensely interested in the well-being of marriage and family therapy as well as in the world around him, and who is as devoted to his family as he is to his chosen profession. It has been an honor to know him.

A systemic orientation for family therapists working with divorcing families can provide considerable resources for assessment and interventions. We know that the ending of a relationship does not end the life of the system, particularly for the children.

The clinician's understanding of the experience of divorce for children must always be placed in the context of the ongoing life and history of the family system. Understanding the child of divorce clinically is not just about "adjustment" but it involves larger issues such as a child's development and maturity, peer and sibling attachments, bonding to parents and intergenerational family-of-origin members, and perceptions of their world as predictable and safe, chaotic, or

When Marriages Fail
© 2006 by The Haworth Press, Inc. All rights reserved.
doi:10.1300/5562_12

threatening. Although the original nuclear family system, following divorce, may never again have the same structure, organization, or predictability, the parent-child subsystem must continue and will face the challenge of reorganization.

Once a family enters the divorce process the role of the family therapist often becomes primarily that of protecting the children. To do this effectively the family therapist must recognize the profound level of disruption and confusion that a child may experience, and understand the range of emotional and defensive responses that may be made to survive the experience. I have written elsewhere that the divorce experience for a family

> is much like a pebble thrown into a moving stream, not into a pond that is quiet and self-contained. For a moment, the pebble creates circular ripples that spread out but are then quickly carried off by the current in contorted patterns downstream. (Everett & Volgy Everett, 1991)

Many stages of the divorce experience have been suggested in the literature (see, for example, Everett & Volgy Everett, 1994, 1991; Kaslow, 1981; Kessler, 1975). From a systemic viewpoint, we have identified three stages that characterize the family's experience of going through the divorce process (Everett & Volgy Everett, 1991; Everett & Volgy, 1983): (1) structural decoupling, (2) network coupling, and (3) structural recoupling.

PROTECTING CHILDREN
THROUGH THE STRUCTURAL DECOUPLING STAGE

This initial stage of *structural decoupling* defines the process of family members withdrawing former loyalties to one another and to the system itself. The parents go through a process of altering their former spousal and parental roles such that each must redefine their identities as single individuals and single parents. This process shapes the early stages of separation and divorce for every family (Everett & Volgy Everett, 1991; Everett & Volgy, 1983).

Clinical Issues

This is the stage in which children are the most vulnerable and at the greatest risk emotionally. Although parents may have been considering and planning a divorce for months, or even years, this information is often kept from the children until the last moment. In these cases the parents have already begun to look past their marriage and even the family as the children know it. When the parents tell the children of their plan to separate and divorce, it is often the first time that the children have been made aware of problems in the relationship and their first opportunity to learn that the family will be significantly changing, often in only a few hours or days. Certainly many children of conflicted families have intuitive fears that their parents may get a divorce, and some even ask about that possibility. But the announcement of the parents' clear intentions is always the most frightening and painful for all ages of children. Whether they express their feelings in an intense manner or act unconcerned after the announcement, this announcement about a separation or divorce is often the most dramatic for children. All of the children with whom I have worked have been able to report, in great detail, who told them, when, how and where they were told. Many adults and children have expressed that the scariest feelings they ever experienced were when their parents told them they were going to separate or divorce.

Clinicians need to recognize the risk for these children because even when the children have been included in the parents' plans, it comes at a time when the parents are preoccupied with divorce attorneys, financial worries, dividing property, and plans to physically separate. Even worse, for most families, the level of antagonism and animosity may be great, and their abilities to be emotionally available to their children is often at an all-time low. The children may experience a more intense degree of conflict between their parents than they have ever seen before. It is often the first time that the children's needs and desires are overlooked or ignored in favor of the parents' needs. No amount of pleading, begging, crying, or sadness on the part of the child is sufficient for the parents to give up their decision to be apart.

Children may have a variety of responses to this traumatic event depending on their age and their personal emotional style. Some children will become more outwardly anxious and dependent. Their behavior may look disturbed and moody. They may cry easily and often, and they may cling to one or both parents and regress in their independent behaviors, shadowing the parent's every move. These children may be more prone to more serious depressive and anxiety disorders, and exhibit such symptoms in a variety of settings. Some children may resist going to school, cry excessively when being dropped off, or go to the school nurse's office complaining of imaginary aches and pains so that the parents will be called to pick her or him up. Often, trips to the nurse's office or counselor's office at school will become excessive. A six-year-old girl with whom I was working was so distraught after her parents' separation that she went to the nurse's office several times a day with vague symptoms of headaches, stomachaches, or dizziness. After a couple of days of this behavior the nurse had to ask the parents to keep the child home until she had received some therapeutic help.

Other children may withdraw from their parents as well as their siblings and peers. They may spend more time in their rooms, riding their bikes, or playing video games by themselves. These are the children who tend to keep their feelings to themselves, and hide their sadness and anger behind a facade of complacency. Often these children may be perceived of as sad or depressed, or they may be described as "moody" by others in the family. A sad five-year-old was found hiding under the teacher's desk when the class returned from lunch. When asked what was going on, he stated that he wanted to run away and hide, and never be found. His parents had announced the prior weekend that they were divorcing.

Other children will openly display angry outbursts, rage responses, and mood volatility. The rages are usually expressed at home but may be acted out at school or in other settings. A ten-year-old boy, who had been told a few days earlier by his parents that they were divorcing, hit another child in the face with his fist while on the school playground. He had no prior history of reactive or violent behaviors at home or at school, and when asked why he had hit the boy he had no explanation and no understanding of why he became so angry. He stated that he barely knew the boy he had hit.

One of the more confusing reactions one might see to the divorce announcement can be the child who appears not to care that the parents are getting divorced. This child will often simply say "okay" and walk away, resuming whatever activities are typical. The parents will

be surprised, as well as often relieved, thinking that the child had handled the announcement unusually well and that perhaps their fears of
the harm they may be doing have been exaggerated. This is the child
who needs time to process and accept the news she or he have heard,
and may often be in a state of denial about the seriousness of the announcement. This child puts the news out of her or his mind and tries
to pretend that everything is normal and that there is nothing about
which to be disturbed. Often, she or he will ridicule other children in
the family who may have more dramatic responses to the announcement and/or will act nonchalantly with her or his siblings. It is important for parents to understand that this child will have a reaction, often
quite a dramatic one, at some point when her or his defenses break
down and it becomes clear that the parents are serious and that the
separation is imminent.

Systemic Interventions and Strategies

The family therapist's primary task during this early stage is to try
to stabilize the family. This is not always possible due to the animosity between the parents, particularly after the adversarial process has
begun. If the case comes to the therapist at an early point in this stage
the focus should be on joint meetings with the parents to stabilize
their parenting roles and to help them develop a plan for continuing to
meet the needs of their children during this very volatile period.
These joint parental sessions are usually best followed with one or
more family sessions spread over several weeks to reinforce the parents' roles and for them to gain feedback from the children. For particularly difficult cases, or where the parents seem unable or unwilling to follow through with these plans, it can be useful to alternate
family sessions which include the children with joint sessions with
the parents to reinforce their roles and assist them with understanding
how their own difficulties in separating are affecting the emotional
adjustment of their children. (See also Nichols, 1985.)

If it is not possible to stabilize the parents during this stage, the
next level of systemic intervention would involve sibling sessions. If
the children are old enough the therapist may be successful in helping
the children to process the divorce together and to learn to support
one another through the ups and downs of the family's transition. Of
course, this would not work well for children under six unless they

have older siblings and would require a healthy functioning sibling system.

Another helpful intervention at this stage is to involve family-of-origin members, if they are available and live nearby. If the grandparents are not involved in the adversarial process they can often fill in for the unavailable parents with support, nurturance, and physical caring for the children. This role can also be performed by aunts and uncles or other extended family members who are familiar to the children and who have an ongoing relationship with them. When these family members live some distance away, it is possible that occasional visits and frequent telephone calls can be helpful. The therapist needs to remember that these children are often desperate for some link to family support and stability which they feel that they have lost due to their parent's decision to separate. In one case, a grandfather who lived in a different state wanted to offer support for his two grandchildren during this period. He came up with the idea of putting a video link on his and the children's computers so that at designated times of the week he could have video chat sessions with them. This became something that the children looked forward to where they had the support of a loved one who understood what they were going through and could offer advice and emotional safety.

If the efforts to utilize the resources of the family system fail, then the therapist must look to external sources of support. Of course these can be used also to supplement the above interventions. Helpful resources may be counseling groups for children of divorce offered by schools or community agencies, new activities for the children to join such as chess clubs, golf lessons, computer classes, or music lessons.

If younger children are offered individual play therapy they will often respond well and be able to work out their feelings of fear, anger, or sadness through the medium of toys or other forms of self-expression. Older children and adolescents will often respond to simply talking individually with an objective and caring therapist about their angry and/or hurt feelings. This can be a useful outlet for keeping the child from acting out in angry or self-destructive ways. It should be noted, however, that separation and divorce are exceptionally painful experiences for children and some level of disruption in their normal behaviors and functioning should be anticipated for a period of time. One should not assume that every child needs to be placed in therapy who is displaying mild symptoms or adjustment difficulties.

PROTECTING CHILDREN
THROUGH THE NETWORK COUPLING STAGE

The second stage of *network coupling* involves the natural development process by which divorcing parents seek to establish and/or renew their relationship ties with both their social and family networks. As the loss of the nuclear system progresses each individual parent will seek to create new social and family systems. This is a transitional period that may involve parents relocating near or moving in with their own parents or other family-of-origin members until their new structure is stable. Their relative progress in doing so will characterize each parent's relative postdivorce adjustment as well as the adjustment of their children (Everett & Volgy Everett, 1991; Everett & Volgy, 1983).

Clinical Issues

By this stage children have usually made some adjustment to the separation and divorce announcement, and they are probably still dealing with ongoing issues of their parents living in separate residences and/or the finality of the divorce. This is the stage in which parents begin to "let go" of the emotional ties of their marriage and look to other sources of support and comfort. Children, however, may still be hanging on to confusing and frightening images of their parents separating and leaving, and may still be having fantasies or nightmares of one of the parents disappearing or dying. Again, this stage, as in the decoupling stage described earlier, tends to be one in which the parents are focused on their own pain and future adjustment. Sadly, for children, the parents' tendency toward self-absorption in these early stages of their own adjustment process can lead to the children feeling emotionally abandoned and alone in their pain. Certainly many parents struggle to readjust during this stage because they were not ready to let go of the marriage and/or were not ready themselves for their partner's announcement. The parents who were "left" and who resisted the separation and/or divorce tend to be the ones who continue to struggle and to readjust to life more slowly as single persons (see Everett & Volgy Everett, 1989).

Here is a useful clinical principle I have learned over the years: the more that parents struggle emotionally postdivorce, the greater will be the unmet needs of their children and the more likely their children will suffer long-term emotional damage.

As in the earlier stage, many parents are simply not able to be attentive or responsive to the needs of their children during this stage, despite their clear wishes to be available to their children. While they are struggling to reconnect with friends and family for support, they often turn to their children for support and even nurturance for themselves. A six-year-old child cried in my office saying that she was sad but could not cry at home because "Mommy cries all the time and I have to take care of her." Many parents do not realize how deeply their children feel the need to protect their parents from their own pain and suffering when they know their parents are having adjustment problems and are not coping well.

The systemic dynamics seen most often through this process are the children who become parentified in their relationships with their now single parents—one or both. As with the six-year-old discussed earlier, these children take on the pain of their parents and are often pulled into inappropriate pseudo adult/parent roles. In all of these cases there exists a clear breach of the boundary between the parent and child subsystems. Older children may actually take on physical parenting of their siblings and greater tasks of household management, e.g., housecleaning and preparing the meals or co-decision making with the parent (Nichols & Everett, 1986). A fourteen-year-old daughter of newly divorced parents was asked why she did not spend more time in activities with her friends since her parents had separated and she replied: "I can't, I don't have time, I have to be home to fix dinner and watch my little brother when he gets home from school." Another adolescent, seventeen years old, said, "I have to give up baseball this season, Dad needs me to pick up my brother and sister after school and take them to their soccer practices. I usually make them dinner before Dad gets home."

This is also the stage in which children move into more "protector" roles with their parents. These are often seen on a cross-sex basis, i.e., male children protecting mothers and female children protecting fathers. I have seen children as young as seven and eight years old giving advice to their parents about their new companions following the parent's dates or offering advice on what they liked or did not like about the person. Children often offer ultimatums on whether the parent can or should see the person again or how to behave and what to wear on the date. It is common for older children to offer advice on how to act, how to flirt, or whether to become physical. Many parents, caught up in their own struggles to adjust, often fail to see the serious breech this creates in boundaries and the inordinate amount of power and responsibility it gives to young children. These types of emotional burdens can sometimes lead to a child who becomes emotionally distraught or symptomatic, such as in becoming school phobic or anxious and depressed.

Many young children, during this stage, will begin sleeping or wanting to sleep in the beds with their single parents—some even as old as twelve years of age. This behavior is either directly or indirectly elicited by the parents—it is about parental need for comfort, not about the children's needs. This is also the time that some children, often young adolescent males, will actually take on the role of "man of the house" for their single mothers. I have worked with twelve- and thirteen-year-old males who have actually waited outside of the home for their mother's date to arrive to confront him. One simply told the date, without the mother's knowledge, upon his arrival that his mother was sick and "can't go out with you tonight." Another boy waited outside and stood on the steps of the porch blocking the date's entrance to the house. When the date refused to leave the boy began cursing and told the date, "If you see my Mom I will get my Dad and we will beat the sh— out of you!" This boy's parents had been divorced for more than three years.

Systemic Interventions and Strategies

The systemic goals here for the family therapist are twofold:

1. Assist the parent's postdivorce adjustment and her or his use of new resources for personal support. This may mean helping them reconnect with their families of origin or specific supportive family members. Many parents who have been through difficult divorces consider and fantasize about returning to the family-of-origin home for comfort and support to heal. Of course, if this is a serious consideration it presents a dramatic complication to the divorce and post divorce legal situation with regard to "move away" issues, i.e., gaining legal permission to move the children out of the jurisdiction. It also adds the whole dimension

of removing the children, shortly after a divorce, from regular access to the other parent in the same community. An important guideline for children's adjustment postdivorce is *the fewer changes the better, the slower the changes required the better.*

2. Help this single-parent system stabilize with clear parenting/adult roles. This means defining ongoing roles and responsibilities for the single parent(s) with regard to day-to-day caretaking. It also provides the challenge for the family therapist of defining and restoring clear boundaries between the parent and the sibling subsystem. As I identified earlier, these boundaries are often blurred or even nonexistent for postdivorce single-parent family systems.

Many of these children have been parentified. The therapist needs to create interventions that will reduce the parentified expectations and behaviors of the children. This may involve strengthening the parent's resources to manage the children better, or it may involve helping the parent to distance slightly from the child (e.g., removing the child from the parental bed at night). It can involve reconnecting the parentified child with her or his siblings in more age-appropriate play and bonding, or removing the child from perceived parental responsibilities by directing them toward friends and other activities external to the family. Often, this may involve recommending that the child spend more time temporarily with the other parent, assuming that this other parent has been able to adjust more quickly to the divorce and not pull the child into the problematic role, until the former parent is stronger and further along in her or his recoupling process. Sometimes, it simply means giving the child "permission" to be a child again. I have conducted many single-parent family sessions in which I have rehearsed and coached the parent in being able to simply say to the child, "I am okay now, I appreciated all of your help, but I will take care of things from here on."

Defining and repairing subsystem boundaries between a parent and children is not always easy. The children often have felt more empowered and have participated in the struggling parent's sadness and grief and recovery. Children empowered in this manner are often reluctant to give up their roles as junior adults. Some children will fight and resist this, while some will respond with relief to the "permission" offered by the parent to get back to being a child. Other children who were parentified or empowered inappropriately at an earlier stage in the decline of the marriage will resist the change in their role. Some of these children may have acquired empowered roles with both their mothers and their fathers because they performed parentified duties for both while the parents were married.

Here the family therapist will have to be creative and firm. Once the parent is convinced of the need to return the child to a more appropriate role, it will be up to the therapist to make it happen. Most parents are concerned that in setting limits they may be perceived by their child as rejecting or distancing. The role of the therapist is to draw boundaries and help the parent enforce them consistently (especially to get them out of the bedroom!); to reconnect the child with siblings and friends; to work together on household tasks so the child will feel that these are family times, not punishment for them; to use day care and babysitters for the parentified child so the parent can "announce" that they are going "out on a date that is just for adults"; to use daycare or babysitters for the younger siblings so the older parentified child is free to return to her/his friends after school and on the weekends.

PROTECTING CHILDREN THROUGH THE STRUCTURAL RECOUPLING STAGE

In this third stage of *structural recoupling* the parents are ready to reconnect as parents by forming a new system (i.e., binuclear family system; Ahrons, 1979) that is clearly focused on their roles and management of their children in separate households. This process of recoupling provides a new structure for new predictable patterns of interaction among the family members and specifically in the parent-child subsystem. Presumably by the time parents are reconnecting they have achieved some healthy emotional separation from their former marital relationship, they have gained some postdivorce adjustment, they have defined new social networks and family ties for personal support and no longer need to rely on their children to provide that. Now they are ready to refocus on the children and the children's needs without their own needs and emotional turmoil getting in the way (Everett & Volgy Everett, 1991; Everett & Volgy, 1983).

Clinical Issues

Children at this stage typically will be relieved at the sight of their parents talking on the phone or being willing to make decisions together. They will feel at ease for the first time in months when they hear their parents interacting without yelling and/or making threats. However, the children's response to these changes will be somewhat dependent upon the emotional damage that occurred over the two prior stages. The more damage the greater will be the need for family therapy interventions and the longer may be task of the structural recoupling.

Some children may still be hurt and scared. They may feel abandoned and rejected or unwanted. They may carry considerable anger and even hatred toward one or both parents who they have perceived as unavailable, unresponsive, and uncaring. Therefore, some of the therapeutic interventions will have to focus on simply renewing ties, being supportive, and eliciting trust again from the children. Some of the clinical needs at this time are often ones that begin a supportive process but may take months to accomplish the task of restoring trust and stability for the children.

If the parents appear to have made progress through the two prior stages and they are on the right track, then the therapist here needs to exercise patience and support, allowing the natural resources of the former nuclear system to reestablish themselves again in the new postdivorce system. This is not a time for the therapist to actively push or pull on the system, particularly the children. It is not a time to encourage the parents to rush this process or to be demanding or impatient. At this stage, following a divorce involving emotionally damaged children, parents may not get many chances to heal the wounds and reestablish their bonds with their children. They need to be on their best behaviors with each other. When therapy at this stage fails, children may carry the hurt and anger into their own adult marriages or remain emotionally damaged throughout their adult lives (Everett & Volgy Everett, 2000).

Systemic Interventions and Strategies

Often, at this stage, blended family sessions can be a useful resource for the family therapist. Sometimes it is difficult for the therapist to interest the divorced parents in considering joint sessions which would involve both parents, sometimes new partners or spouses and all of the children from the original biological nuclear family. It is not usually a good idea to involve stepchildren in this process, particularly in the beginning, as this can become complicated and often volatile.

If the parents are concerned with the emotional development of their children and how they are coping, typically the therapist can enlist them together in considering these sessions for the welfare of the children. It is important that the therapist delineate guidelines for these sessions and place clear parameters on what will be discussed and the goals that appear to be useful for the children. It is often helpful to start such a process with a joint session with the parents to create the guidelines and goals mutually so that both feel involved in the process of creating a helpful environment for their children in therapy.

There may also be some benefit derived from meeting with the children as a sibling subsystem to prepare them for what the sessions will entail and to discuss the goals and guidelines previously developed for the sessions with their parents. The children may prefer to not have stepparents or new partners involved in this process at first. This should be discussed with both the parents and the children in advance of creating the blended sessions and a decision made regarding when to involve these other participants. However, it is important that they be involved at some point because they may sabotage the process and the decisions obtained if they feel left out of the process altogether.

Another useful strategy at this stage of intervention might be to entertain the notion of creating an intergenerational intervention when members of the families external to the nuclear family are involved in the day-to-day caretaking with the children. In some cases these external caregivers may represent possible obstacles to the maintenance of stability for the children in the decisions made by the parents in the sessions. Often grandparents or aunts and uncles can be instrumental in improving the emotional climate between the divorced parents and can play mediation roles that can be valuable for the therapist. In their concern regarding maintaining their roles with the children, they can be peacemakers and create connections which allow the parents to maintain some distance while still creating a sense of solidarity for the children. However, the therapist must recognize that these figures can be powerful enough to sabotage even the best intentions of the parents.

AUTHOR'S REFLECTIONS

Recognizing these clinical stages of divorce has been helpful in my practice over the years because it identifies certain tasks as well as underlying issues that most divorcing families experience. I use it as sort of a map to let me know where the family is, how far they have progressed, and what remaining tasks need to be addressed. Family therapists bring a unique role, based on their systemic understanding of the family, which allows them to help restabilize divorcing families and to protect the ongoing adjustment of the children.

REFERENCES

Ahrons, C. (1979). The binuclear family: Two household, one family. *Alternate Lifestyles, 2,* 499-515.

Everett, C., & Volgy, S. (1983). Family assessment in child custody disputes. *Journal of Marital and Family Therapy, 9,* 342-353.

Everett, C., & Volgy Everett, S. (1989). The assessment and treatment of polarizing couples. In J. Crosby (Ed.), *When one wants out and the other doesn't* (pp. 67-92). New York: Brunner/Mazel.

Everett, C., & Volgy Everett, S. (1991). Treating divorce in family therapy practice. In A. Gurman and D. Kniskern (Eds.), *Handbook of family therapy,* Vol. II (pp. 508-524). New York: Brunner/Mazel.

Everett, C., & Volgy Everett, S. (1994). *Healthy divorce.* San Francisco: Jossey Bass.

Everett, C., & Volgy Everett, S. (2000). Single-parent families: Dynamics and treatment issues. In W.C. Nichols, M.A. Pace-Nichols, D.S. Becvar, & A.Y. Napier (Eds.), *Handbook of family development and intervention* (pp. 323-340). New York: John Wiley & Sons.

Kaslow, F. (1981). Divorce and divorce therapy. In A. Gurman and D. Kniskern (Eds.), *Handbook of family therapy,* Vol. I (pp. 662-691). New York: Brunner/Mazel.

Kessler, S. (1975). *The American way of divorce: Prescription for change.* Chicago: Nelson-Hall.

Nichols, W.C. (1985). Family therapy with children of divorce. *Journal of Psychotherapy and the Family, 1,* 55-68.

Nichols, W.C., & Everett, C.A. (1986). *Systemic family therapy: An integrative approach.* New York: Guilford Press.

Chapter 13

Surprised by Divorce: Working with the Spouse for Whom the Rejection Was Unanticipated

Dorothy S. Becvar

Tribute to William C. Nichols

I knew about Bill Nichols long before I had the opportunity to become acquainted with him and later be able to work with him. From the first, I knew Bill to be a person of integrity, one whose views I respect and whose friendship I value. I am truly grateful that I was invited to participate in this tribute, one that is so richly deserved. My thanks to you, Bill, for all that you have contributed to the profession of marriage and family therapy and for what you stand for as a human being.

Having provided therapy for couples for more than twenty-five years, I have learned that there are several paths that ultimately may lead to the same final end point, the dissolution of a marriage[1] through divorce. For some couples, divorce represents a mutually agreed upon resolution to marital difficulties, while for many others one member of the couple is more desirous of a divorce than is the other. Although the parties to the divorce in these two instances are likely to have entirely different kinds of experiences, in both cases, they have in common the fact that divorce follows various efforts to save the marriage. They also have had an opportunity to discuss their problems, perhaps attempt to find solutions, and to digest the fact that a divorce may occur, however much it may not be desired.

By contrast, there is a third scenario in which one member of the couple is presented with a *fait accompli* as she[2] learns that her partner

When Marriages Fail
© 2006 by The Haworth Press, Inc. All rights reserved.
doi:10.1300/5562_13

has already decided upon divorce and is not open to other options. In this case, the nonconsenting spouse is faced with the challenges associated in becoming a divorced person, re-creating life as a single person, and perhaps also as a single parent. At the same time she must come to terms with the added pain of a major rejection for which there was no warning or preparation. Helping clients in such situations to navigate some very turbulent waters requires understanding of this specific context and awareness of various factors that may affect a successful outcome to the therapy process.

CLINICAL ISSUES FROM A SYSTEMS PERSPECTIVE

Divorce disrupts the system no matter how much it may have been desired by both partners. All roles, rules, relationships, and responsibilities, both within the family as well as between the family and other systems, must be renegotiated and redefined. The old family and related dreams and expectations must be mourned even as the business of re-creating family life in the context of divorce is undertaken. Depending on the circumstances, feelings of anger, sadness, alienation, and/or guilt may emerge and require appropriate attention. For mothers who receive custody of their children there may be a substantial reduction in standard of living that occurs concurrently with a significant increase in the demands on their time. And for those who have been rejected, there may be the additional challenge of regaining a sense of one's own worth. However, if rejection has come "out of the blue," another layer of complexity often may be added, one that I find similar in character to the experience of a sudden death (Becvar, 2000). The following are two examples of such a situation.

Case Example: Theresa and Bob

Theresa and Bob had been married for ten years and had two children, ages seven and nine. Bob was a successful lawyer and an avid sports enthusiast. Theresa was a stay-at-home mom who thoroughly enjoyed her role as a homemaker and willingly supported Bob and his career. Theresa and Bob owned their own home, had two cars, took regular family vacations, and seemed to have everything going for them. They had some squabbles over the years but usually managed to settle them fairly quickly.

Theresa's main complaint was that, given the demands of his work and Bob's participation in sports, he was not at home as much as she would have liked. For his part, Bob often became irritated with what he considered Theresa's lack of independence and overreliance on him. However, their problems had always seemed manageable and therapy had never even been mentioned, let alone considered. Nevertheless, on her thirty-fourth birthday, Bob took Theresa to dinner at one of their favorite restaurants, and before the meal was over announced that he thought he was going to have to leave the marriage.

For the next month, Theresa, who was shocked and stunned, told no one what Bob had said and tried everything she could think of to be the wife she thought Bob wanted her to be. She also begged him to tell her why he was leaving, but Bob could not. Finally, during a late evening conversation that lasted into the small hours of the morning, Theresa asked Bob if there was another woman and Bob acknowledged that there was. Theresa was heart-broken but still wanted to work on the marriage; Bob was silent. The next day, Bob went to work and never came home again. After several days he let Theresa know that he was now living with the other woman.

Example: Case of Marie and Greg

Marie and Greg had lived together for several years before deciding to marry. Although Marie was older than Greg, they agreed that they did not want children, so this was not an issue. They were confident in themselves and their respective careers, and felt good about the fact that their relationship had successfully weathered the test of time.

Shortly after the wedding, Greg's job as an engineer took him to Germany, for what was supposed to be a brief stay. However, after several months, it became clear that he would need to remain for at least two years, and perhaps more. On very short notice, they decided to sell their home and have Marie join Greg in Germany, where they would reside in a rented apartment. Although Marie missed her work as a nurse, she was excited about this new adventure and enjoyed the opportunity to learn a new culture and a new language. Greg often had to work long hours, but the couple traveled to different parts of Europe on weekends as Greg's schedule permitted. Greg was finding great satisfaction and success in his current assignment.

They experienced periodic conflicts about money, with Marie wanting to save and Greg often spending beyond their means. Ultimately, however, Marie tended to go along with Greg despite the fact that she disliked creating debt and continued to worry about their lack of planning for the future. Greg, in turn, often criticized Marie for nagging him about money, but otherwise they generally got along pretty well. It therefore came as an unbelievable shock to Marie that as Greg's duties were nearing completion and they began making plans for their return home, Greg informed Marie that once they were back in the United States, he intended to file for a divorce.

As with a sudden death, the coping system of the rejected spouses, in instances such as those described above, is severely challenged. In addition to the various feelings associated with the loss of the relationship, they must deal with shock, disbelief, and extreme disruption in all areas of their lives. In a moment, their world has been shattered, often bringing about a sense of unreality as they find themselves projected into a totally new realm with no directions on how to proceed, indeed, often with no idea even of how or where to begin to move.

SELECTING POSSIBLE SYSTEMIC INTERVENTIONS AND STRATEGIES

When meeting with a client such as Theresa or Marie, in the aftermath of unanticipated rejection, I believe it is very important to allow her to share the details of what has happened and to be willing just to listen. This requires that the therapist be able to sit with and acknowledge the pain, the shock, the anger, and whatever other emotions the client is expressing. The client needs to be able to tell her story and to have her experience validated as normal, given the circumstances. Along the way, the therapist may gain valuable information as she or he listens attentively not only to the details of the client's story but also to her use of language, and the manner in which various events are framed and explained.

The therapist must also be attentive to the requirements of the family system for stability in the context of change (Becvar & Becvar, 2003). Although the client may be experiencing a sense of urgency about figuring things out and getting on with life, I do not believe the process should or can be rushed. Therefore I may speak about the importance of taking whatever time is necessary to regain a sense of balance before attempting any radical changes. Not only do I believe this to be true, but I also recognize that such restraint from change may have a paradoxically effective impact, facilitating the ability of the client to start sorting things out and taking appropriate next steps. In addition, I am aware that giving the client permission to feel what she does may alleviate secondary guilt responses related to her emotional reactions, i.e., feeling crazy because she cries at the drop of a hat.

Theresa (mentioned previously) had been referred to me for therapy by her sister, a former client. By the time of our first meeting, Bob had been gone for two weeks and Theresa had lost at least ten pounds. She related the details of what had happened and indicated that she seemed to be moving through her days in a kind of haze, doing what was necessary for her children but otherwise unable to focus on anything meaningful. She knew she wasn't taking very good care of herself—she was barely eating and found herself alternating between numbness and tears.

As with clients who are bereaved, I listened to Theresa's story, normalized her reactions, and suggested that she consider designating a specific block of time each day to allow herself to grieve, to experience her feelings fully, and perhaps to write in a journal. After the designated period of grieving time each day, I suggested that she continue on with her regular routine, knowing that she would have a similar block of time the following day. I also tried to help her understand that it is natural for her to bounce around emotionally, vacillating between feelings of sadness and anger, feeling guilty and blaming herself one moment and feeling angry and blaming Bob the next moment. Since she indicated that the children seemed to be doing okay, I decided to pursue that subject in greater detail at another session. However, I did emphasize the importance of taking care of herself so that she could continue to do a good job of caring for the children during this very crucial time.

As therapy continues, I believe it is also important to help the client begin the process of re-creating life as a divorced person. This includes assessing her resources and prioritizing the tasks that need to be accomplished in several areas. In the emotional realm, as in the case of the sudden death of a loved one, the client who is surprised by divorce may benefit from conversations that help her to come to terms with her grief, deal with her anger, and transform whatever guilt she may be experiencing. Helping her find ways to forgive herself and her spouse also may be appropriate and useful at this time. In addition, it may be helpful for her to recognize the cyclical nature of grief such that a "good day," e.g., feeling confident and reconciled to the situation, may be followed by a "bad" day, e.g., one in which she reverts to patterns characteristic of the initial period following the departure of her spouse.

Given the sudden disruption in their lives, it also becomes important to consider some very pragmatic challenges with which clients may be faced. As with a sudden death, there are likely to be many loose ends that require attention since the separation has occurred without prior preparation. Has the client spoken with a lawyer? Will there be adequate financial support? Will a move to a new residence be required? Will it be necessary to find a job? Are there other people in the client's world who would be willing to assist with the details of daily living if help is needed? If there are children, how will visitation with the noncustodial parent be structured? I believe the therapist may provide assistance as the client begins to consider such issues, helping her explore options and figure out the best way to proceed. This, too, may require patience as the client is required by circumstances to move more slowly than she would like.

When Marie returned to the United States from Germany, she had a great deal of debt and very little money. She also no longer had a home and had to accept her parents' invitation to live with them until she could find a job, save some money, and move out on her own. She felt ashamed not only that her marriage had failed but that, as a woman in her early forties, she was once again having to depend on her parents for financial support. The situation was further complicated by the fact that despite having kept her license current, Marie had not done any nursing for several years and was feeling a little shaky about resuming her career.

I suggested that Marie start by looking for part-time work while she did whatever was necessary to hone her nursing skills. I also encouraged her to reconnect with old friends in the area and to use this time of living with her parents as an opportunity to solidify her relationships with her mother and her father, and to help them with household tasks that were becoming more difficult as they aged.

RECOGNIZING THE FAMILY SYSTEM'S RESPONSES AND DYNAMICS

Grieving the Loss

Throughout the process of helping clients to re-create their realities in the wake of an unexpected divorce, I believe it is important for the therapist to pay attention to any challenges to their belief systems they may have experienced. For example, even in today's society with its high rate of divorce, most couples expect that their marriages represent a lifetime commitment. Therefore, when circumstances prove otherwise, they may find themselves grieving, not only for the end of their marriage, but also for the loss of some of the ideas and convictions that comprised the foundation for their lives. This phenomenon may be more obvious when religious or spiritual beliefs and behaviors are called into question, but it also merits attention even when dealing with views about marriage and divorce from a secular perspective.

For example, the client may question whether the marriage ever had meaning for her spouse, or whether "everything was a lie." She is likely to express feelings of failure, and also may doubt her own judgment and perceptions. If religious/spiritual dimensions emerge, she may puzzle about or even blame God, perhaps believing that she is being punished for some supposed wrongdoing. She also may worry about violating the tenets of her religion, perhaps committing a sin, by being party to a divorce. I have found it essential to discuss such issues with clients thoughtfully and carefully, and to provide suggestions as appropriate to facilitate their process of examining and discarding ideas that no longer fit and incorporating beliefs that are consistent with their new lives. I may recommend readings, suggest attendance at support groups, and/or encourage conversations with clergypersons.

At some point, I also may offer my interpretation of the dynamics of divorce, which when accepted, may positively reframe the situation. What I often share with clients is that marriages may end when the partners have learned everything that they can from each other. Accordingly, while the experience certainly is painful, and while we may not be able to see it in the moment, there may be some way in which the divorce and its circumstances "make sense." If nothing else, this may offer a perturbation to the family system that yields interesting reflections and responses.

Becoming an Effective Single Parent

There are two additional considerations that I also believe require attention. The first applies to divorcees with children and involves becoming an effective single parent. Parenting is a demanding job even when two partners share the responsibilities and it can seem overwhelming when the entire burden falls on the shoulders of one person. However, when one becomes a single parent in the context of unanticipated rejection, the family may be at even greater risk for extreme disruption. Indeed, children are likely to be confused not only by the loss of their father's regular presence but also by the emotional absence of their mother at a time when they are most in need.

As Theresa began taking some first steps toward coming to terms with what had happened and successfully regained some feelings of stability, I decided to devote some of our time together to a consideration of her children. Although she had continued to report that the children seemed to be handling the situation fairly well, I encouraged her to spend one-on-one time with each child on a daily basis, if at all possible. I suggested that she use this time for an enjoyable activity and to answer questions as they arose rather than trying to focus conversations in a particular way.

I also emphasized the importance of never speaking negatively about their father and of avoiding triangulation. I shared my belief that one of the benefits of an otherwise horrendous experience was the opportunity to forge relationships with each child in ways that might not have been possible had the marriage continued. Finally, I encouraged Theresa to recognize that as she demonstrated her competence and parented effectively she would provide her children with the security they needed, not only during this period of adjustment but also in the future. Indeed, it likely would prevent her from seeking a new relationship in order to find someone to take over the responsibilities for parenting, a situation that generally is doomed from the outset.

Becoming a Competent Single Person

In these situations, the issue of new relationships generally emerges, often rather early in the process when a spouse is coming to terms with a divorce. For me, regardless of whether children are involved, the second important topic for consideration involves becoming a competent and confident single person. That is, I believe it is extremely important for clients to get to a place where they feel good about themselves and their lives, and know that they can make it on their own. They can then move toward creating a new relationship from a place of desire rather than of need, recognizing that they will be fine even if they do not find another partner and ultimately remain single.

As we begin to consider the topic of new relationships, I have found that some clients initially may feel that they never want to marry again, while others may express fears around the possibilities for remarriage. Some may want to find another person with whom to share their lives but distrust their ability to make wise choices. Others may worry about where they will meet someone and if they do, whether they can ever again be fully trusting. Some may be looking for persons who "make" them feel better about themselves or who will share some of the burdens they are carrying. However, I have found that if they focus first on achieving a sense of wholeness for themselves before entering into a new relationship, many of these fears and concerns will disappear, and if they do find a new partner, it will be a person who complements that wholeness in a positive manner.

Marie was successful in finding part-time work that enabled her to take some continuing education classes in nursing. While doing this she continued to live with her parents and often felt frustrated by her circumstances, as well as by the emotional roller coaster she seemed to be riding as she and Greg negotiated the details of their divorce. She also had a tendency to beat herself up and to lament the mistakes she had made in her life. At the same time, she was anxious to begin dating, despite a variety of concerns about finding a new partner. I advocated patience and understanding of the need for healing before getting involved with someone again. I suggested that when she had achieved her personal goals for herself the likelihood of finding someone with whom she could create a meaningful relationship would be much greater.

I also talked with her at length about finding ways to recapture a sense of joy in her life, despite the sadness she was likely to continue to feel about the end of her marriage. I suggested that she do something nice for herself every day, and that she explore her talent for music, which had been dormant since high school, by joining a local Bach chorale group. I encouraged her to spend time with her female friends and to begin thinking about where she might want to work and live once she was able to move in these directions.

AUTHOR'S REFLECTIONS

Just as there is no bereavement experience that is necessarily more difficult for survivors, I do not believe that there is one type of divorce experience that is inherently more painful than another. Rather, what is important to recognize is that each experience is different, with varying stresses and challenges. And while divorce is rarely considered anything but a negative event, there may also be some aspects unique to each situation that may be considered to be "positives." Thus, for example, those who have been surprised by divorce certainly may be angry at the lack of opportunity to work on resolving problems and perhaps saving the marriage. At the same time, the definitive end to the relationship precludes many of the tumultuous ups and downs that often characterize the days and months leading to a decision to divorce. Avoided are the doubts, the questions, the recriminations, the uncertainties, and the vacillation between hope and despair.

While one has not had a hand in its creation, nor does one necessarily like it, the agenda is set and the client knows from the outset that she is once again to be an unmarried woman. The therapist, therefore, also must be careful not to engender false hope. Although the possibility of a reconciliation always exists, at least implicitly, helping the client re-create her life as a single person is a priority. Should her ex-husband express a desire to get back together at some point in the future, the client will be better prepared to consider this option in a healthy manner. And if such an option does not emerge, she also will be better equipped to forge new paths on her own. As with other painful experiences of loss, if they can be handled appropriately, unanticipated rejection may become a catalyst for growth for which the client one day may feel gratitude.

NOTES

1. The terms marriage, marital, divorce, and spouse, as used here, refer to all committed relationships as well as to those that are legally sanctioned.

2. While unanticipated rejection certainly may occur among men, I have encountered this phenomenon primarily among women, who therefore will be the focus of this chapter.

REFERENCES

Becvar, D. S. (2000). *In the presence of grief: Helping family members resolve death, dying, and bereavement issues.* New York: Guilford.

Becvar, D. S., & Becvar, R. J. (2003). *Family therapy: A systemic integration.* Boston: Allyn & Bacon.

Chapter 14

Rebalancing the Postdivorce Family When the First Spouse Remarries: Systemic Family Interventions

Craig A. Everett

Tribute to William C. Nichols

I arrived at Florida State University as a new doctoral student in Fall 1974. I had a masters degree and five years of mental health experience, both inpatient and outpatient. I was a little older than most of the students and certainly had more clinical experience than the others—I was confident and a little cocky. Bill Nichols' first words to me in Tallahassee were, "Well, you have about one year of experience repeated four times."

*As colleagues and friends, Bill and I have taken on many challenges, but all had a flair of adventure. When he and I began to write our textbook (Nichols & Everett, 1986) together in 1983, we did so in a rustic cabin at 9,000 feet in the Santa Catalina mountains outside of Tucson. More recently, in working on our present project (*The Teaching and Learning of Family Therapy*), we recorded hours of audio reflections on our experiences in the field while driving through western North Carolina and the Blue Ridge Mountains.*

Historically, Bill often single-handedly shaped the definition and future of the marital and family therapy field as a profession from his work with the Journal of Marital and Family Therapy *and early standards for training and education, and through political initiatives for MFT licensure and ethical standards of practice. His voice has always been one for professionalism, competence, and integrity. Although he has stirred controversies and been viewed often as stubbornly holding onto his views for the field, it has been a privilege to have my career so closely tied to his as a mentor, colleague, and friend.*

When Marriages Fail
© 2006 by The Haworth Press, Inc. All rights reserved.
doi:10.1300/5562_14

DISCUSSION OF THE CLINICAL ISSUE
FROM A FAMILY SYSTEMS PERSPECTIVE

As clinicians we know that the life of a family system continues following a divorce, particularly with regard to the parent-child subsystem. All postdivorce family systems go through a process of rebalancing and stabilizing in order to survive. Some families accomplish this more successfully than others. The more dysfunctional the predivorce family system and/or the more problematic the emotional health and stability of the parents, the greater will be the difficulty of the postdivorce system's restabilization.

As therapists we are aware that even when postdivorce family systems appear to have rebalanced and the divorced parents are working well as coparents, the potential for events and conflicts to suddenly unbalance the system remains. One of the most prominent and predictable dynamics for creating such an imbalance occurs when one of the parents announces her or his decision to remarry. This step in the evolution of the postdivorce system carries an underlying threat to the stability of the rebalanced system that many clinicians fail to recognize.

In fact, the tenuously balanced postdivorce systems may be threatened just by the continued serious dating of one of the parents or when a dating partner has been invited to move into the parent's residence. The threat to these systems magnifies when the first of the former partners announces plans to remarry. Sadly, the other parent often learns of this plan initially through one of the children. Sometimes it seems that former spouses have a way of knowing when certain behaviors or decisions may trigger a serious reaction in their former partner and mistakenly believe that the potential reactivity to the announcement may be softened if the news is delivered by a child. Of course, some former spouses may delight in provoking their former partner with this news while others may be able to communicate the information in an adult conversation.

From my own experiences, this is a time where attorneys may become involved quickly. Often the "offended" single parent threatens to return to court to modify custody of the children and/or restrict the children's access to the remarrying parent and her or his partner. It should not be surprising to the therapist when the offended parent involves family-of-origin members, particularly grandparents, in destructive coalitions against the former partner. These grandparents may also finance the attorneys for court proceedings.

It is important for the systemic therapist to be able to look at the *bigger picture* of these dynamics. The ensuing conflict that may result between the former spouses is never simply about the character or traits or history of the new partner. It may not just be about "a new partner coming into my children's lives." In my experience the underlying issues that emerge here are about prior marital dynamics of *territory, jealousy, and the fantasy of reunion*. It may also be about more primitive internal dynamics of a partner regarding *attachment and loss, and especially abandonment* (Everett & Volgy, 1991).

Systemically, a postdivorce balanced system of single parents maintains an equilibrium that can be experienced as "safe" and familiar. The system can exist in this state in a reasonably healthy manner for years—to the benefit of the children. The "intrusion," inevitably, of a new partner—no matter what she or he may be like—immediately threatens this equilibrium and balance of the system (Everett & Everett, 2000, 1994). Unfortunately, I have found that these underlying dynamics can lead to even more unpleasant and primitive *charges* by the one partner that may range from erroneous allegations of abuse and molestation of the children to unfounded accusations of past offenses of drug abuse, sexual affairs, or the use of pornography. One of the more damaging consequences may involve false charges by the offended parent that the other parent is alienating the child against them. In some cases the offended parent may withhold the children's access to the other parent and even attempt to directly alienate the children by telling them false stories that cast the parent or new partner in a negative light (Everett, in press).

SELECTING POSSIBLE SYSTEMIC INTERVENTIONS AND STRATEGIES

In working with an imbalanced system, as described earlier, the earlier the therapist can become involved the better will be the prognosis. Unfortunately, the legal system and adversarial process offers a conducive arena to play out this drama of anger, hurt feelings, and even revenge. Many well-meaning attorneys and judges can easily become seduced by these allegations due to their zeal and well-intentioned attempts to protect children. Many of these cases will be in courts before they will be in a therapist's office.

The earliest goal is for the therapist to develop a careful and thoughtful strategy because of the potential volatility of the family's situation. The systemic therapist needs to look initially at the resources and dynamics of the larger family system. From my own experiences I always try to create—at least as a start—the most straightforward and direct of interventions. Here are some early interventions that have worked with regard to rebalancing postdivorce systems.

Joint Sessions with the Remarrying Parent, New Partner, and Child

Invite the remarrying parent and her or his new partner into a joint session to see whether straightforward ways exist to ease their transition into marriage and make their new relationship more acceptable to the children and palatable to the other parent. For example, I worked with a father and his new wife of six weeks, one year after his divorce from the mother of his seven-year-old child. I saw the mother and child in an initial session since the child was refusing to visit her father if the new wife was present. I learned from the child that her father had filled his apartment with pictures of him and his new wife (many in kissing poses) and they had actually removed some of his daughter's pictures from his bedroom. He had also insisted that the child call his new wife "Mom," to distinguish her from the child's use of "Mommy" for her biological mother.

One would think that any caring parent would be able to anticipate these issues and the resultant pain to the child. I did not think that he was uncaring but simply caught up in the excitement of his new relationship and focused on pleasing his new partner. Fortunately this case resolved itself after a couple of sessions with the father and stepmother by helping them to recognize and to think through these issues and make some practical corrections in their home. A final session with the father, stepmother, and the child allowed the airing of feelings, provided the father with a setting to formally apologize to the child, and allowed all three family members to develop a new game plan for their time together. The only session necessary in this case with the mother was at the very beginning to gain her support of me and assess her level of animosity.

Joint Sessions with the Remarrying Spouse and Former Spouse; Then Introducing the New Partner

A more conflicted case involved a father who was making threats of returning to court to modify custody because of the mother's involvement with a new partner. The parents were about three years postdivorce and while both had dated some, neither parent had been in a serious relationship up to this point. The strategy here involved two sessions with the biological parents (former spouses). My goals were as follows:

- clear away some animosity that was left from their predivorce period;
- process and facilitate the spouses' further emotional letting-go of each other;
- help them actually say "good-bye" to each other and acknowledge verbally that they were no longer expecting to reunite (this was very difficult for the father); and
- help them to understand the needs of their children (two adolescents) in their postdivorce adjustment and the potential damage of their pursuit of a court battle.

In these early sessions the father admitted to his former wife that he "never wanted the divorce" (though he had initiated it because he was involved with another woman) and that he not only had pictures of her in his apartment but that he had saved some articles of her clothing that he kept in his chest with his own clothing.

I should note this case was referred to me by an attorney and that both of these parents had their own individual therapists. Both of the therapists had refused to meet with the parents jointly. These sessions were so successful that I cautiously suggested a meeting with Dad, Mom, and mother's fiancé (I would not suggest this in all cases). To my surprise the parents agreed and the following session focused on communication for the future and some access issues. A follow-up session that included the three adults and the two adolescent children was held primarily to demonstrate that in "public" (at least in my office) the adults could interact and behave respectfully.

Combined Subsystem and Intergenerational
Family Sessions

Another more dramatic and highly conflicted case involved the early stages of Parental Alienation (see Everett, in press; Gardner, 2001). In many of these cases, as illustrated earlier, I tend to start with strategies that involve working primarily with subsystems rather than the whole family. This is helpful in bypassing potentially explosive situations, sometimes altogether, and at least until I have a better sense of risk.

This was a case that involved two young adolescent girls who were refusing to see their father because he had invited his fiancée, whom he had been dating for over a year, to move into his home. He had prepared the girls for some time and did not do this abruptly. However, the underlying animosity had been building in this family since before the divorce. The mother and her parents blamed the father's travel and business on the divorce and had often stated to the girls that the divorce had been "his fault."

The alienation began a few months earlier when they all realized that he was quite serious about this relationship and when he told the girls four months in advance that he was planning to ask her to move in. At this point the mother and grandparents pulled the girls into a destructive coalition against the father and his girlfriend. They now accused the father of having had "an affair" with this woman before the divorce (he had only known this woman for the past fourteen months, the divorce had occurred three years previously). They even went on the computer and found two traffic citations that the woman had received more than ten years ago. They said to their attorney (paid for by the grandparents), "We cannot allow the girls to be in a car with this woman."

Due to these allegations and a brief time frame before the case went further toward court, I decided to jump right in and begin this case with a family meeting. Those invited were the father and his fiancée, the mother, the maternal grandparents (who lived up the street from the mother and who were clearly reinforcing the alienating behaviors and message), and the two teenage daughters. There are certain family conflicts that can only be addressed and potentially changed by involving ALL of the "players," and family therapists must understand that hours and hours of therapy with pieces of a family may never accomplish what can be done in just one or two hours with everyone.

This is where it is important to understand the powerful nature of systemic coalitions and scapegoating. Also, in this case it would have been naive and futile to plan interventions without the grandparents' involvement because they could continue to sabotage the children's relationships with their father from the "safety" and relative "anonymity" of their background role. Including them in the first session gave them a chance to be heard and also made them accountable for their behaviors and messages. This case resolved itself after three family sessions because the two daughters actually liked the fiancée and identified with the fact that she was a buyer for a large women's clothing store. The girls needed to hear from her and their father that they were still welcome and loved. They also needed to hear from both their mother and grandparents that they had permission to like and enjoy their time with the father and his fiancée.

The reason the mother and grandparents were willing to support this in a relatively short time was because the daughters were mature enough and old enough to express their feelings in the relative safety of the therapy sessions. Younger children may not have been able to either express themselves or gain the support of their mother. The other factor, as is often true in these situations, was that neither the mother or the grandparents had ever met the fiancée, even though the father had offered to get together with them socially some months earlier. The fiancée was able to acknowledge the ongoing roles and continuing authority of the mother and grandparents, and her personal style and demeanor did not elicit any reactivity on their part.

RECOGNIZING THE FAMILY SYSTEM'S RESPONSES AND DYNAMICS

To be effective in working with complex cases such as these the systemic therapist must be able to visualize in one's clinical mind what a *rebalanced system* looks and feels like. The therapist must be able to conceptually "see" the interactions among the postdivorce systems, understand the intersystem balancing dynamics, and recognize the power of feelings of loss, fear, abandonment, and even the need to hurt the one that was once loved.

The systemic therapist must ask:

- What change is realistic in a case such as this, given the "players" in the family system?
- What are the respective resources and/or deficits in each of the systems?
- What are their motives behind the conflicts?
- What are the sources of emotional stability?
- Where do the children fit into the alliances and coalitions?
- What are their relative levels of attachment with each parent and their partners and their former spouses?
- How do the children fit into the reestablished subsystems?
- How rigid are the external boundaries surrounding each of the postdivorce subsystems? How rigid are the internal boundaries around the parent-child subsystem?
- Who is the most fragile family member—the offended parent or a child?

In many of these cases where the conflict was triggered by the first remarriage, the underling dynamics are often tied to the vulnerability of the parent who is not getting remarried. This parent may be the most fragile. She or he may have held onto the hope of reuniting with the former spouse. Or she or he may still be struggling with her or his own postdivorce adjustment. The remarriage may trigger a range of issues for this parent from practical fears of financial loss to grief regarding the loss of the marriage. However, perhaps the most dramatic issue often involves fears of potentially losing a child, either literally or emotionally. This powerful fear is characterized in thoughts such as these:

- Maybe the children will like "her" more than me.
- They may want to live with "them" instead of me.
- They may feel sorry for me because I don't have a life of my own.
- I always knew she/he would take them away from me.
- She is just doing this to get back at me for the divorce.
- He is just doing this so the children will live with him and he won't have to pay child support.

In the first case just mentioned, the system rebalanced after the father and future stepmother learned and understood the child's needs. They were able to make changes that alleviated the child's fears and created a more normal transition for them as a new family. This was a pretty straightforward intervention!

In the second case the system rebalanced after the former partners gained some closure on issues left over from their prior relationship and divorce, and after the father met the potential stepfather, which diffused his reactive behaviors. The stability of the newly organized, blended system (i.e., with a stepfather) was further solidified by the family session involving the children. This intervention was somewhat risky, but not if handled straightforwardly one step at a time.

In the third case the decision to include all of the "players" right at the start worked—but it could have been quite risky, particularly if the grandparents had refused to participate or had come to the sessions in a confrontational mode. However, everyone's participation in several family sessions clearly extinguished the alienation messages and behaviors from the grandparents, diffused the mother's concerns about the new future stepmother, and was solidified by the children's involvement and support (even though rather guarded) of the new stepmother. This intervention had more unpredictable risks, but I tend to err on the side of inviting more family members than fewer. There are always underlying live dynamics to process with multiple family members that can redeem interventions—and, I probably got a little lucky here, too.

AUTHOR'S REFLECTIONS

Systemic family interventions represent the majority of my practice and clinical orientation. I am often asked by students or at workshops, "Don't you just use 'regular' interventions like behavioral or cognitive therapies?" After thirty some years of practice I find that I really do not use those types of interventions explicitly, though I would acknowledge that some are probably blended into my interactions with clients. When I am questioned about this I usually say that I rely on my understanding of systems theory and the clinical knowledge of how families behave to identify the target points for interventions and to select the least offensive intervention that may work. I think this is how *Integrative Family Therapy* really works (Nichols & Everett, 1986).

The therapist learns to think about the system and to "see" the interplay of patterns and dynamics within families. When you learn to do that you can relate to the family in ways that cause the dysfunctional elements of their interactions to change; or at least you can cause these dynamics to be called into question. If this level of intervention does not work, then you move to the next level of challenging and/or correcting the interactions. If that level does not work then you move to the more complex level of connecting with the system in ways that more directly challenge the behaviors of either individuals, subsystems, or the entire nuclear system. Sometimes the therapist has to perturbate the system to create change. However, I really prefer to work more indirectly with the system.

I find that if I take my time and look at the presenting case situation from the "bigger picture" systemically, I can identify several dynamics and intervention strategies that I wish to pursue. This may involve having a child sit next to me to tell me about the family, or separating the sibling subsystem from that of the parents. It may also involve inviting a grandparent in to change the balance of the dynamics or to diffuse levels of conflict. I learned years ago that you do not need to take on the primary presenting issues of the dysfunctional family system from the start. Then I learned some years later that a good systemic therapist can create change in a system without even addressing the sensitive or fragile dynamics of the system. If you really believe in concepts such as systemic balance, reciprocity, circularity, perturbation, homeostasis, and, of course, if you know how to recognize them and use them in your therapy, there will always be more choices and resources for clinical interventions than one ever needs to use in any one case.

REFERENCES

Everett, C.A. (in press). Family therapy with Parental Alienation Syndrome. In R.A. Gardner, R. Sauber, & D. Lorandas (Eds.), *The parental alienation syndrome: Legal and clinical issues.*

Everett, C.A., & Volgy, S.S. (1991). Treating divorce in family-therapy practice. In A.S. Gurman and D.P. Kniskern (Eds.), *Handbook of family therapy,* Vol. II (pp. 508-524). New York: Brunner/Mazel.

Everett, C.A., & Volgy Everett, S. (1994). *Healthy divorce.* San Francisco: Jossey-Bass.

Everett, C.A., & Volgy Everett, S. (2000). Single parent families: Dynamics and treatment issues. In W.C. Nichols, M.A. Pace-Nichols, D.S. Becvar, & A.Y. Napier (Eds.), *Handbook of family development and intervention* (pp. 323-340). New York: John Wiley & Sons.

Gardner, R.A. (2001). *Therapeutic interventions for children with parental alienation syndrome.* Cresskill, NJ: Creative Therapeutics, Inc.

Nichols, W.C. & Everett, C.A. (1986). *Systemic family therapy: An integrative approach.* New York: Guilford Press.

Chapter 15

Cognitive-Behavioral Therapy in the Wake of Divorce

Frank M. Dattilio

Tribute to William C. Nichols

William Nichols' development of integrative couple therapy has served to help couples and family therapists broaden their perspective on the use of varying approaches to treatment. Virginia Satir was reported as once saying: "It behooves all of us to continue being students. My recommendation is that we free ourselves to look anywhere to what seems to fit. This makes each of us continually growing entities" (Satir & Baldwin, 1983, p. ix).

William Nichols is the epitome of this statement in that he truly professes the idea that individuals need to look wherever necessary to broaden their perspectives. Nichols, admirably, always embraces various approaches to couple and family therapy, trying to find the best that each had to offer. He is notorious for never denigrating any particular brand of therapy, but accepting that every approach has something unique to offer that may be helpful when working with the difficult population of couple therapy. It is his authenticity as a human being as well as his astute qualities in observing human behavior that have made William Nichols the fine professional and scholar that he is today.

Cognitive-behavioral therapy (CBT) has been frequently utilized in various modalities of couple therapy (Nichols, 1988, 1998). It is especially useful in clinical situations involving divorce, which, unfortunately, has become a relatively common event in the United States and other countries throughout the world. The rates in many countries represent an enormous number of individuals enduring emotional upheaval and resulting dissolution of relationships. In the

United States alone, the divorce rate has skyrocketed. In 1999 the United States Census Bureau indicated that the divorce rate has approached the 50 percent mark, which is up from 43 percent in 1988. What this means, essentially, is that there currently is a 50 percent chance that most individuals are likely to end up in divorce in the United States, with a lesser, but substantial rate abroad.

Despite the traumatic effects associated with the onset of terrorism in this country, divorce continues to rank as the second most severe form of distress that one can undergo (Granvold, 2000). The first is the death of a loved one, particularly a child. This finding continues to be regarded as an accurate reflection of the accommodation demands of divorce. Divorce has a profound impact as a crisis situation on individuals and clearly needs to be addressed vigorously. Even if an individual desires the divorce, the attendant changes and adaptations may have both positive and negative outcomes. Although the positive consequences of these life-changing events may be predominant, some negative outcomes may reach crisis proportions.

In all circumstances, the individual's cognitive functioning and the availability of social and instrumental resources play critical roles in determining what may be considered manageable stress. How well individuals accommodate to a divorce situation also may be expected to be inversely proportional to the intensity of its demands. Some of the demands associated with divorce beyond the actual physical and emotional separation processes include coping with infidelity, custody determinations, health issues, and so on. When the accommodation demands of the situation exceed the coping resources of the individuals, additional serious problems develop in their lives. These additional stressors may be experienced as cumulative.

In the midst of this bleak picture evidence is mounting that many individuals who experience serious aversive events also may realize some positive changes in the process (McMillen, 1999). One such positive change might be the stress inoculation effect that results from overcoming adversity. Nevertheless, individuals who are proceeding through divorce will likely experience several discrete events of crisis proportion at various points during the arduous process. These repetitive waves of emotional turmoil are what may be appropriately addressed through the use of CBT.

COGNITIVE-BEHAVIORAL APPROACH
TO DIVORCING COUPLES

CBT as applied to couples in a divorce situation draws its strength from a schema-based information-processing paradigm that comprises structures, processes, and products (Clark, Beck, & Alford, 1999). The focus on cognitive structures comprises symbolic meaning networks and associative linkages, the leading matrix into which stimuli are processed (Ingram & Kendall, 1986; Granvold, 2000).

Epstein and Baucom's (2002) introduced an enhanced CBT approach that integrates aspects of family stress and coping theory (e.g., McCubbin & McCubbin, 1989) with traditional cognitive-behavioral principles. A couple or family is often faced with a variety of demands to which they must adapt, and the quality of their coping efforts is likely to affect satisfaction and stability of their relationships. Demands on the couple or family may derive from three major sources:

1. Characteristics of the individual members. For example, a family may have to cope with a member's clinical depression.
2. Relationship dynamics. For example, members of a couple may have to resolve or adapt to differences in the two partners' needs, as when one is achievement and career oriented and the other is focused on togetherness and intimacy.
3. Characteristics of the interpersonal environment (e.g., needy relatives, a demanding boss) and physical environment (e.g., neighborhood violence that threatens the well-being of one's children).

Obviously, divorce is clearly one of these stressors. Cognitive-behavioral therapists assess the *number, severity, and cumulative impact of various demands* that a couple or family is experiencing during the course of divorce, as well as their available *resources and skills for coping* with those demands. Consistent with a stress and coping model, the risk of couple or family dysfunction increases with the degree of demands and deficits in resources. Given that the family members' *perceptions* of demands and their ability to cope also play a prominent role in the stress and coping model, cognitive-behavioral therapists' skills in assessing and modifying distorted or inappropriate cognition can be very effective in improving families' coping strategies.

This theory is highly relevant to individuals facing divorce, particularly because maladaptive or dysfunctional self-schema that have remained dormant may become activated as consequences of the stress demands of the process (Granvold, 2000). A perfect example of this is with individuals who experience low self-esteem or feel unlovable and fear rejection. They may come to engage in the strong belief, "I am not worthy of anyone's love and, therefore, will never be able to remain married." Therefore, in this respect, an individual who experiences extreme emotional pain of rejection may construe their spouse's quest for a divorce as being just another reaffirming measure that they are worthless. The intensity of feelings of rejection and the pervasive consequences of the divorce are capable of providing a state of crisis. The notion of a divorce may also facilitate a crisis because it violates some of the ingrained schemas that individuals hold about marital relationships. For example, one of the typical areas of conflict is the notion that, "once married, one must remain married no matter what." Therefore, if individuals divorce, they fall from grace with others and, therefore, view themselves as "failures" and as marked individuals. Such beliefs may spawn all sorts of catastrophic thought content such as, "I'll never be able to maintain another relationship if I divorce," "I can't stand life without the love of a spouse," "People won't respect me," "I'll never be a good parent," and so on.

Consequently, the role of CBT specifically addresses ingrained beliefs that individuals maintain that are based on distorted information and are unable to be adapted to a situation that may be out of one's control. Hence, the process of helping individuals restructure their thinking is what CBT approaches are all about.

CLINICAL VIGNETTE

The following is an excellent example of how the finalization of the divorce process exacerbated a woman's stress level to the point where she engaged in distorted thinking. This particular client was raised to believe that a marriage is forever and she felt morally obligated to remain in the marriage despite any level of dissatisfaction or turmoil. Interestingly, in the following dialogue the therapist uncovered a line of thinking that clearly indicated how such distortions contributed to a major depressive reaction in a crisis situation for her:

THERAPIST: What are you thinking about?

CLIENT: Nothing really [smiles].

THERAPIST: No, come on—what—say it.

CLIENT: I don't know—nothing good.

THERAPIST: Share it with me. Don't keep it all to yourself. You have such an intense look on your face.

CLIENT: It's just that I feel like such a failure.

THERAPIST: Why?

CLIENT: Because—I'm getting divorced. I mean, that's unfathomable to me. I never, ever thought I'd be divorced.

THERAPIST: You know what—I don't think that most people ever do plan on becoming divorced, but it is unfortunately something that happens to people in life.

CLIENT: I know, but I'm the first one in my family—in fact, for generations. So, it's just . . .

THERAPIST: So, that means you're a failure?

CLIENT: Well yeah, you know—I'm the one and only. The spotlight is on me.

THERAPIST: How does it make you feel?

CLIENT: Like shit! Like a real loser!

THERAPIST: That could tend to make a person pretty depressed.

CLIENT: Ah, yeah. You could say that.

THERAPIST: But it sounds as though you failed an exam or something—all by yourself—because you didn't study, or didn't know your material.

CLIENT: Well, sort of. I failed at marriage you could say.

THERAPIST: All by yourself?

CLIENT: No; my husband helped. Actually, he's the one that wanted out of the relationship.

THERAPIST: So, it wasn't all your fault, was it?

CLIENT: Hey, I wanted to work at things, he didn't.

THERAPIST: It sounds as though your hands were tied, but if it were up to you, you would have liked to really work to salvage the marriage, correct?

CLIENT: Yeah, but I still feel like the loser.

THERAPIST: Look, you've definitely lost something important, but it doesn't mean that you're a loser. And how much did you really fail if you wanted to try and he didn't?

CLIENT: I don't know. I just have this thing in my head about being a failure.

THERAPIST: Sounds like it's been there for a while?

CLIENT: Yeah, all my life.

THERAPIST: I wonder how much you feel like a failure because you tell yourself that you are a failure or a loser? In fact, it sounds as though you may have been reciting that message to yourself long before you were married.

CLIENT: I don't know.

THERAPIST: Give it some thought. The messages that we give to ourselves are probably more powerful than we are aware of. What's more, if we were to examine the real evidence that supports the statement of being "a loser" or a "failure," my guess is that there is little substantial evidence.

CLIENT: I'm not sure. Perhaps I just know what I feel.

THERAPIST: That's right, but, my question to you is, can you trust that your feeling is based on solid evidence?

CLIENT: No.

THERAPIST: Okay, so then let's examine the evidence to see if it validates your feelings. If we determine that the evidence is erroneous, then we can begin to consider restructuring your thinking. If not, then I might suggest that you try an experiment. Take a piece of masking tape and make the form of a large "L" on your sweater. When people ask you what the "L" stands for, tell them it stands for "loser" and tell them why you think you're a loser. Let's see what people have to say about that.

CLIENT: Oh boy, now I'm in for it!

THERAPIST: What do you think about trying this as an experiment?

This is a classic example of how CBT encouraged a client to examine the content of her thoughts and weigh her self-statements. These no doubt were extremely powerful in contributing to her depression and sense of failure and needed to be addressed.

In the dialogue, the therapist uncovered the woman's negative automatic thoughts such as, "I am a loser" and helped her to understand how this thought was a result of underlying beliefs that she "failed." Identification and analysis of the consequences of her thinking, which included both feelings and behaviors, were examined and posed to her in a way that encouraged her to challenge her self-statements. The personal appraisal of the consequences, "Do you like how you feel when you think about this?" was food for thought. The generation of alternative constructs as a means of challenging active automatic thoughts was the first step in helping this woman consider taking a different perspective on the circumstance. Selection of one of the alternative constructs was used to demonstrate the benefits of cognitive elaboration and how her thinking was distorted. Finally, the identification and analysis of the consequences within a construct that involved feelings and behaviors were considered. These were made particularly evident by having her consider walking around in public with the letter "L" on her sweater. In essence, it exaggerated the erroneousness of her thoughts in order to force her to think more about the validity of her statements. In a sense, it reified the notion so that she could examine it better.

The previous dialogue is just a glimpse of what the cognitive-behavioral process is about, particularly when dealing with a crisis such as divorce. Below is a more detailed case study of a couple who were, unfortunately, unable to salvage their marriage. In this vignette, the husband could not get over his wife's infidelity and eventually the couple decided to end the marital relationship. Consequently, this couple needed help with how to let go of the marriage and reclaim their lives separate from each other. This, in time, actually resulted in being a good outcome for both.

CASE EXAMPLE

Tom and Karen were a young couple in their early- to mid-thirties, married ten years, with two children, a seven-year-old girl and a five-year-old boy. They were referred for marital counseling by a friend because of a trauma that had occurred in their relationship. Tom recently learned that Karen had been involved in an extramarital affair with a co-worker. He had learned of this after Karen broke down one night in a moment of weakness and divulged that she had had an indiscretion that had just ended. Tom's emotional reaction of anxiety and depression required him to see the family physician the next day for medication to help him sleep. During the course of Karen's revealing of the affair, it also surfaced that she had had a brief affair with someone else earlier in the marriage. Tom stated that this news "simply blew my mind . . . I had no idea, no clue. This hit me like a ton of bricks."

During the initial evaluation, Tom confessed that he was initially in a state of shock. However, he subsequently began to manifest many symptoms similar to those of post-traumatic stress disorder (PTSD). Even though extramarital affairs do not formally constitute enough criteria for a diagnosis of PTSD, this was nonetheless an acute stress reaction (Dattilio, 2004). Tom stated that he obsessed about the idea of his wife being with another man. He would experience recurrent, intrusive, and distressing thoughts on a regular basis and he identified specific triggers for these thoughts. For example, one time he was lying down in their bedroom waiting for Karen to come out of the shower. As she exited the shower and he watched her dry off, he became sexually aroused. However, his sexual arousal was quickly thwarted by the intrusive thought, "I'm not the only one who has seen her naked." When this type of reaction occurred, it soon escalated into anxiety attacks, other emotional distress, and uncontrollable crying.

During my initial interview with Karen she made it clear to me that it was not her intention to become involved in an extramarital affair. She had become involved with a supervisor at work over a period of time because he listened to her and showed her attention. There was a great deal of tension in Karen's marriage because Tom was always very critical of her. She claimed that she felt good while she was involved in the affair, but did experience guilt once Tom began to suspect that something was going on.

During the course of treatment the focus was helping both individuals understand the dynamics that contributed to the violations in the relationship. These included areas wherein one or both spouses felt unfulfilled. Interestingly, Tom eventually admitted that he had at times thought about ending the marriage because he simply was not satisfied with his wife. However, a great deal of Tom's distress was because he felt "had" by the fact that his wife went behind his back and became involved with another man. In addition, when Tom found out that there had been other affairs, he felt like a "fool."

Unfortunately, marital therapy was unsuccessful in that neither Tom or Karen could forgive the other, reconcile their differences, and put the past behind them. After much work and contemplation, this couple decided that it would simply be best if they filed for divorce and went their separate ways. They did attempt to remain cordial for the sake of the children. However, this was a struggle for them in the beginning.

The divorce therapy phase began with what Tom and Karen were able to forgive in the other. The idea was to accentuate those aspects of the relationship that were compatible and congenial. Therapy also focused on the idea that the dissolution of their marriage was a relief to both parties. Much mutual discontent had contributed to Karen venturing outside of the relationship, which ultimately ended their marriage. Interestingly, as we began to discuss this matter Tom stated that in many ways he now believed that he may have set his wife up to be unfaithful. He admitted that, because of his discontentment with her, he didn't give his wife as much attention as he should have. Once the two of them were able to accept the fact that there were shortcomings in the relationship and that they were operating their relationship on some false pretenses, the tension reduced. This also probably was because they were no longer under pressure to make the marriage work. Tom and Karen also recognized that they had some irreconcilable differences in their personalities that really did not make them very compatible with each other. Eventually they both admitted that they would have separated long before had they not had children.

Much of the cognitive-behavioral interventions involved helped Tom and Karen to restructure distorted beliefs about force-fitting this relationship into something that worked. Much of our work also helped them to reconsider some of the guilt and shame that they experienced about the divorce. We also included the children in some of the family therapy sessions to help orient them to their parents' new relationship. Overall, the children actually handled the situation quite well because Tom and Karen were civil with each other in their divorce proceedings and explained things to the children together.

Once this couple had the opportunity to restructure their thinking and consider some of the distorted thoughts that they both had become embroiled in over the years, their tension reduced and they actually developed a fairly good friendship. Each went on to meet other individuals and, surprisingly, Tom was the first to remarry.

AUTHOR'S REFLECTIONS

This is an interesting case that portrays how cognitive-behavioral techniques can be used as a crucial ingredient of an integrative attempt to ameliorate the distress of divorce. Extramarital affairs, albeit almost always destructive by nature, are sometimes a forerunner to breaking things open in a relationship and forcing couples to start to address issues that otherwise may have remained covert for years. Much of the power of CBT with couples and families is based on the fact that it is employed against the backdrop of a systems approach (Dattilio, 2001; Dattilio & Epstein, 2004, 2005). Systemic approaches situate people's feelings, thoughts, and psychodynamics in the major systems and subsystems in which they function. (For example, see those proposed by Nichols, 1998.) If it were not for therapeutic approaches such as integrative marital therapy, CBT strategies alone might be too linear and miss many of the intricate system dynamics that are important in facilitating change (Dattilio, 1998).

This point is elaborated in a recent case study by Nichols (1998) in which cognitive-behavioral techniques also were an integral part of the therapeutic intervention. The case involved an attractive, middle-aged couple. The wife was in her third marriage and the husband was in his second. Nichols had constructed a genogram for both individuals and determined that the family legacy of each was that of a lower-middle-class Protestant family in the Midwest. His use of genograms was quite compatible with what cognitive-behavior therapy indicates is important when working with couples and families. Genograms are an important tool for couples to recognize and understand the individual belief systems that have such great influence on each of them and their marriage.

Both spouses in this case were retired. They had done well economically and had amassed a nice sum of money for their retirement years. This could have been the perfect relationship. However, each spouse perceived problems in the different way each related to the world and to each other, and in how they dealt with those differences. Specifically, the husband had wanted to take life at a slower pace, sleep late, and spend most of his waking time with his wife. His wife, however, even though she was retired, wished to spend her days essentially as if she were still employed. She preferred to get up early, work seriously at some volunteer activities, and get together with her husband only at the end of the day. Consequently, the couple's energy levels were much different and their differing views elicited conflict in their relationship. These differing views were experienced as a violation of their expectations of life with each other.

In this case, Nichols very nicely conducted an assessment and shaped the interventions of his integrated approach in order to address the couple's respective ideas about their interaction and perceptions of the situation. This approach dovetailed nicely with the cognitive-behavioral approach, which also suggests the use of a number of inventories for assessing specific cognitions and perceptions. In so doing, Nichols laid the groundwork for the exploration of schemas that trickled down from each of their families of origin and how these might be coming into conflict with each other. The basic tenets of cognitive-behavioral psychotherapy allowed Nichols to effectively address the "five Cs" in marital tasks and interactions, namely

(1) commitment, (2) caring, (3) communication, (4) conflict and compromise, and (5) contract. These five Cs are central ingredients to both Nichols' and the CBT approach to couple therapy.

The integrative approach to marital therapy is wide open for augmentation with cognitive-behavioral strategies and vice versa. Both may serve to enhance the already effective track records that each have accumulated to date. It is important to recognize that Nichols' focus in integrative marital therapy is on integration of theory and not integration of techniques, as in eclectic therapy or technical integration. Most important, both approaches aim to tailor their interventions in accordance with the assessment of the needs of the situation. This makes them both extremely user friendly. In this age in which relationships are more complex than ever, therapists have much to gain by considering the integration effects in their clinical work.

REFERENCES

Clark, D. A., Beck, A. T., & Alford, B. A. (1999). *Scientific foundations of cognitive theory and therapy of depression.* New York: Wiley.

Dattilio, F. M. (Ed.). (1998). *Case studies in couple and family therapy: Systemic and cognitive perspectives.* New York: Guilford.

Dattilio, F. M. (2001). Cognitive-behavior family therapy: Contemporary myths and misconceptions. *Contemporary Family Therapy, 23,* 3-18.

Dattilio, F. M. (2004). Extramarital affairs: The much overlooked PTSD. *The Behavior Therapist, 27*(4), 76-78.

Dattilio, F. M., & Epstein, N. B. (2004). Cognitive behavioral couple and family therapy. In T. L. Sexton, G. R. Weekes, & M. S. Robbins (Eds.), *The family therapy handbook* (pp. 174-175). New York: Routledge.

Dattilio, F. M., & Epstein, N. B. (2005). The role of cognitive behavioral interventions in couple and family therapy. *Journal of Marital and Family Therapy, 31,* 2-6.

Epstein, N. B,. & Baucom, D. H. (2002). *Enhanced cognitive-behavioral therapy for couples: A contextual approach.* Washington, DC: American Psychological Association.

Granvold, D. K. (2000). Divorce. In F. M. Dattilio & A. Freeman (Eds.), *Cognitive-behavior strategies in crisis intervention* (2nd ed.) (pp. 362-384). New York: Guilford.

Ingram, R. E., & Kendall, P. C. (1986). Cognitive clinical psychology: Implications of an information processing perspective. In R. E. Ingram (Ed.), *Information processing approaches to clinical psychology* (pp. 3-21). New York: Academic Press.

McCubbin, M. A., & McCubbin, H. J. (1989). Coping. In C. R. Figley (Ed.), *Treating stress in families* (pp. 3-43). New York: Brunner/Mazel.

McMillen, J. C. (1999). Better for it: How people benefit from adversity. *Social Work, 44*, 455-468.

Nichols, W. C. (1988). *Marital therapy: An integrative approach*. New York: Guilford.

Nichols, W. C. (1998). Integrative marital therapy. In F. M. Dattilio (Ed.), *Case studies in couple and family therapy: Systemic and cognitive perspectives* (pp. 233-256). New York: Guilford.

Satir, V. M., & Baldwin, M. (1983). *Satir step by step: A guide to creating change in families*. Palo Alto, CA: Science & Behavior Books.

Chapter 16

Using Maps and Vision
in Family Therapy with Remarriage

Noga Rubinstein-Nabarro
Sara Ivanir

Tribute to William C. Nichols

My first encounter with Bill Nichols was as the editor of the Journal of
Contemporary Family Therapy. *Already, I noticed the amazing way in which
he supported professionals, encouraging them to make their contributions.
We served together on the board of the IFTA and collaborated on an edited
book about family therapy (still unborn). Bill and his wife Mary Anne were
invited to be on the faculty of our advanced International Program of Family
Therapy at The Israeli Institute for Systemic Studies. Throughout my ac-
quaintance with Bill, I came to know him not only as a person with the highest
personal integrity, but also as a rare combination of a person who has
succeeded to integrate knowledge, success, the highest professionalism,
vision, humbleness, kindness, and friendship. His writing is amazing in his
ability to embrace many theoretical frames and to incorporate them, like
stringing beads together into a beautiful necklace. His systematic supervision
materials became indispensable in our teaching. His books are loved by our
students and trainees because of their lucid language and their sensible and
systematic progression. We, at the Israeli SHINUI Institute, are but one group
of family therapists out of many worldwide, who are grateful for Bill's contributions to the field. On a final note, I feel lucky to have gotten to know both
Bill and Mary Anne, and to witness their loving, respectful, and professionally collaborative relationship. I feel privileged to contribute to this work in
his honor.—NR-N*

Remarriages encompass a cornucopia of complexities. Imagine
two separate families, which broke up under unhappy circumstances,
coming together to create a new family while at the same time their

When Marriages Fail
© 2006 by The Haworth Press, Inc. All rights reserved.
doi:10.1300/5562_16

members hold contradictory expectations for this union. These families often carry the expectation of becoming a new "happy and united family" (Visher & Visher, 1988), while, at the same time, expecting that this can never be like (or replace) the original "real family." Moreover, although the spouses may be happy and pleased with the new life arrangements, others (e.g., children or grandparents) may be displeased with it. As time passes, unresolved issues from previous marriage(s) intrude into the new one, eroding the couple's and family's new relationships (Nichols, 1996, 1988).

In remarried family systems, there are multiple subsystems that are directly and indirectly involved (Nichols, 1996, 1988) and may complicate family roles and dynamics. Every change in one subsystem immediately reverberates throughout all of the others, often shifting relationships and alliances. These dynamics can curtail the family's capacity for effective problem solving.

In remarriages, unresolved issues develop exponentially into larger dysfunctions while the flexibility essential for problem solving is reduced. As one client described, "When it doesn't work, it really doesn't work [in a big way] and then it radiates onto all other aspects, like an inflammation that spreads throughout all the relationships."

At developmental junctions (e.g., adolescents leaving home or marriage of an offspring), problems that were regarded as resolved or nonexistent tend to erupt again, greatly amplifying existing problems. Unresolved issues in the "step" subsystem may continue into the children's adulthood, overshadowing the couple's relationships. These are often experienced as "cutoff" relationships. In such cases couples may survive from one crisis to another, applying "more-of-the-same" solutions (Watzlawick, Weakland, & Fisch, 1974) that only exacerbate the problems and diminish the possibility of resolution.

The family therapist working with remarried couples must develop a "systemic insight" (Rubinstein-Nabarro, 1996a, 1996b). This involves grasping a panoramic view of the remarried family's different subsystems, including the therapeutic system, and their delicately balanced influences. Hasty interventions by an inexperienced therapist designed to contend with just one symptom or problem, or one part of the larger system, may create a short-lived solution and elicit problems elsewhere in the larger system.

In this chapter we will describe and illustrate two working concepts, or tools, that we have found facilitate our clinical work with remarried couples for both short- or long-term marriages: (1) The concept of *invisible maps* and (2) The process of *joint vision* for the remarriage. Utilizing these concepts enables the family therapist to move the spouses from their habituated reactive stances of "putting out fires" to a broader, more expansive outlook that offers better solutions.

THE METAPHOR OF INVISIBLE MAPS

We have found it tremendously useful to utilize visual metaphors and symbols that can assist our therapeutic thinking and conversations in complex therapeutic situations. A "map" is a natural metaphor, as people repeatedly use "maplike" expressions when referring to relationships. For example: "my way is shorter/quicker"; "a dead-end situation/one-way street"; "there are too many roadblocks"; and "detouring the conflict."

Every person seems to have her or his own "map" in a relationship. We use the "personal map" to connote the clear and set paths of actions and directions that guide a person's voyage within a relationship. The personal map is the culmination of past experiences in meaningful relationships and is also an expression of that person's worldviews, cognitive schemas (Dattilio, 1998), emotions, and perceptions. It represents one's laborious efforts (conscious or unconscious) to translate those experiences into a coherent territory of modes ("roads") of actions and reactions in present relationship circumstances.

The map allows one to navigate and plot a course of action in order to reach "desired destinations" or to avoid certain "undesired destinations." The "map" can become increasingly sophisticated with experience. Some of the pathways may include helpful structures, such as bridges, while some have very deep ravines laden with obstacles that are difficult to overcome. Both partners enter remarriage "navigating by their own personal map," which represents the outcome of their previous relationships.

In working with remarried couples, the therapist can now understand that as long as each partner is routed on her or his map (their own territory), neither can see the other's map. The partners' maps remain *invisible* to each other unless they are willing to temporarily leave their own map and explore the other's. The mutual maps may also be observed if both are juxtaposed by a third party, such as the therapist. All too often partners try to decipher each others' maps through their own coordinates, only to find that they have superimposed their own map on the other's. This results in a partial view or distortion of the other map (Berenstein, 1999).

The reader is invited to imagine a remarried couple with two maps, each containing a "togetherness" destination. On the wife's map there are three roads leading to "togetherness": (1) "Share intimate or hurtful details of her previous marriage"; (2) "Her children will always join them on vacations"; and (3) "They will make joint decisions." There are also roads on her map that lead away from "togetherness": (1) The road of "making decisions alone" marked with a huge "beware!! No Entrance" signpost; (2) "Doing things separately" marked with a "dangerous curve" sign; and (3) "Leaving her kids with the ex-husband," which is a hanging bridge that can only be crossed with much support.

The husband's map looks quite different. The wide roads to the destination of "togetherness" are: (1) "Keep the previous marriage out of couple's joint life"; (2) "Vacations should be taken only with his spouse"; and (3) "Surprise his partner by making big decisions on his own."

Imagine this couple after five years of marriage, when the husband decided to once again surprise his wife with an expensive prepaid vacation for two, arranged for her kids to stay with their father, and bought her a new car of *his* choice that awaited them at the vacation resort.

USING MAPS WITH REMARRIED FAMILIES

Partners in first marriages leave their familiar families of origin and unite to work together on creating their own family life. They are usually more willing to view each other's maps and to expose/share their own maps. Remarried partners, on the other hand, tend to continue using the map from their previous relationships rather than taking the risk of paving new pathways and developing new maps. Discarding the old map may be reminiscent of bad past experiences.

Moreover, one cannot totally discard the old map, as it entails "losing sight" of one's previous family (e.g., children).

Metaphorically speaking, the interaction between partners occurs in the "space" between each partner's personal maps. Within that intermap space, a third map is created—that of the relationship. A common destination on this "relationship map" of remarriage is "not failing." As one of our clients put it, "The first objective is not to fail. In the first marriage you go 'blindly.' In the second marriage I wanted very much to know and make sure that the same thing doesn't happen again."

Unfortunately, many remarriages do fail. Much like young parents who vow "never" to raise their children as their own parents did, spouses in remarriages may consciously disavow anything that might remind them of unhappy memories from their previous marriages.

If either one or both spouses view the remarriage territory as treacherous, they will make sure to designate only those few pathways that are presumably "safe courses" for them. This limits their joint map's alternative directions and destinations. They will create many "dead end," "no exit," "no entry," and "dangerous curve" roads for each other, rather than spending their energy creating alternatives that could lead to desired destinations. On the other hand, if one partner is blind to the obstacles, that partner will not build the necessary structures to overcome rough terrains and will repeatedly fall into unexpected traps. This bind is very common in remarriages. On the one hand, there is an adamant determination to "not fail" (rather than "to succeed") and on the other hand, one does not do what it takes to succeed because of continuous scouting for signs of potential failures to preempt.

WORKING WITH MAPS IN FAMILY THERAPY

Working with the invisible maps of remarried couples can be, at times, a confusing endeavor for the family therapist since so many things are hidden from view and often consciousness. Many interactional dynamics may not be apparent at first until the map becomes visible to the partners. This is why the therapist must help the partners, as soon as possible, create a safer environment that will enable them to disclose their own maps and then begin to study each other's maps. The therapist, through well-thought-out questions, can help the couple identify their differing maps and acknowledge the wisdom inherent in each.

In our practices, once the clients are familiar with using the map metaphor, we often help them to draw their maps on paper, filling in the details as treatment progresses. This can reveal more routes that were hidden from the eye and consciousness. We also use a technique called the Reciprocal Empathic Response (Ivanir, 1999) in which couples are taught to transform conflicts triggered by personal anxiety into opportunities for self-exploration, personal growth, and increased intimacy. Here we focus on moments of conflict and train partners to empathically stimulate each other to discover conscious and unconscious elements in their internal maps. This will allow the maps to become visible and "roadblocks" (i.e., obstacles to intimacy) can be removed.

These maps are then used to co-construct a new remarriage map of the relationship with roads leading to joint destinations. The new map will also include an infrastructure for dealing with the entire family.

In family therapy, using this map metaphor enables spouses and therapists to move away from a language that focuses on conflicts and introduce a more playful resource.

Case Example: Debbie and Alex

Debbie and Alex entered therapy in a state of severe marital crisis related to Alex's son from his previous marriage. Debbie felt desperate and on the verge of separation. Debbie (fifty-six), is a physician and Alex (fifty-six), is a software engineer. They had been married seventeen years. Although Debbie had no children from her first marriage, Alex had two children: Guy (thirty), from whom Alex has two grandchildren, and Maya (twenty-seven). Alex and Debbie have a son together, Jonathan (sixteen). While Debbie's divorce was relatively simple, Alex's divorce was traumatic as his wife left him for another man. Four years later, Alex and Debbie were married.

Alex's children were very fond of Debbie. They developed good relationships with her and were happy when Jonathan arrived. All went very well until Alex's son, Guy, turned 16. He became increasingly aggressive verbally toward Debbie, instigating fierce arguments and inventing stories of emotional abuse. His perplexing "vengeance" rendered Alex helpless and torn. The deterioration of Debbie's and Guy's relationship continued into Guy's adulthood. Alex's requests from Guy to change his behavior caused several "cutoffs" between them. Every time this happened, it was Debbie who pushed Alex to reconnect with Guy.

However, the resumption of the father-son relationship always left her out of the loop. When the first grandchild was born, both spouses were excited and hoped for a positive change. However this did not happen and joint visits were infrequent. Although Debbie never prevented Alex from visiting Guy alone, she did express her pain. Since they lived far away and visits were a whole day affair, Alex began to lead "a double life," visiting his grandchildren mostly when Debbie was away, concealing his intentions to visit till the last moment, and sharing little about his grandchildren. Debbie was concerned about the future and about Jonathan's learning to "cut off" as a means of dealing with conflicts as he distanced himself from his half-brother, Guy.

Deciphering and Exposing the Maps

From the start, as Debbie and Alex related the details of the crisis that led to therapy, we began to decipher each spouse's map. We introduced the metaphor of the map as soon as possible. Debbie described the event in which Alex suddenly announced: "I'm going to visit Guy and the grandchildren! You can come if you want to but if you don't, that's fine! When she asked if she was invited, he became furious and said, "I have no intention of asking Guy to call and invite you," and he stormed out. Debbie, who never had such a wish, felt completely misunderstood and was so hurt that she seriously contemplated separation for the first time.

The therapist began by exploring Alex's map:

THERAPIST: What did you have in mind that prompted you to inform Debbie about the visit at the last minute, telling her that you didn't mind if she joined you or not?

ALEX: I wasn't thinking about how she felt . . . because this is a battle situation. The current constellation is such that this issue becomes a battle and you've got to watch out for "mines."

THERAPIST: One goes into battle to in order to win . . . ?

ALEX: Yes!

On Alex's map this relationship area has become a battleground with mines in which one either wins or loses. It is familiar ground from his previous marriage. Defending his territory necessitates keeping his map invisible and sometimes being harshly insensitive.

Further discussion revealed that the destination at stake was "grandchild-grandfatherhood." Alex explained that he felt stuck in a biblical "Solomon's Trial," exclaiming to Debbie: "What's your sacrifice compared to mine . . . ? It's my tangible grandchild that I have to give up, while for you it's merely your feelings. I feel that your sacrifice is solely related to our couplehood while I'm risking losing my real-life grandchild."

THERAPIST: So you are on a map in which there is only a two-way junction: either overruling Debbie's feelings or losing your grandparenting. . . . Is there a third way?

ALEX: Right! . . . So instead of going there four times a month, I go twice a month to spare myself the conflict. Of course it's a far cry from what's desirable for me. . . .

Alex tried to pave another road that did not take him to the desired destination, leaving him resentful and frustrated. It was a solution that coincided only with his own map, and it remained invisible to Debbie. She had no way of seeing that this was the best alternative on his map. Debbie could only be confused and disheartened by his reactions.

On her map, we discovered that destinations of security and inclusion were crucial. For her relationship was a ground for security, and Alex's roads (if placed on her map) were leading to very undesirable and unsafe destinations. On Debbie's map the roads which led to destination security were: togetherness, visibility (information), and collaboration in problem solving. On Alex's map security was reached by autonomy, resolving problems alone, vigilance, and caution. For him, togetherness and collaboration led to possible loss of autonomy and endangered the unity of his first family and grandchild. Thus, when Debbie wanted to be informed and collaborate on decisions about the family, Alex's "warning lights" flickered.

Following the therapeutic session in which both maps became more visible, Alex invited Debbie to join him of the visit. She felt more relaxed and found herself playing and enjoying Alex's grandchildren. Although Alex felt tense at first, he recalled visualizing how on Debbie's map this led to destination security and he was able to relax. Interestingly, Guy relaxed, too, and the whole visit was experienced as rather positive.

Developing a Joint Map

As Debbie and Alex became more conscious of their own and each others' maps, they could untangle some of the complexities of their situation. They were able to converse about their relationship with his children and grandchildren without Debbie's unduly interfering. The therapist showed them that they must co-generate an alternative map with routes that take both personal maps into account; otherwise they would never reach their desired destinations. They realized, for example, that Debbie could reach *security* and *togetherness* through *visibility* only if she removed all the mines on her map. Alex's roads could lead to *security* and *autonomy* only by creating more *visibility*. Thus, their joint map should entail a safe and visible route to *security*.

This was demonstrated as Alex began visiting his son at his own discretion while informing Debbie of his plans and occasionally inviting her along. When she accompanied him they played with the grandchildren together but she also allowed him time alone with his son and grandchildren. As these urgent issues were dealt with the couple was ready to move on to the next phase which entailed working on their *marital vision*.

In the next section we will elucidate the concept of the vision specifically as it relates to remarriage and proceed to illustrate the process in therapy with the continuing case of Debbie and Alex.

THE MARITAL VISION IN REMARRIAGE

Bader and Pearson (2004a) defined "vision" as "A strong desire that is aligned with partners' values and supported by a plan" (p. 1). A joint marital vision defines aspirations the spouses have as a couple and for their family; the values they both share; and their common interests and goals. A vision is always oriented toward the future—the horizon on a map. However, the work in therapy is always done in the present.

In a first marriage couples do not usually allocate time to develop their shared vision and dreams of their future life together. To quote a client: "The first time around [first marriage] we were so innocent. Everything was so clear—it was obvious that you had kids, raised them well, developed your career, saved your money to buy a house, and eventually had grandchildren." Investing time and energy, and sacrificing individual needs to achieve the common goals seems almost automatic. Many aspects of the vision automatically cross over from both spouses' respective families of origin.

In contrast, individuals whose marriages have ended in divorce or widowhood do not carry into remarriage the same natural vision they had in their first marriage. Members of remarried families that include children from previous marriages have difficulty feeling rooted, even after many years of marriage. The roots and legacy are often associated with their first family, causing a sense of impermanency in the present family. Furthermore, there is a sense of disappointment and pain in harboring a vision that was shattered.

Often a partner's personal vision may not even be known to the remarried partner and the vision of the remarried spouses may not really encompass the whole newly formed, blended family. In cases in which the relationship had begun as an extramarital love affair, for which spouses left their previous marriages (Rubinstein-Nabarro & Ivanir, 1999), the couple's vision may express an egocentric encapsulation of their love more than a well-thought-out and planned joint vision.

In another case, David (fifty-two) and Judy (forty-six), both married to other partners, had been involved in an extramarital love affair for several years before David's wife died from a chronic disease. A year later David pressured Judy to leave her husband, promising her marriage and wealth. Relying on David and following what appeared to be a joint dream, Judy left her husband. She even left him all of their joint property. She dreamed of building a new home and family with David, including her two young adult children and David's two grown children and grandchildren. When they married, a crisis related to David's children brought them to therapy.

In the first two therapy sessions the discrepancy between both their visions became apparent. David was extremely involved with his son and daughter who greatly resented Judy for the affair. He was also quite attached to his deceased wife's family of origin who lived nearby on the family estate. His vision was to build an extensive multigeneration estate where his children would build a home, living in close proximity to him and his in-laws, who had not accepted Judy either. This vision had included Judy with him, but not her children. He dreamed of being in her arms forever, free at last, without having to pay any price other than expressing his love. Their individual visions were so rigidly different and overpowering that no joint vision was possible, and they eventually separated.

A goal of the therapist in working with cases such as this is to facilitate a joint vision that is neither the accumulation of their previous family visions nor merely the egocentric encapsulation of their love and unity as a couple.

The Importance of the Vision Process in Working with Remarriage

We share the opinion of Bader and Pearson (2004a) that bringing larger dreams into focus gives partners an incentive. Many remarried couples, when they are confronted with the complexity of their situation, experience the future as vague and uncertain, lacking the sense of security and unity of a first marriage. As one client expressed it, "Couples who have kids and grandkids together have a clearer picture. When it comes to a second marriage, everything is so uncertain. . . . And then, when you get into a crisis you become skeptical about the whole system and tend to give up easily."

The most important functions and objectives of the *vision process* in remarriages are

1. predicating the relationship on common goals and rooting it in the present and future rather than in the past;
2. uniting personal and family resources on both sides for the sake of the blended family;
3. Going beyond the symmetrical and competitive struggles of "mine" and "yours";
4. creating a sense of security and permanence in the new relationship; and
5. Fueling the relationship with new enthusiasm by revealing a new horizon.

In remarriages it is essential that the vision and the common goals permeate all areas of life, such as: family, couple/marital, personal growth, financial, spiritual, physical, hobbies, work/career, community/social, and health. In doing so, even simple aspects of daily living can be viewed as a natural extension of the couple's vision. Moreover, if a vision of remarriage does not include family aspects, it may provide temporary couple satisfaction but will eventually become problematic as the stepfamily will always have strongly bound subsystems to which members remain loyal (Keshet, 1980).

Ordinarily, the process of generating this joint vision entails several major steps:

1. clarifying the concept of the vision;
2. defining common values;

3. determining common goals in the different areas of their life: personal, couple, and family goals; and
4. evaluating the resources and skills needed to achieve these goals.

For the therapist, developing a clear and detailed vision identifies both complexities encountered by the couple and important destinations on their relationship map. It also functions as a compass that points them in the right directions.

Dealing with Hindrances to Creating a Shared Vision in Therapy

The work of creating a shared vision in therapy of remarried couples typically blends feelings of love and enthusiasm with frustration, fears, and despair. These require the therapist to skillfully recognize several fundamental hindrances and help the couple move past them. Here are several typical hindrances that we have encountered in therapy, with suggested therapeutic responses:

1. Spouses do not recognize the significance of a shared vision as a unifying resource that can guide them in mapping out their new family life. The therapist must highlight what the couple *does* want for themselves rather than remaining focused on what they do not want.
2. One or both spouses may feel disloyal to their children from the previous marriage, as the joint vision strengthens their intimate bond (Visher & Visher, 1988). The therapist must ensure that the couple understands that the vision will include the children of both spouses.
3. One or both spouses may fear that a shared vision would curtail their personal freedom and jurisdiction over their families from the previous marriage. As a client professed, "I can't commit myself fully to a vision that might add to or limit my commitments to the first family." The therapist must identify the source of the fear and challenge its contention by helping the couple agree to clear rules rather than curtailing the vision.
4. One or both spouses may fear impermanency of the relationship. (See the following case of Debbie and Alex for further explanation and therapy.)

5. There may be an inherent inequality that typifies remarriage when one spouse has children from a previous marriage and the other is childless or living apart from offspring. In an attempt to correct the imbalance, the "disadvantaged" spouse may utilize distancing, threats of separation, or divorce (Rubinstein-Nabarro, 1996a; Iwanir & Ayal, 1991). These promote insecurity and encourage the spouse to cling to separate visions instead of a joint, shared one. The therapist must identify the meaning of these threats and reframe them as the spouse's attempted declaration of significance within the marriage. Subsequently the therapist may challenge the threatening partner to empower her or his status in the relationship.

6. Some remarriages occur out of convenience rather than romantic love (e.g., a widower marrying someone to care for children, a marriage that eliminates financial concerns, or remarriage for the sake of business building). In such cases a shared vision pertaining to the couple may be difficult to achieve. The therapist can assist the couple to launch the process with what they *do* have in common. However, a vision that is not based on romantic love can nevertheless include common goals relating to their choice of partners, to building a good family or business, personal and spiritual development, or contributing to the community.

Working on a Shared Vision with Debbie and Alex

As Debbie and Alex exposed more of their personal maps, they became more comfortable with each other, which alleviated their crisis (discussed earlier). Alternative solutions began to appear on their joint map. A more balanced atmosphere fostered hope. After a few sessions, the foundation was laid for working on the couple's *joint vision.* We chose to begin by identifying both overt and covert wishes that each of them had in entering remarriage. Debbie shared that she was deeply impressed by Alex's devotion and paternal investment in his children, and she was convinced that he would be a wonderful father to their own child. She dreamed of creating a close, warm family together with Alex, including his children from his first marriage, whom she was willing to regard as her own. Alex recounted: "My dream was that the children would love Debbie, and there would be a close-knit, harmonious atmosphere. . . . But that proved to be a lost cause. It could never become the home, or the family."

They had never discussed their dreams or visions. Given their sense of recurrent failure and disappointment, it was obvious that without a clear joint vision this second marriage for both could collapse.

As we initiated a discussion about the concept of the *joint vision,* we quickly saw their divergence: Debbie, seeking the security of "togetherness," attempted to create a clearer future for a more cohesive family. Alex, on the other hand, felt resistant at first, stating two major reasons: (1) Fear of impermanency of the relationship: "My past experience has taught me that she may not be there forever. If my children's own mother bailed out, why couldn't the same thing happen with her? It is scary to commit to some vague horizon." (2) Fear that committing to a shared vision would curtail his personal freedom, particularly regarding his relationship with his children and grandchildren. The more Debbie showed investment in the shared vision on their home and family life, the more Alex felt threatened.

We challenged them to think of the existential role that each of them holds in the life of the other. Alex immediately answered: "She's like my 'anvil'; she stimulates me to keep growing and moving forward . . . not to settle for where I'm at." Debbie said: "He teaches me, bit by bit, how to receive love in ways that are different than what I'm used to . . . and much more. . . ."

It was apparent that affirming their mutual roles raised their sense of commitment and increased their cooperation. We began the discussion on the vision by taking a nonconflictual approach, enlisting the values they held in common and how these were already present in their joint activities. As they spoke about a joint project with a group of underprivileged patients, Alex said: " . . . the value that both of us are inspired from is optimism . . . that no matter how bad the situation is—how bleak—one should always search for a ray of light and pass it on to others. Sometimes a little help from the outside goes a long way . . . together we can create a sense of hope." Debbie added: "We have a mutual commitment to spiritual development . . . in that sense there is a strong connection between us; beyond the experience of daily life . . . it's bigger than both of us . . . something that can only come from our togetherness. We both desire to realize the gift that has been given to us, to make a difference in this world. We don't always use it well, but it's a very meaningful vision."

Alex happily agreed: "When it's just the two of us, that's when and where our creativity really flows . . . it's like the two wings of a bird." He continued: "There's a kind of excitement, pleasure, transcendence beyond the ordinary or the mundane; little leaps out there and back again—but those leaps make all the difference."

In the next session we expanded the dialogue on the values and vision to encompass the entire family so that it would become a link aiding in overcoming their prior difficulties. We began with their joint son Jonathan. This was the first time they had a "parent talk" discussing how to create a setting that would ensure his growth based on their shared values and visions. Debbie was relieved as she sensed Alex's growing commitment. Further discussion was geared toward clarifying their aspirations and plans for the whole family. Alex became less vigilant and suspicious as he learned that he did not have to be torn away from his son and grandchildren. The couple was able to achieve a realistic vision in which there are two families, practicing different types of affiliation, bound by fondness, compassion, respect, love, and mutual interests.

Later in therapy Alex reported that he shared the work on the vision with his daughter, Maya, who had just announced her plans to be married. She immediately suggested that the whole family meet together and discuss it: "We can take the position of a tribe, where rivalries do exist, yet there are also common goals and joint activities." With that, Maya took it upon herself to invite Guy, who hesitantly agreed, "As long as we don't have to pretend anything." Clearly, this family was off to a new start.

AUTHORS' REFLECTIONS

As teachers and trainers of family therapists, our goal is to research and develop working principles and tools that enable family therapists to tackle complexities, such as those inherent in remarriages. We find that complex human situations demand two major skills: (1) To experience simultaneously the family system from the "inside" and be able to view it from the "outside." The "inside" gives the affective-interactional information while the "outside" enables seeing the system's patterns and the rules (Rubinstein-Nabarro, 1996); (2) To see the uniting threads that connect all the elements into a new and functional whole.

In working with remarried families it is our task to help them find ways to relieve their anxiety and helplessness, acquire a sense of direction, and develop more stable and predictable relationships. We have found that the metaphor of the "maps" and the process of the joint vision presented in this chapter has proven to be very useful in our clinical work. Working with the maps gives the entire therapeutic system a clearer field of work, illuminating directions in which the spouses and the therapy can progress. The vision-building process is the "unifying thread" through which we come to know our clients' deepest values as people and as couples. Co-creating the shared vision helps to ground the therapeutic alliance and makes the horizon visible. The shared vision points to the desired direction and the maps show the way.

REFERENCES

Bader, E., & Pearson, P. (2004a). *Practice development dispatch.* www.couples institute.com.

Berenstein, A. C. (1999). Reconstructing the Brother Grimm: The new tales for stepfamily life. *Family Process, 38*(4), 415-429.

Dattilio, F. M. (1998). *Case studies in couple and family therapy.* New York: The Guilford Press.

Ivanir, S. (1999). Restoring and cultivating reciprocal empathic responsiveness (RER) as an alternative couple therapy. Unpublished PhD dissertation submitted to The Union Ins.

Iwanir (Ivanir), S., & Ayal, H. (1991). Mid-life divorce initiation: From crisis to developmental transition. *Contemporary Family Therapy, 13*(6), December.

Keshet, J. K. (1980). From separation to stepfamily. *Journal of Family Issues, 1,* 517-531.

Nichols, W. C. (1988). *Marital therapy: An integrative approach.* New York: Guilford Press.

Nichols, W. C. (1996). *Treating people in families: An integrative framework.* New York: Guilford Press.

Rubinstein-Nabarro, N. (1996a). "Systemic insight" and the couple "seesaw effect" in couple and family therapy. In M. Andolfi, C. Angelo, & M. De Nichilo (Eds.), *Feelings and systems* (pp. 195-215). Milano: Raffaello Cortina Editore. Published in English at: www.noga-nabarro.com.

Rubinstein-Nabarro, N. (1996b). Systemic insight in family therapy. *Contemporary Family Therapy, 18*(1), 19-40.

Rubinstein-Nabarro, N., & Ivanir, S. (1999). Terapia delle coppie di mezza eta in crisi per una relazione extraconiugale (The therapy of extramarital affair crisis in long-term midlife marriages). In M. Andolfi (Ed.), *La crisi della coppia—una prospettiva sistemico-relazione* (pp. 177-225). Milano: Raffaello Cortina Editore. Published in English at: www.noga-nabarro.com.

Visher, E. B., & Visher, J. S. (1988). *Old loyalties, new ties: Therapeutic strategies with stepfamilies.* New York: Brunner/Mazel.

Watzlawick, P., Weakland, J., & Fisch, R. (1974). *Change: Problem formation and problem resolution.* New York: W. W. Norton.

Chapter 17

Family Therapy for the Postdivorce Adjustment of Women Left by Their Husbands for Another Woman

Sandra M. Halperin

Tribute to William C. Nichols

Bill Nichols changed my life forever. We met on a dreary February afternoon in 1975 when he was the clinical director of the Interdivisional Doctoral Program in Marriage and Family Therapy at Florida State University. I was being interviewed by him and others, hoping to be admitted. As the interview progressed, I was so excited because he was teaching exactly what I wanted to learn. I very much wanted to be his student! Alas, he told me at the end of the interview that, although he would like to admit me, he could not do so because of my age: twenty-seven years old. He explained that he felt that candidates for this program needed to have more maturity and life experience, and thirty years of age was the "cutoff." I implored to him, arguing that I was bright and mature for my age and would he please consider me an exception. I promised that he wouldn't be sorry. I left that day heartsick—fearing I would have to wait to be admitted. However, and to my great delight, two weeks later I received a letter of acceptance into the program. I later learned that he had discussed my interview with his first wife, Alice, who encouraged him to "take a chance" on me. And he did! Consequently, not only my career but my life has been enriched by this very gifted and generous man who has been my teacher, mentor, and friend over the years. Thank you, Bill, for taking a chance on me!

It has been said: "No adultery is bloodless." When it leads to divorce, its effects are traumatic! Whatever the circumstances, divorce is difficult and painful. However, for women who have been left by their husbands for another woman, the process can be devastating and, in some cases, debilitating, from which they may never recover. I

When Marriages Fail
© 2006 by The Haworth Press, Inc. All rights reserved.
doi:10.1300/5562_17

have treated many, many women over the years who were going through divorce—for a variety of reasons. However, adultery on the part of the husband appears to me to be the most damaging of reasons for the wife.

This chapter describes a pattern I have observed in my practice, particularly relevant to the postdivorce adjustment of women in this situation. I am especially interested in helping the reader understand the importance of assessing and treating the woman who has been left by her husband for another woman as one who has been traumatized. I believe that the trauma aspect for the treatment of these women has been neglected in our field, a fact somewhat amazing to me as there are so many divorces in which the husband's infidelity is a factor. Nevertheless, this distinction is critical. If the trauma is not recognized by the clinician, and the post-traumatic stress reactions are not treated as the divorce process moves forward, the trauma colors how the practical settlement of issues, such as finances, living arrangements, child custody, and informing family and friends, are negotiated for the woman. The affair and subsequent experience of abandonment will permeate and contaminate the entire process.

DESCRIPTION OF THE CLINICAL PATTERN
OF TRAUMA

When the husband has left the relationship for another woman, the wife experiences a number of typical reactions during the divorce and adjustment process. (Of course, similarly difficult recovery may be also true for husbands who have been left by their wives for other men. I am not addressing this because I do not have as much clinical experience with men in this situation as I do with treating women.) This is a powerful, deadening reality that no amount of "reframing" can comfort or soothe. The shock of suddenly finding out for certain—either by being told by the husband or someone else (e.g., private detectives or a friend)—is the critical beginning of this often shattering traumatic process for the woman. Many times the wife has been suspicious and has confronted the husband, and the husband has denied an affair. Zemon-Gass & Nichols (1988) elaborated on this pattern, calling it "gaslighting," which refers to the actions of a husband who repeatedly lies to his wife and denies he is having an affair, attempting to convince her she is imagining things. They also stressed the impact of the husband's lies and rationalizations on confusing the wife's sense of reality. So there is often a period of "feeling crazy" before the actual "discovery," which ends with "proof." This proof initiates mixed emotions of relief at "not being crazy," yet at the same time, the harsh truth of the betrayal and abandonment elicits deep feelings of anger, depression, sadness, or other emotions that interfere with her ability to maintain a routine with family and/or work.

Often the husband "trashes" what was good in the marriage and/or blames the wife in an effort to justify his behavior. This response causes the wife to "feel crazy" again, questioning her experience of her reality about the marriage, her husband, and herself. A flooding of self-doubt erodes her self-confidence and her perceptions of her experience, her interpretation of reality. How could she have not known? She no longer trusts what she knows, thinks, or feels. She experiences the husband as someone she thought she knew, but does not know now: "I'm amazed! This is just not like him. Just not him!" Again, she doubts her perceptions of her past and present reality, and the present state can even feel very chaotic.

Sometimes the husband and wife have even come to marital therapy together, but often the husband's intention is not to work on the marriage. Instead, his intent is merely either to drop off the wife at the therapist's doorstep "to take care of" and/or to look good before the judge (suggested by his attorney), or for other reasons designed to absolve him of any responsibility for her pain. The cruel point here is that his willingness to go to couple therapy may raise the wife's hopes for reconciliation, when the husband has no intention of working on the marriage and he is already "out the door" with the other woman. The use of therapy for his personal gain further erodes the wife's confidence in her own emotions and perceptions: "What is real?" "What can I believe?"

This sudden onslaught of confused and chaotic reality is second only to the exquisite pain of being cut off by the most important person in her life, having no recourse, no say in the matter, and being replaced by another. Nichols (1996) identified this "separation distress" resulting from the loss of the attachment to the spouse. As one woman put it: "It was bad enough that he tossed me aside like a worn-out toy, but that he just went and replaced me with a new and improved model is more than I can bear." Of course, it is during this time that the wife questions her own value and self-worth. "What did I do wrong? I must not have been good enough." She questions and compares herself with the "other woman." At this point she may experience an obsessive need to find out more about the girlfriend, she may fantasize about what the girlfriend and her husband had shared together, and/or she may embark on a torrent of self-criticism and self-scrutiny.

This phenomenon of confusion, self-doubt, and questioning of her reality is actually quite common among those experiencing trauma; it is an experience of feeling or being disoriented—thrown completely off balance (Heller & Heller, 2001). As such a deep and intense experience, it takes more than simply "reality testing" and reframing to pierce its hold over the person.

The husband's potentially unilateral decision to divorce and his attachment to another woman certainly contribute further to the wife's trauma (Nichols, 1996). This further traumatizes the wife, and she, like "a deer in the headlights," is stunned and freezes—neither able to successfully fight to "get her husband back" or even able to flee from him. She is trapped by being out of control of these major decisions that will affect her and her children for the rest of their lives. At this point helplessness, hopelessness, and rage become prominent for the wife and these emotions are directed at the husband. These feelings are heightened as the couple negotiate financial and child custody arrangements. The wife's financial vulnerability may prompt additional feelings of desperation and bitterness, which, if unattended, could become quite self-destructive.

In an attempt to deal with the confusion of the trauma and her sense of being out of control, the wife begins to reorient herself by trying to understand and to make sense of the chaos and confusion that has entered her life. The reflection, "How could this have happened to me and I not know it?" becomes a common refrain. At this point she begins an often desperate search for a coherent understanding, narrative, or story of what has happened to her and why. It is an attempt at making sense of what for her is "nonsensical." The search for meaning is also an attempt to gain some control of her life using understanding as a tool. Her journey toward healing the trauma begins by removing herself from the trap of "no control." She can, at least, try to understand and make order out of chaos.

An additional aspect of the trauma for the betrayed wife, as in all trauma, are elements that affect her body. She may feel "prohibited feelings" of anger and rage in such intensity in her body that they feel like part of the trauma. She also may exhibit any number of other symptoms: depression, anxiety, sleep and eating disorders; physical symptoms such as headaches, stomach problems; and numbness or hyperalertness. These aspects of her therapy may be addressed with other body-oriented approaches, additional therapeutic interventions, and/or medication that can help her deal with the tensions from the trauma that remains stored in her body.

CLINICAL ISSUES AND TREATMENT STRATEGIES

This section uses aspects of the developmental tasks for divorcing spouses developed by William C. Nichols (1988) as a framework for discussing the clinical issues and therapeutic approaches in treating and facilitating the traumatized wife. These are helpful because they delineate the "normal developmental" tasks for adults in the divorce process.

Acceptance

Among the first tasks in the divorcing process, identified by Nichols (1988), is "acceptance." As stated earlier, the wife upon learning that she is being left for someone else and that she has no control over the decision, experiences the traumatic stress reactions of "freezing" and the inability to think clearly. Thus, her ability to progress in this initial developmental task is greatly compromised by feelings of shock and numbness.

It is at this time, if she has not already been in therapy, that she comes into therapy with symptoms of depression, feelings of being overwhelmed, shock, terror, and confusion. Of course, she needs considerable support from the therapist who must be particularly sensitive to her need for empathy around the trauma of losing someone to whom she is very attached. This experience may feel worse to her than if he had died because she is being replaced by another woman.

Although reality testing is often needed at this time, she may be too emotionally numb or emotionally flooded to be able to take it in. This is a time for the therapist to be patient and to listen compassionately, to help her begin to sort, figure out what she is experiencing here and now, and acknowledge the reality of her confusion and inability to trust herself and her perceptions. This is the beginning of a long process of helping her slowly to create an "emotionally rich and coherent narrative" (Wylie, 2004, p. 35) of what has happened to her and why. This phase of treatment requires a deep sense of empathy and patience on the part of the therapist, as the wife may need to go over and over the same incidents of the past.

As the wife deconstructs, constructs, and reconstructs her story, she will integrate her feelings over and over again under the guidance of the same caring and concerned therapist. The therapist needs to help her by listening, asking her questions, pointing to other data, interpreting (Nichols, 1996, p. 148)* reality testing, and suggesting reframes. The goal is to help her create a more illuminating and meaningful story of what happened. Listening to and affirming her narrative—with all of its details and repetition—is essential for her to begin to feel understood and safe. This therapeutic process soothes her emotionally, helps her become reoriented, and supports her while she increases her ability to trust herself again. This, in turn, further empowers her and soothes her, helping her be able to think even more clearly again and therefore become more amenable and less afraid of accepting that the divorce is actually happening.

Coping with Emotional/Psychological Reactions

Coping with emotional/psychological reactions is another of the developmental tasks Nichols (1988) described. The fact that the wife in this situation has experienced trauma simply underscores both the importance and the difficulty of helping her deal with emotional and psychological reactions. They are by definition "bigger than life," as she is flooding with emotion and confusion.

Healing trauma requires a coherent narrative or self-story to help explain the traumatic events for the wife to feel soothed, clear-thinking, and reality oriented. Just as important, the body must be enlisted in the healing process, as the body is a major container for the locked-in tension and energy she was unable to release when the trauma happened (Levine, 1997).

---

*Nichols' concepts of pre-ambivalent, ambivalent, and post-ambivalent stages in the decision to divorce may be useful in helping the wife understand that her husband is in the negative post-ambivalent stage while she is in the pre-ambivalent stage.

It is common in the very beginning of therapy for the wife to report feeling "nothing," "numb," or "dead." This is the predictable experience of the "frozenness" of the initial stage of trauma (Levine, 1997). She really does feel nothing. Yet, at the same time she is usually hyperalert, but unaware of it. Of course, what she needs first is to feel safe—physically, emotionally, and psychologically. Thus, the predictable, empathic, holding environment of the therapist is critical. As she reports what she has experienced, I have learned to watch carefully for her body to tell me what she might be feeling but may be consciously unaware of. For example, she may be unconsciously clenching her fist as she talks. I will call her attention to her fist and ask her to "stay with it" to see if she can connect with what her fist is communicating. Then slowly and eventually, her body and her consciousness move from "feeling nothing" to "feeling something" and finally to "feeling flooding."

As her feelings become more conscious, there is then a tendency toward this flooding of feelings. I find that a variety of conscious breath-work and imaging techniques are useful in helping the body release this locked-in energy. For example, when she becomes aware of her body flooding, I will ask her to stop and notice her body, and what is happening in it. This is a way of her honoring her body and the feelings within—whatever they are. I invite her to soften and relax her breath and notice what happens. I teach her to consciously deep breathe—breathing along with her. Another technique I have found useful is helping her create her own "safe place" in her imagination, using at least three of her senses. I teach her to oscillate from her flooding experience, for example, to "her safe place" and deep breathe until her body feels safe and relaxed and then return to the feelings. This structure helps her begin to move from feeling overwhelmed to more clearly recognizing and delineating vis-à-vis her body just what feelings she is experiencing in a safe and contained manner. This allows these feelings to be experienced, honored, and present in her body. This exercise further provides her with skills or tools to deal with the flooding of emotions when they occur outside the protected therapeutic environment.

It is important to note here that the therapist must be keenly sensitive to the woman's pace and allow and encourage her to experience and move at her *own* pace through intense emotions, such as rage, and not "relax" them prematurely. If she is encouraged to soften too early, it may give her a sense that the intense negative feelings are shameful or threatening. This careful tracking calls upon the therapist's skill in observation and empathy, but it is critical to the healing process.

Although these breath and imagery techniques can be useful, I have observed that due to the intensity of these feelings these interventions may not be sturdy enough to manage some types of anxiety and depression. It is helpful for clients to know this possible limitation; otherwise this work may become another arena in which the woman is likely to experience "failure" or shame. If the depression and anxiety continue to be overwhelming, a consideration of additional therapeutic support (e.g., more frequent sessions, support groups) and possibly medical consultation may be warranted.

Sometimes the wife is so traumatized that simple breathing and soothing do not break through the numbing or flooding. I have observed that when this happens, it is not uncommon to find this may not be the woman's first experience of abandonment. Often I find that she has had other experiences of being abandoned by those she loves. When this is the case I utilize an approach to treating trauma, called somatic experiencing, introduced by Peter Levine and Diane Heller (Levine, 1997; Heller & Heller, 2001). This is a body-centered approach which I have found extremely helpful with these women. Of course, a number of other effective therapeutic approaches are available for treating trauma: eye movement desensitization reprogramming (Taylor, 2004), thought field therapy, and Naperstak's guided imagery. The important point for the therapists is to recognize that this type of divorce situation has produced trauma that it must be dealt with clinically. Less experienced therapist must be careful not to simply dismiss her emotional numbness and/or overreactions as "drama." Zeman-Gass & Nichols (1988) discussed the danger of the therapist mislabeling the wife's reactions to her husband's affair as jealously, insecurity, or masochism.

Informing Others, Including the Children

Another aspect in Nichols' (1988) paradigm of divorce adjustment is the need for the divorcing person to be able to inform others, including one's children. Two areas here are especially problematic for the wife left for another woman. First, each spouses' perceptions of the reason for the divorce may not coincide. In fact, they may disagree completely on what and how to tell others about the divorce, "the other woman," and her part in the dissolution of the marriage. Second, no matter what they decide to tell others, this process will be particularly difficult for the wife since it identifies the reality of the "other woman" in the husband's life. It also identifies the end of the marriage in a more public and undeniable manner. This process of informing others leaves the wife at risk to retraumatization through public humiliation of being left for another woman or not being "good enough" to keep her husband. If anger and rage have not been predominant in her feelings, this announcement certainly can amplify them. It is very important, therefore, that the therapist, while remaining empathic, supportive, and containing, also be able to help the wife refrain from taking this opportunity to act out her rage in inappropriate ways that could be self-destructive and/or destructive to her children.

As therapy progresses, the wife will become more able to contain her emotions, think more clearly, and have a sense of her own internal power. This will allow her to be able to engage in negotiating with her husband about what to tell the children and others. A specific agreed-upon plan for this process will help prevent triangulation of the children, the divorcing couple, and the other woman. The occurrence of this dynamic is quite common early in the treatment process.

Other underlying clinical risks exist if the wife's trauma goes untreated. For example, the angry wife may use her sense of power to threaten to tell others and the children that "the real reason" for the divorce is the other woman. The husband may not view the affair as the reason for the breakup of the marriage. In fact, many husbands wish to keep that a secret, especially from the children, family members, and family of origin. The wife may feel real power over her husband in this situation and be tempted to triangulate others, especially the children, in an "acting out" of her anger and helplessness. This is a critical time for her in therapy due to the range of emotions she is experiencing.

Nichols (1988) delineated the later developmental tasks for the divorcing person to include: restructuring relationships with the spouse and children, adapting to new living patterns, and completing the mourning process and moving on. As the wife heals from the traumatizing events of the divorce, she is better able to master these later developmental tasks.

Restructuring Relationships with Spouse and Children

The wife's task of restructuring relationships with her husband, when he has left her for another woman, is difficult, at best. If there are no children, a woman can work toward a more complete disengagement from the relationship than when children are involved. Of course, when children are involved the mother must come to some type of working relationship with the father. This task places her in a situation in which she cannot avoid potential "triggers" of her traumatic experience.

I have noticed that one of the most important, if not *the most important* variable in this process, is the father's willingness to sacrifice for the financial security of the mother and the children. If he is willing to do all that he can so that the mother and children are not deprived financially, it is easier for the wife to assuage her anger in the interests of the children, thereby not undermining their relationship with their father via the triangle. If this is the case, the mother often feels that she has been dealt with more respectfully and fairly in financial matters. This may, in some cases, offset some of the feelings of betrayal.

If, on the other hand, the wife does not feel that the husband has treated her fairly and if she feels financially deprived, she will experience this as yet another trauma he is inflicting upon her which, again, she has no control over. Financial trauma can affect her on a day-to-day basis over a long period of time. It may interfere with or delay both her adjustment to the divorce and the formation of a workable relationship with the father. In fact, if the mother views the divorce settlement as unfair, and if she and her children experience a decrease in their standard of living, therapeutic work will be necessary to help her work through her bitterness if she is to construct a workable relationship with the father.

Another retraumatizing factor which women in this situation experience occurs when the wife becomes aware that while her standard of living has dropped that of the "other woman" has increased in her relationship with the ex-husband: "She has what was mine or should be mine." "She's living the retirement that he and I always talked about!" "I have get an additional job just to care for my children."

Not surprisingly, women who have their own financial means and do not drop in their standards of living (e.g., are professionals themselves or who have money of their own or from a substantial divorce settlement) fare better in the divorce adjustment process. It should be noted that the experience of a more precarious financial standard of living only adds insult to injury—injury that can have long-lasting effects for the entire family system's future.

Adapting to New Living Patterns

Even when the wife is able to remain in her residence and is more financially secure, she is painfully aware of the loss of status as a part of a couple "in a couples' world." This is yet another trauma the woman must face. For an older woman who had been in the marriage for many years, this is even more traumatic and difficult to adjust to because much of her identity was founded in being part of a couple. Nichols (1996) observed about the wife: "To the extent that she has been accustomed to being 'the wife of' her husband, she finds that she is missing her identity as well" (p. 269).

Helping the wife adjust to her new postdivorce status can pose quite a challenge for therapists—precisely because the wife did not choose this role or experience! Of course, it is a reality she must accept and to which she must adjust. The therapist must continue to be supportive and reality test, helping the woman navigate a middle ground between isolation and jumping into another relationship too quickly. As she continues to resolve and heal the trauma, the therapist will see that she is beginning to integrate her "new story." There will be other evidence that she has come to know and understand herself better as a separate person, creating her own new identity as a single woman. Gradually she will gain more confidence in reaching out and forming networks with old friendships and making new ones. Often the therapist will need to raise issues with the wife who is at risk for jumping too quickly into another relationship. The therapist needs to recognize that this is a common tendency for some women to try to quickly repair their loss and ease their trauma. It can create detrimental effects of her avoidance in getting closure on her trauma and moving through the grieving process of her marriage. Nichols (1988) described this type of relationship or marriage as the "bridging" or "sandwich" marriage.

Completing the Mourning Process, Integrating the Loss, and Moving On

According to Nichols (1988), completing the mourning process is the beginning of the end of the adjustment process for the divorcing person. Along with accepting that her marriage is over, the wife must grieve and redefine what she thought was to be her future with her husband. As described earlier, she must also grieve for the loss of her partner. The goal of therapy is to help her work through the various traumata encountered in the divorce process so that as she moves through the painful, yet healing process of mourning, she will be able to integrate her loss. Her grief-work may be complicated by the waves of trauma she has experienced. The healing of her trauma and the subsequent confidence she gains from not just grieving her "old story" but creating and empowering herself with her "new story" greatly facilitates her ability to mourn appropriately and find her own "new" identity. At this point the woman is able to live in the present. She has mastered what Nichols (1988) described as the postdivorce stage where her "emotional energy no longer is invested in past objects and relationships, but in current and future attachments" (p. 270).

AUTHOR'S REFLECTIONS

I have presented a neglected and sometimes minimized aspect of the divorce adjustment process for a betrayed wife—her trauma and postdivorce adjustment. Based on my clinical work I have described how I understand the experience of a wife who has been left by her husband for another woman as a traumatic event within which waves of trauma come crashing down on her throughout her experience of the divorce itself and the subsequent divorce adjustment. I have suggested therapeutic approaches and techniques that are commonly utilized in treatment of trauma, adapting them to the unique situation of the betrayed wife.

REFERENCES

Heller, D. P., & Heller, L. S. (2001). *A self-healing guide to auto accident and recovery*. Berkeley, CA: North Atlantic Books.

Levine, P. A. (1997). *Waking the tiger: Healing trauma*. Berkeley, CA: North Atlantic Books.

Nichols, W. C. (1988). *Marital therapy: An integrative approach*. New York: Guilford Press.

Nichols, W. C. (1996). *Treating people in families: An integrative framework*. New York: Guilford Press.

Taylor, R. J. (2004). Therapeutic intervention of trauma and stress brought on by divorce. *Journal of Divorce and Remarriage, 41* (1/2), 129-135.

Wylie, M. S. (2004, September/October). Mindsight. *Psychotherapy Networker*, 28-41.

Zemon-Gass, G., & Nichols, W. C. (1988). Gaslighting: A marital syndrome. *Contemporary Family Therapy, 10*, 3-16.

Chapter 18

The Systemic Treatment of Affairs:
A Multicontextual Relational Approach

Kenneth V. Hardy

Tribute to William C. Nichols

Mere words, no matter how much time I had or how many resources available to assist with the task, would never allow me to adequately express the regard, gratitude, love, and warmth that I have for you Bill. I have listened to you, observed you, accepted much from you, patterned myself as a human being and marital and family therapist after you, laughed with you, grieved with you, rejoiced with you, conferred with you, consulted with you, been unconditionally supported by you, and admired by you for thirty years now. . . . and for it all . . . because of you, I am who I am. My heartfelt thanks and I look forward to another thirty years. A very proud and grateful former student—"Mr. Hardy"

Of all the clinical issues addressed by couple therapy, the treatment of affairs is among the most difficult. The devastation that the broken trust, deceit, and betrayal of an affair impose on a relationship often makes the healing process challenging at best. For the couple coping with the pain and relational wreckage following the aftermath of an affair, rebuilding a viable relationship often requires relational resources that most partners find difficult to access in the midst of such a crisis. Finding effective ways to address the onslaught of the relentless raw emotions that follow the affair is critical to the healing process. For any clinician who has provided in-depth comprehensive and intensive therapy with a couple trying to recover from the trauma of an affair knows that working with these clinical issues is much easier stated than done.

When Marriages Fail
© 2006 by The Haworth Press, Inc. All rights reserved.
doi:10.1300/5562_18

Even for the well-intentioned, dedicated couple determined to "hold it together" in spite of the transgression, "moving on" can be difficult. Most affairs, unless they are of the one-night-stand, "only-for-sex" variety, are difficult to recover from because they not only injure the nonoffending partner, but they also often culminate in an injury to the relationship. A relational injury is one of the most difficult issues for clients to recover from and the most challenging for family therapists to treat.

THE AFFAIR AS A RELATIONAL INJURY

Relational injuries can be a by-product of any type of intimate relationship but are particularly prevalent among those in which an affair has occurred. The concept of relational injury is a systemic one. It refers to the substantive and often believed to be irreparable damage that occurs within the relational bond that connects individuals or groups. In many regards, an injury to the relationship is far more salient and destructive than it is to a given individual within a given relationship. These types of injuries are particularly damaging because they assault virtually all of the essential relational properties that are integral to healthy relationship formation and maintenance. Hence, relational injuries erode and weaken the "glue" that is necessary for effective bonding. Moreover, they prevent the establishment of the type of foundation that provides for relational resiliency and the kind of coping skills necessary to overcome adversity.

Johnson (2001) coined the term *attachment injury* to refer to a similar process which "occurs when one partner violates the expectation that the other will offer comfort and caring in times of danger or distress. An attachment injury is characterized by an abandonment or by a betrayal of trust during a critical moment of need" (Johnson, 2001, p.145). It is likely that this type of injury would be associated with affairs, although as Johnson acknowledged, "some incidents involving some form of infidelity might be experienced as attachment injuries, whereas other incidents would not" (p. 146).

Relational injuries, while certainly involving attachment issues, tend to have a far more pervasive impact on relationships and are not exclusively confined to intimate connections. With regard to groups, Hardy's (2004) discussion of the strained relationship that exists between whites and people of color is based on the notion of a long-standing race-related relational injury for which limited opportunities for healing have been provided. Whether applied broadly to societal transgressions, such as racial oppression, or to smaller systems such as infidelity in an intimate couple relationship, relational injuries are characterized by the confluence of several central factors.

Deceit and Betrayal

In a sense both deceit and betrayal are the hallmarks of relational injury. *Deceit* systematically destroys basic trust, undermines a sense of good will and one's faith in the sanctity of a relationship. It not only calls into question the integrity of the individual who has been deceitful but it also places the integrity, trustworthiness, and legacy of the relationship under unrelenting scrutiny as well. Deceit obscures the consensually validated realities that have been constructed within the context of a given relationship. The beliefs that were at one point considered unquestionable and irrefutable "truths" are destroyed in the face of deceit. *Betrayal*, like deceit, also injures relationships and culminates in an attachment-type injury resulting in a basic and pervasive mistrust in the relationship's ability to provide an emotional and psychological home.

When betrayal and deceit are introduced into the psychosocial interior of a relationship they disrupt and destroy security, safety, and that which was once considered predictable and guaranteed. Deceit and betrayal are often linked inextricably, although there are circumstances in which one can exist without the other, at least within a given time frame. They have in common a respective and collective capacity to function as relational legacy and ritual erasers. *Relational legacy* refers to the unique accumulative experiences that develop between partners over a period of time—the unique history that is created and shared between two people. It is comprised of the good and bad times, the anniversary experiences, and the unique, tailor-made way in which partners in a relationship have engaged in meaning making. *Rituals*, on the other hand, are the patterned and predictable events that partners establish and engage in to celebrate and honor their connection and legacies. Not surprisingly, rituals help shape and contribute to relational legacies. In a powerfully destructive and disconcerting way, deceit and betrayal not only have the capacity to restory the past but also have the potential to erase existing legacies and rituals. In the face of deceit and betrayal, the past is often quickly stripped of the unique meaning that was once romantically, lovingly, and/or significantly attached to it. The following case provides a brief example of this phenomenon.

Case Example: The Lie

Bridgette, thirty-eight years old, learned in our therapy session that her forty-two-year-old husband, Matt, had been involved in a two-and-a-half-year affair with his office manager, Collette. She was someone whom they had socialized with and entertained as a guest in their home. Moments after Matt disclosed this very painful and unanticipated information to Bridgette, she was devastated as tears streamed uncontrollably down her face. She shook her head slowly from side to side reflecting her disbelief and her initial refusal to believe what he was saying.

Moments later, after refusing efforts of comfort and solace from Matt, she began to express anger. Matt reached out again to embrace her, but she stated belligerently " . . . get your dirty, disgusting, fuckin' hand off me . . . don't you ever touch me again!" Matt backed off and was clearly confused as to what he should do next. After glancing over at me for a few seconds, he approached Bridgette again, attempting to touch her hand, stating, "I am *really* sorry. . . . I love you . . . and I never wanted to hurt you. . . ." Bridgette erupted, stating, "I don't believe you. . . . I don't believe anything you say. . . . I don't know you Matthew. . . . You are a liar . . . it's all a lie. . . . I have been living a lie. . . . Our new house, our children, vacations, all of our so-called plans for the future. . . . They are all lies, nothing but all lies built on nothing but more lies." As she cried and grimaced, she continued: "Everything. . . . It is all lies. . . . I will never ever believe another word that comes out of your mouth about anything."

This case vignette provides a brief illustration of the deleterious effects that deceit and betrayal have on the viability of a relationship. During the ensuing sessions with Bridgette and Matt, the quality of their relationship continued to deteriorate for awhile. Virtually every solitary moment that Bridgette had or created for herself was infiltrated with intrusive thoughts about what else Matt had lied about, whether he had had other affairs, and how stupid she was to believe in him. She played back, several times a day, every detail that had occurred between them in their relationship over the years, each time with strong conjecture as to whether any of it was "for real." She now wondered about the times he worked late, several of his business trips, the times that Collette had been in their home, and so forth. There seemed not to have been any immediate relief from the incessant questions that she was left to contemplate about the past as well as the future.

Unfortunately, and predictably, as time went on Matt became progressively less patient with Bridgette's "obsession with Collette and the past." His impatience began to spill over into anger and subtle threats that he should leave the relationship since they seemed unable to move forward. Matt's behaviors helped Bridgette to realize that if she wanted the relationship, she had to find new coping strategies. She understood that the implicit dictate underpinning Matt's expressed displeasure with getting stuck in the past was that she had to find ways to "let it go" or at the very least to exercise more restraint with her outbursts.

In this relational injury Bridgette discovered ways to deny her innermost vulnerable feelings, as often occurs with women and members of oppressed groups, while concomitantly trying to heal from the trauma of the affair. As the violated partner, Bridgette, wanted to emote, reflect, and find relief from a pain for which there appeared to be no remedy, Matt wanted to move forward and forget about the transgressions for which he had assumed responsibility. In a sense, both Matt and Bridgette were engaged in a type of denial that was tightly interwoven with the relational injury.

Denial

Another factor associated with relational injury is that of *denial*. It refers to a conscious effort to dismiss, disavow, and/or ignore salient information that is believed to be harmful to the well-being of a relationship. Ironically, the more prevalent denial is in a relationship the greater is the potential for harm. With regard to relational injures, denial is often used as a vehicle to avoid difficult dialogues and intense emotional interactions. It allows the couple to move on and make pseudo progress because conflict is usually suppressed. As long as the denial persists the quality of the relationship actually deteriorates, although the actual presence of overt conflict may be minimal. This dynamic constitutes the essence of a relational injury, significantly stifling healing.

Relational injury denial is sustained by the collusive efforts of the involved partners. Both the violator and the violated assume active and specific roles in this process. The violator engages in the denial process, usually through a host of dismissive behaviors. Although it is not uncommon for the violator to express remorse and contrition, seldom are the expressed views and feelings of the violated acknowledged or validated. Through a myriad of sophisticated acts of denial, the violator often abdicates responsibility for his or her behavior. Among the most potent acts of the violator is that which involves denying the violated the power and authority to make decisions about what the latter needs with regard to a process of healing and recovery.

The violated individual typically denies his or her "self." This frequently involves denying the authenticity and legitimacy of his or her feelings, thoughts, perceptions, and general worth (this latter point will be discussed in greater detail later). In so doing, the violated, with the collusive assistance of the violator, denies himself or herself the right to dignity, respect, and integrity. These are major assaults to the soul of the individual that both contribute to and exacerbate relational injury. The following case provides a poignant illustration of the intersection between an affair, relational injury, and denial.

Case Example: The Extreme Makeover

Efriam, age thirty-eight, and his thirty-four-year-old wife of eight years, Miranda, were high school sweethearts. By their account they had the perfect relationship. They did everything together both during their courtship and during their marriage, they reported rarely being apart. Both were avid skiers and enjoyed camping. Miranda asserted that she loved Efriam's "natural instincts for the outdoors." He commented that he always appreciated how Miranda gave him the best of both worlds: "She was my lover and best friend. . . . She was every man's dream. . . . She was beautiful, sexual, and feminine . . . and yet she was like one of the guys. . . . You know, she never worried about not doing things because of her nails . . . or all of that other prissy stuff." Miranda stated that she always felt free with Efriam: "He was like a godsend. . . . I know it's weird but he loved that I didn't shave my legs, or feel compelled to wear makeup."

Miranda and Efriam entered therapy because "things had begun to change." While they could not agree when the shift began, they did agree that their marriage was changing and that Efriam's relationship with a mutual friend, Crystal, was becoming problematic. Miranda felt the change shortly after Crystal had joined them on a camping trip. After consistently questioning Efriam about Crystal, he admitted that he had kissed her after their trip. He assured Miranda that they both had been drinking and that it was a mistake. He begged Miranda for forgiveness and to not tell either Crystal or her husband about the incident. Miranda reported that after struggling with the issue she decided to "let it go and move on."

According to Efriam, their relationship began to deteriorate after Miranda began constantly questioning him, calling him repeatedly at work to check on him, and demanding that he report his whereabouts. Miranda attributed the change in their relationship to Efriam. He, according to Miranda, had become "more emotionally distant, and totally disinterested in sex. . . . All he ever does is talk about Crystal."

Several weeks later, Efriam admitted to Miranda that he and Crystal had actually been having an affair for several months. Miranda seemed to be in a catatonic state in therapy. She cried and seemed petrified, though she never yelled or expressed any anger, only disbelief, shock, and unrelenting curiosity about what was wrong with her. She tried constantly to reassure Efriam that she wanted their marriage and that she thought that "things could once again be the way they used to be." Efriam, on the other hand, stated that he needed some time. "I feel bored and I need to figure out what is going on with me. . . . I honestly think the thing with Crystal was more about the excitement I felt from our conversations than it was about sex."

The more reticence that Efriam expressed about the future of their marriage, the more Miranda tried to assure him that it was salvageable. Finally Efriam stated: "I am tired of all this. . . . It takes too much energy. . . . It's not fun . . . the same old talk day in day out. . . . I don't know how much longer I can do it. . . . I am not giving up on us, I am just tired of the same old conversations."

In the next therapy session Miranda was virtually unrecognizable physically. Her long straight hair had been replaced with a slightly shorter, permed and curly style. She had French manicured finger nails. She was wearing bright red lipstick that seemed to match perfectly the red, low-cut V-neck sweater that she proudly, but seemingly uncomfortably, wore. Efriam smiled and looked approvingly. Miranda agreed with Efriam that "things had become boring and that she had a major role in that. . . . After all, I have had the same old look since high school. . . . I can see why he is bored. . . . I had gotten bored with my same old look." She then turned to Efriam and asked somewhat coquettishly, "Should I tell him our big news or do you want to?" With Efriam's encouragement, Miranda stated that, "We have decided to get breast implants! I think he will really like them and they will really help me feel better about myself."

This case vignette provides an example of the inextricable connection between denial and a relational injury. While Efriam *acknowledged* his affair once it was exposed, he really neglected to take responsibility for little else. In some ways, he "allowed" Miranda to assume full responsibility for the difficulties of the marriage. His declarations of agitation made it difficult for Miranda to feel safe enough to engage in a meaningful conversation with him. So while they were successful in colluding to minimize the intensity and conflict in their relationship regarding the affair, they were less successful at taking some important first steps to heal the injury to the relationship.

Miranda, on the other hand, was not only unwilling to see the relationship between Efriam and Crystal as it was, but she could not hold Efriam accountable. She exhibited the kind of *denial of self* that is often characteristic of a relational injury. While Miranda's physical makeover did provide a spark for the relationship, it did not address the underlying emptiness, loneliness, and lack of safety she was experiencing in her marriage. She even acknowledged that while they were having sex more frequently, "It is really for him. . . . Most times when he touches me, I can only think about the fact that he probably touched Crystal the same way. . . . I don't bring it up because I don't want to spoil things. . . . I just have to find a way to deal with it within myself." Miranda's denial of self was pervasive, denying that she had needs, expectations, and desires, or even that it would be healthy for her to have and express her needs. Either way the result was the same: devaluation, relationship strains, and ultimately deeper injuries to the relationship.

Devaluation is a process that systematically strips an individual or group of the essentials of their humanity (Hardy & Laszloffy, 2005). Devaluation assaults ones' sense of dignity and sense of self. It is integral to relational injuries. The accumulative effect of betrayal, deceit, and denial is that it erodes one's sense of worth and well-being. This is why it is so common in relationships in which one partner has had an affair.

Relationship strain is the culmination of unresolved conflict that persists in a relationship over time. A strained the relationship is usually characterized by a surface-level tolerance for a relational connection that harbors intense unacknowledged conflict that is historical and perceived unresolvable. When a relationship is strained the participants "walk on eggshells." The longer a relationship strain is permitted to exist, the greater the injury to that relationship. A recursive relationship exists between relational injuries and strains such that the greater the relationship injury, the greater the magnitude of a relationship strain.

It has been my experience that many of the issues associated with a relational injury are systemic. Despite a proliferation in the number of relationally based treatment models devoted to treating couples there remains a dearth of systemically based models of treatment for addressing complex relational issues from a multicontextual perspective.

THE MULTICONTEXTUAL RELATIONAL MODEL

The multicontextual relational model is a systemically based approach to therapy that focuses on the intersection between difficulties in living and the multiple and varied context in which our lives are embedded. It is based on the assumption that relationships occupy a central role in our lives and that they significantly influence our quality of life. It is a relational approach that takes into account the dynamics of oppression, issues of power, the dimensions of diversity, and the salient principles underlying relationship formation, development, and maintenance. This model is based on the following core values and assumptions:

1. the centrality of relationships;
2. the notion that power is a salient but often unacknowledged factor in relationships;
3. all participants in a relationship have a responsibility to heal relational injuries and strains;
4. betrayal, trauma, and oppression redefine the distribution of power in relationships; and
5. healing relational injuries and strained relationships occur within a five-step process: acknowledgement, validation, apology, deliberate targeted action, and a request for forgiveness.

TREATING AFFAIRS AND HEALING RELATIONAL INJURIES

Treating a couple who have experienced an affair and consequently an injury to their relationship takes time and patience by the therapist and clients. The stages of treatment are fluid, and innumerable variables can affect its length, the couple's commitment to therapy, the severity of the problem, scheduling logistics, joining, and engagement difficulties. The stages are: (1) assessment; (2) preparation for surgery; (3) engagement; (4) integration; and (5) termination.

The Assessment Phase

During this phase, the therapist must make a concerted effort to gain a thorough understanding of the couple's relationship dynamics, both through self-report and by observation. Creating a context in which the couple's dynamics are enacted in the therapy is a critical aspect of the phase. Yet, it is important clinically to establish a delicate balance between allowing them to "fight as usual" and intervening when necessary to inspire feelings of hope, safety, and optimism.

Although the couple is the unit of treatment, it is also standard procedure during this phase to meet with each partner individually as a means of acquiring additional information that may not be initially disclosed in the conjoint sessions. However, in these individual sessions, the therapist must be careful to avoid being triangled by either partner into hearing and keeping secrets related to the affair. Generally speaking, honesty and disclosure of secrets with regard to the affair are essential, if the couple is to genuinely engage in a process of healing.

The therapist can assess progress in this phase by observing the following issues:

1. The couple feels that the therapist has a good understanding of their relationship;
2. The therapist believes that a good working understanding of the couples' relationship has been obtained;
3. A secrecy contract has been established; and
4. The couple reaffirms its commitment to work diligently on their relationship.

Once these general benchmarks have been achieved, the therapy moves to the next phase.

The Preparation for Surgery Phase

A major premise of this model is that affairs can break, or at the very least fracture, the relational bond. Relational-oriented "breaks and fractures" cannot completely heal independently—they require attention and restructuring. The mending of important relationship bonds disrupted by an affair requires a kind of "surgical procedure."

This phase includes a psychoeducational component that occurs over several sessions involving both conjoint and concurrent individual sessions. The primary goals of this phase are: (1) to assist the couple in gaining a better cognitive understanding of what has occurred in their relationship; and (2) to explicate the grounds rules and tasks that will facilitate the couple healing.

An implicit clinical goal is to help the couple move beyond non-productive hostile interactions. For example, it has been useful to offer the following reflection: "Based on my experiences, affairs are one of the most difficult relationship issues to recover from. . . . It requires a lot of tenacity, patience, and hard work. . . . If you are really committed to working this out it will probably be one of the most challenging issues you have had to confront as a couple, and it can be extremely rewarding if/once you accomplish your goal." At this time the couple is encouraged to acknowledge and discuss some of their strengths as a couple. They are also encouraged to consider how the affair has impacted their relationship and their efforts to move on in their lives. Finally, I offer them an invitation to examine the dynamics of power, privilege, equity, and fairness in their relationship with consideration to how these may impact their current crisis.

Once these tasks have been achieved, the couple is then divided and treated individually for several sessions. The focus of the work at this point is to help the couple position themselves to have a different kind of conversation about the affair. This process is a critical prerequisite to repairing a relational injury. The major organizing principle of this phase resides in the belief that both partners have a responsibility in transforming, repairing, and healing the relationship, albeit their roles in this may not be equal.

Because affairs tend to imbue the violator with an increase in power (within the relationship) regardless of the amount or degree of social power that was held previously, this partner has a greater responsibility for repairing the relationship. The increase in power is a result of a "perceived" (or real) reduction of the violator's interest in the relationship. There is always the fear on behalf of the violated that one's partner could either leave or have another affair at any time, which in a rather perverse way assigns more power to the violator. Following this rationale, each partner is given a set of tasks that he or she is expected to adhere to in the interest of promoting change. The effective execution of these tasks constitutes the foundation of the intensive couple work that follows.

The partner directly involved in the affair occupies the role of violator and is assigned the tasks of the violator: (1) Resist the equalization of suffering; (2) Resist dialogues designed to negate; and (3) Develop "tough" skin. The execution of and adherence to these tasks are essential to moving the couple toward more functional interactions.

Resisting the equalization of suffering is necessary because it helps the violator to appreciate that "pain and suffering" is not the exclusive domain of the violated. This process allows for the recognition and validation of the intense feelings (guilt, anxiety, grief, etc.) that the violator may be experiencing while simultaneously dispelling all notions that the "suffering" is equal. If a couple is to begin a process of healing from an affair, it is necessary that the violator create space for the violated to openly and freely discuss the matter without interruption, correction, or a sense of competition. Too often these conversations break down, escalate, or become stifled when the expressed suffering of the violated is matched with an expression of the violator's pain. Thus, it is imperative that the treatment process, at least initially, provide a forum for the violator to provide a detailed discussion of his or her hurt and pain.

Resisting dialogues designed to negate is a task for the violator to resist the disclosure of information (directly or indirectly) designed to negate the experiences and testimony of the violated. This process is often the preferred method for equalizing suffering. In the first clinical vignette case, Matt often negated his partner's experiences and feelings by noting that "he was tired of the same old conversations and Bridgette's obsession with Collette," the woman with whom he had an affair. He also implied that "the stuck conversation and the obsession with Collette" caused him considerable discomfort; a pain that was equal to or greater than that experienced by Bridgette as a result of the affair. During this phase, the violator is introduced to strategies and "ways of being" that make it possible to be more emotionally present and less defensive during intense conversations.

Developing tough skin is a task designed to help the violator address a host of emotional and psychological issues that impede vulnerability. In addition this phase is devoted to equipping the violator with skills that will increase her or his capacity to hold a partner's vulnerability, even in the face of what feels like rejection, personal attack, or an expressed lack of gratitude. By developing thick skin, the violator is in a much better position to tolerate the conflict and intensity that eventually has to be dealt with if healing and repair are to take place. By developing and exhibiting thick skin, the violator essentially grants the violated implicit permission to get off of the "eggshells." Once this occurs, the couple can cease and desist their tentative, conflict-avoidant, nonauthentically engaged interactions with each other.

Since both partners, according to the model, are responsible for repairing the relationship, the violated also has specific tasks that must be executed. The tasks of the violated are: (1) Exhale, and (2) Exercise Voice. Although these tasks appear simplistic in nature, they are formidable undertakings for those whose sense of self has been decimated by an affair.

Exhaling refers to a conscious process of expunging one's self of all the negative self-definitions that become internalized as a consequence of a trauma such as an affair. It involves resisting the internalization of constructions of self that assault and deflate one's self-esteem. Miranda and Efriam provided a moving case illustration of how powerful negative messages can become internalized and shape one's behavior. Miranda's decision to pursue a physical makeover was triggered by a host of negative self messages that she had internalized. She had become convinced that she was inadequate and incomplete without larger breasts and makeup, the latter of which she had resisted most of her life.

Exhaling is a relatively easy task to achieve when one "has a voice." The concept of "voice" is a metaphor for becoming an advocate for one's self. It involves personal agency and advocacy—standing up for one's self, reclaiming one's dignity, and establishing appropriate boundaries on behalf of one's self. The real test for the violated is to be able to exercise her or his voice in the presence of the violator, especially when much appears to be at stake. The next stage of the therapeutic process is designed to provide a platform for this and other types of potentially transformative interactions.

The Engagement Phase

At this phase the couple is reunited in treatment and one of the major goals is to promote constructive engagement—promoting honest, open, and painful dialogue. It is during this phase of the treatment that the first steps toward healing the relational injury must occur. Thus it is vital that the violator take steps toward demonstrating *acknowledgment* and offering *validation.*

Acknowledgment is knowledge that involves a deep level of empathic understanding. It is what the violator uses to convey to the violated that he or she understands the gravity of hurt and devastation that his or her actions have caused—both to the individual, and to the relationship between them. Before this can be genuinely and empathically expressed, the violator must gain a deeply internalized sense of this "knowledge." If is not readily present, the process of therapy must advance to this stage before the couple can proceed with intensive conjoint work. If on the other hand, the violator has developed a sense of acknowledgement, it paves the way for both offering validation and participating in intensive couples work.

Validation is an act of affirmation. It is a way of communicating compassion, understanding, and affirmation to someone else about his or her thoughts, feelings, and perceptions about the world. Offering validation is fundamental to creating a safe space for couples to talk openly, especially about those topics that are difficult to discuss. Once the couple, especially the violator, can demonstrate acknowledgment and offer validation they have taken the first critical steps toward creating a context to mend their relationship.

During this treatment phase the couple is encouraged to take risks with each other and a premium is placed on positioning each partner to be vulnerable with the other. Establishing a forum where the couple can be encouraged and supported in their efforts to confront their deepest emotions is of paramount significance during this stage. Expressions of anger, rage, and despair are particularly encouraged during these sessions; the one caveat of course, is that the couple avoids the destructive interactional patterns that have existed between them.

The work occurring during this phase is often generates a plethora of raw emotions and uncertainties about the relationship. The "mask" covering all of the difficult dialogues and intense interactions that the couple has collusively and assiduously worked toward avoiding is removed during these sessions. The couple's capacity to express and tolerate increasing levels of vulnerability is usually a reliable indicator that they are ready for the next stage of the treatment process, the integration phase.

The Integration Phase

During this phase, the goal of the treatment is to assist the couple in integrating new interactional strategies into their behavioral repertoire. This is mainly achieved by the therapist working actively with issues that are generated in the sessions, and building on "lessons learned" from the previous stages. Assisting the couple to develop a more comprehensive and complex understanding of their relationship dynamics is also important during this phase. It is not uncommon for there to be an in-depth exploration and integration of family-of-origin issues, attachment considerations, and underlying cultural issues throughout this segment of the treatment process. In some instances, external support systems of the couple (parents, siblings, and friends) may be incorporated into parts of the therapy for specific, time-limited initiatives.

Here the therapist plays an instrumental role in assisting the couple to refine and solidify the requisite targeted action that is necessary to promote the type of change that is desired. As the treatment continues, it is expected that the couple's work will progress to the point at which the violator can offer an apology that is buttressed by specific targeted actions. When an apology is offered with intimacy and vulnerability, it can pave the way for the violator to request forgiveness. The violated may be much more amenable to receiving a request for forgiveness once an apology is initiated. The therapist explains that the act of forgiveness has no predictable timetable and authentic forgiveness is not attainable prior to the termination of therapy. This latter point is one that cannot be reiterated and reinforced enough with couples during the final phase of therapy.

The Termination Phase

The final phase of therapy is used to conduct a comprehensive review with the couple regarding their strengths, weaknesses, and areas of potential future growth. Since most relational injuries are not completely healed by the end of therapy, couples are provided with guidance and direction regarding how to continue to nurture the growth and healing processes of their relationships. As stated earlier, the couple is reminded about the perils of moving to forgiveness prematurely. Forgiveness can be desired, craved for, and requested by the violator, however it can only be extended by the violated at a time and pace dictated by his or her unique healing cycle.

AUTHOR'S REFLECTIONS

This chapter examined the impact of affairs on intimate relationships. It introduced the concept of relational injury as a way of describing the systemic deterioration of relationships ravaged by betrayal and deceit. The anatomy of relational injury and strains were described. It was posited that since the relational consequences of an affair are systemic, the remedy employed for redress from an affair should also be systemic and take into account a host of sociocultural issues.

The multicontextual relational model was introduced as a systemic approach to treatment with couples maligned by an affair. The five stages of treatment: assessment, preparation for surgery; engagement; integrative; and termination were discussed in detail. These were also accompanied by a discussion of the five steps for healing relational injury and strained relationships: acknowledgment, validation, deliberate targeted action, apology, and seeking forgiveness.

REFERENCES

Hardy, K.V. (2004). Race, reality, and relationships: Implications for family therapists. In S. Madigan (Ed.), *Therapy from the outside in* (pp. 87-98). Vancouver, BC: Yaletown Family Therapy.

Hardy, K.V., & Laszloffy, T.A. (2005). *Teens who hurt: Clinical interventions for breaking the cycle of youth violence.* New York: Guilford.

Johnson, S. (2001). Attachment injuries in couple relationships: A new perspective on impasses in couples therapy. *Journal of Marital and Family Therapy, 27*(2), 145-155.

Chapter 19

The Futile Quest:
Parental Loss and Serial Relationships

David Moultrup

Tribute to William C. Nichols

Bill Nichols is one of the unsung heroes of the world of marriage and family therapy. Standing tall for critical thinking and common sense, Bill has offered a consistent voice of reason over the years. Whether it be in the realm of theory, practice, academics, or politics, Bill has been there with his keen mind and perceptive vision. Certainly my life has been deeply enriched both personally and professionally by having Bill be a part of it. Indeed, the entire field of mental health has been deeply enriched by his countless contributions.

The words were so familiar. It seemed like they probably had been handed down over the ages. Certainly I had heard them almost verbatim countless times before. But for Tom they were new ideas, and new words. And it was Tom who was sitting with me now, exploring the implications of these new feelings and experiences. He was describing in great detail the way he felt with Betty. It was clear she understood him. It was clear she was available sexually on a more profound level. It was clear he felt different with her than he ever had before. He felt better.

But, there was a problem. Tom was married to Debbie. He had been married to Debbie for almost twenty years. And Debbie, once she found out about Betty, told Tom she did not want a divorce, she wanted to work things out. Tom was now in a quandary. He had assumed Debbie did not want him at all, and certainly did not want him enough to work through his transgression with Betty. Tom was now in entirely unexpected territory.

When Marriages Fail
© 2006 by The Haworth Press, Inc. All rights reserved.
doi:10.1300/5562_19

INITIAL TREATMENT CONCERNS

There is no shortage of questions posed by Tom's situation. On a seemingly simple level, Tom needs to make day-to-day decisions. There are inevitable questions, such as which woman to see when. The answers to these questions trigger rashes of feelings among the three of them, and others close to the drama. Although those questions seem to be earth-shaking at the time, in the overall evolution of the drama, they are minor questions.

More substantive questions include: should Tom get divorced from Debbie and begin a new life with Betty? Ultimately this needs to be answered. Finally, there are fundamental questions that are not readily apparent but which are the most critical layer to understand. These fundamental questions are rooted in the meaning and timing of the crisis.

Fairly quickly it became apparent to everyone, including Tom, that he was totally clueless about any abstract meaning to this crisis. He simply could not see past the "good" feeling with Betty, and the "not good" feeling with his wife Debbie. But that difference in feeling did not translate into clear decisions. He was notably inconsistent about answering the questions concerning daily contact, and found himself in the impossible position of trying to please both women simultaneously.

This translated into paralysis on the question of divorce. While Tom could muster considerable certainty about any given answer at any given moment in time, invariably he would be equally convinced of the opposite answer within minutes or hours of that moment. Tom was like a ping-pong ball, bouncing from one side of the table to the other. As soon as he hit one side, he was on his way back to the other.

SHAPING THE ONGOING TREATMENT

Engaging in a therapeutic endeavor with Tom in this type of quagmire is not a project suited to brief therapy. The usual course of these dramas in life is slow and agonizing, easily taking more than a year to play itself out. This time period is not a sinister manipulation. It is not an indication of a failure of therapy. It is, in a very fundamental way, a sign of the human forces of confusion and ambivalence which must be encountered and resolved before concluding this type of chapter.

Likewise, it is not a therapeutic project suited to any one theoretical lens. Many a zealot could argue persuasively that a certain model of therapy would be ideal for Tom. However, the ambiguities and complexities of his situation are particularly amenable to being viewed with the power of an integrated model of psychotherapy. In that way, the insights and perspectives from multiple sources can offer Tom and the therapist the opportunity to invoke the concepts and images which most resonate to Tom in his situation.

Seemingly endless themes and nuances invite serious contemplation in regard to Tom's situation. I have explored many of these previously (Moultrup, 1990, 2005). One worthy of further exploration is the complexity of terminating one relationship, which had been considered to be "til death do us part," and engaging in another one with the same premise. This phenomenon of divorce and remarriage is one of the central social structures of contemporary society. Tom's situation exposes some of the potential ambiguities of that transition.

Tom was convinced early in the therapy that his marriage to Debbie was over. He had considerable data to substantiate that hypothesis. Indeed, Tom's and Debbie's history was a painful example of a poorly functioning relationship. Debbie corroborated the history, but maintained her belief that with work the relationship could be rehabilitated. Both of them recounted an early history together in which Tom was, at best, marginally committed to the relationship. He had become involved with Debbie in the wake of ending another long-term relationship with Ellen. Actually, the relationship with Ellen was not truly over when Tom and Debbie became involved. But even after that first relationship officially ended, he had a continuing concern for Ellen which caused considerable friction with Debbie. Beyond that, both Tom and Debbie struggled with substance abuse and found a wide array of trigger points for conflict.

The story the couple related was characterized by a clear ability to successfully create a material life together, covering a deep sense of emptiness and lack of connection. They created a home life with a considerable social network, and both recovered from the period of substance abuse of the earlier years. However, frequent and severe flare-ups marred many different occasions, both private and public. And even in the absence of significant conflict, the discontent and fundamental emptiness between Tom and Debbie was constantly lurking just below the surface.

In that light, Tom's retreat from Debbie, and his new liaison with Betty would seem to be understandable, perhaps even justified. Why not move away from a relationship which simply "wasn't working," and move on? Why not be in a relationship with someone who seemed to be more tuned in and able to engage emotionally?

Answering those questions depended on identifying and answering many other questions, and expanding the field of view beyond the threesome of Tom, Debbie, and Betty. It calls for a comprehensive view of the broader emotional system, complete with multigenerational patterns and themes. The more those factors are understood, the more depth can be brought to the seemingly simple question of moving on.

Tom continued to fit the classic picture of confusion and ambivalence. He alternately proclaimed that the marriage was over, and then told Debbie that he loved her. He chose to see Betty, leaving his wife Debbie alone. Then he would find himself in a fight with Betty, and use Debbie as a confidante, expressing his deep sadness and confusion. Clarity and definition were simply not to be found in Tom's life during this period.

THERAPEUTIC ARTISTRY

Working with Tom in the middle of this confusion, for me, is an art. The art of psychotherapy involves the balancing of broader tasks with the need to attend to the anxiety which is present every day. The combination of behavioral and cognitive lenses with the broad systemic lens gives the therapist the tools to both pursue the bedrock issues while simultaneously maintaining calm on a daily basis. Each situation will lend itself to a different intervention, or even range of interventions. Ultimately, however, balancing the compelling daily drama with the need to explore the broad system will yield the most comprehensive understanding of the forces which are propelling the situation.

Several key points emerged in the exploration with Tom. First, there was an intriguing similarity between Betty, his new friend, and Ellen, his first relationship. He described both of them as being more tuned in to emotions than Debbie. He was unclear as to why he had left Ellen, but believed it had to do with his frustration at her lack of organization and lack of motivation. Betty was easily described with the same images. Debbie, conversely, though less emotional, was highly organized and motivated.

It became increasingly clear that Tom, on one level, was struggling with forces that alternately pushed him into two different types of relationships, one which was more emotionally resonant, and one which was more functionally successful. Notably, this struggle was now in its second major eruption in his life. The simple addition of history prior to Tom's relationship with Debbie created an entirely different light in which to view the current crisis.

THE LETHAL DYNAMIC OF TOXIC GRIEF

Further exploration revealed another, even more impressive factor to consider in this crisis. Tom's mother had died when he was a young boy. He had grown up without really knowing her. He had seen the trouble he and his older brother had in coping with the loss, and the trouble both of them had in bonding with the woman who became their stepmother.

Careful, gentle, and slow exploration of Tom's sense of his mother exposed a complicated schism. One image Tom carried was of his mother as the perfect emotional nurturer who was there for him when he needed her. This particular version of his mother was the "wished for" version. He yearned for much nurturing that he had missed. The other image was of the competent mother who was not there. Clearly, her death left her unavailable. Tom carried that sense of disconnect with him as a defining experience of how close relationships function.

Unearthing these two major images gave a thematic core to the therapy. They offered limitless opportunities to plumb the depths of unresolved feelings of loss and emptiness. Even more, they were easily traced into seemingly minor current interactions, in which Tom's inability to make decisions about his current relationships with Debbie and Betty were able to be seen as echoes of confusion and uncertainty about his mother.

THE CURRENT CAST AS A REFLECTION
OF THE INNER EMPTINESS

The two women in the current triangle offered intriguing counterpoints to Tom's dynamic portrait. His wife Debbie came from a family of high achievers with a father who, in subtle ways, scorned weakness. Debbie learned to be strong in the face of his constant challenges, so strong that there had been no room for a healthy attention to feelings. It became clear to her over time that the relationship with Tom had suffered greatly with something she began to identify as her own obtuseness about feelings. Learning about feelings in the therapy was a new experience for her.

Betty, Tom's new paramour, was a notable contrast to Debbie. Her parents were not really able to care for themselves, and in turn did not care for Betty and her brother. And in what seemed to be stunning symmetry with Tom, Betty's father had died when she was quite young. She then found herself attending to the needs of both her brother and her mother. She became unusually adept at tuning into the needs of those around her. She learned to be nurturing in a way which, at times, seemed to go to extremes of her ignoring her own needs and attending to others. This style could be described as having very indistinct boundaries between Betty and those closest to her. As it worked with Tom, it was clear that in some ways they felt almost melded together.

The chemistry in the Tom—Debbie—Betty triangle was impressive. Multigenerational patterns, profound loss, and incontrovertible evidence of a poor initial relationship between Tom and Debbie might seem to support the notion that the "best" option for all of them would be for Tom to move on, and build a new life with Betty. Certainly that was the premise that Tom was focused on early in the therapy.

But there were two questions which loomed large, even at the outset. First, why had Tom engaged with Debbie in the first place, and why had it lasted such a long time? Clearly there was the sense of Tom wanting something which Debbie offered, despite an obvious sense of ambivalence about it. Second, what does his continuing inability to decisively separate from her reveal about the fundamental bond between them?

Wholeness of self surfaced as the predominant theme in the quest to answer these questions. It became clear that Tom had an uncanny way of showing his emotional side in the relationship with Betty, and his practical and functional side in the relationship with Debbie, his wife. His sense of self and sense of being in the world were in some way a reflection of his view of the dominant characteristics of the woman in his life. As this pattern emerged, it became painfully clear that the path to a healthier life was to be able to integrate both the functional and the emotional into one relationship. This was a considerable challenge. Tom had been operating on the premise that the answer to making life better was to get out of a bad relationship and get into another "good" relationship. With all of the pain and difficulty of recasting a damaged relationship, he thought that just starting with a clean slate would be a more feasible option.

This premise had been exposed as a futile quest. His sense of what made a good relationship with Betty was now seen as yet another incomplete, disintegrated attempt at recapturing the impossible. His cloudy sense of what his mother was like, and his deep sense of incompleteness, had thrust him into relationships which had been decidedly incomplete. Debbie had colluded in the incompleteness over the years, again very much a function of the culture of her family of origin. She, however, was very interested in growing and rehabilitating the relationship.

AUTHOR'S REFLECTIONS:
CONTINUING THE JOURNEY

Being able to articulate these dynamics does not necessarily translate into immediate change. Tom's indecision acted as a catalyst for both him and his wife. The process continued with Tom and Debbie continuing to learn about the many different ways that their lives are shaped by the interaction of their inner worlds, and the emotional system in which they live.

For my part, the privilege of engaging with people in a therapeutic relationship is a treasure of incalculable proportions, and one that I never cease to appreciate. It offers the opportunity to join with people at a moment in their lives when they are ready to do battle with whatever forces have pushed them into previous self-destructive choices. The intention to change course into a positive direction is powerful and invigorating. It offers the opportunity to contemplate many of the ambiguities and enigmas of life. This, too, is invigorating and calls for constant creativity on the part of the therapist. It also elicits profound humility. Encountering life's enigmas yields questions more often than answers, and it lays bare the massive discrepancy in power between the therapist and the fundamental human forces which shape thoughts, feelings, and behavior. It is not the therapist who occupies the position of power in this equation.

REFERENCES

Moultrup, D.J. (1990). *Husbands, wives, and lovers: The emotional system of the extramarital affair.* New York: Guilford Press.

Moultrup, D. (2005). Undercurrents. In F.P. Piercy, K.M. Hertlein, & J.L. Wetchler (Eds.), *Handbook of the clinical treatment of infidelity.* New York: Haworth Press.

Chapter 20

A Therapeutic Look
at "Gray Divorces"

Marcia E. Lasswell

Tribute to William C. Nichols

My association with Bill Nichols goes back over forty years and has been a rich friendship professionally and personally. We have seen each other through some joyous times and some times of sorrow and pain. We have served on numerous professional committees, commissions, and boards together and I have always valued the wisdom and good humor he has brought to whatever task we set out to accomplish. Bill has contributed so much to the field of marriage and family therapy and I can think of no one who deserves the gratitude and honors he has been given from his students, supervisees, and colleagues more than he does for his lifetime of service.

An elderly couple appeared before a judge in divorce court. The husband hobbled toward the bench using a cane and his wife followed holding on to her walker. The surprised judge asked how old they were and they reported that they were in their eighties. He then asked how long they had been married. "Sixty years," they answered. "Why in the world do you want to get a divorce now?" the judge inquired. The husband replied, "The time just never seemed right before." "Oh, were you waiting until your children were grown?" asked the judge. Whereupon, the wife piped up, "No, we were waiting until they died."

The first experience I ever had with an older couple (retirement age) who were contemplating divorce came many years ago. It was such a novelty that I remember it to this day. The wife was sixty-six and her husband was seventy-one. They had been married forty-two years and had raised three children. I was young enough at the time to be one of their children and I was inexperienced with older couples. I am afraid I reacted to their announcement in a very unsophisticated way. I probably looked shocked as I asked why, after all these years, they wanted a divorce. In fact, I am embarrassed to say, I may have wondered aloud why they were not able to work things out since they had made it this far. Probably also in my thoughts was that they surely did not have all that much time left to live. The man gave me his answer: "I just want to have some peace in my last years." Of course, the couple's combined stories spelled out a much more complex picture than his words implied.

The husband, a small business owner, had retired several months before, much to the delight of his wife. She had been waiting years to travel and enjoy some time with this man who had always been working. Over the years she had pretty much raised their children alone, kept the house and, as time allowed, worked in the business. However, her husband gave up his short retirement to start another company. Once again, he was gone almost all of the time and she was fed up with putting her plans on hold. They both said that they wanted "out" to do what they pleased in the years left to them.

The husband appeared to be looking at the alternatives outside his marriage. The wife's plan was to change their life within their marriage. The husband needed a reality check focused primarily on how much his wife had enabled his success in business up to that point, and how well he could pursue a new business while taking care of personal needs he had delegated to the wife for years. He also was unrealistic about their financial situation after the even split demanded by state divorce law. In contrast, the wife was more realistic about taking care of her personal needs and had formed a wide circle of supportive friends to help take care of any problem of loneliness. Actually, she had been lonely for years within the marriage and did not see that being divorced would bring about a dramatic change. However, she was not well informed about her financial prospects. Even with her share of the community property and a fair amount of spousal support, she would have to change her lifestyle. The travel she had envisioned might be minimal.

In spite of my inexperience at the time, I was able to convince this couple to try a few sessions of marriage counseling to look critically at their expectations of what freedom from each other might bring. As often is the case with older couples, financial security was paramount to my two clients. The husband came to realize that living apart would be more expensive, and it might be unrealistic to count on his new business to do as well as the old one. Both parties decided that what would be lost financially in the division of assets was a powerful motivator to try to work things out. They also discovered feelings of guilt and concern for their children's reactions.

As you can see, my values were very traditional, and the mere fact that this couple had come to therapy instead of heading right to divorce court gave me hope that there was still a way they could work out their differences. It is here that marriage therapists are tested when working with the older couples who are on the verge of divorce. Caution is needed to ensure that the therapist's own values are not being used to influence the couple into staying married.

WHO ARE THESE DIVORCING ADULTS?

I first heard the term *gray divorce* about the time I saw this couple (circa 1983). It referred to a small percentage of individuals over sixty-five years of age who were ending long-term marriages. Apparently, for them, their generation's inhibitions against divorce had somehow been weakened. They often stood up to the dismay and strong disapproval of their children. They viewed any hardships of going it alone (e.g., probable economic decline for the wife) as being better for them than remaining in what they saw as lifeless or conflicted marriages. Most seemed to be in good health and financial condition. They had waited to see their children grown and independent. Both they and their children were concerned about the impact of the grandparental divorce on the grandchildren. Ironically, some of these divorcing elders had watched as their own children, and even a few grandchildren had divorced. I think of these brave, unstudied few as "the first wave" because I expect increasingly larger waves to follow.

The Current Older Generation

Generalizing about generations by age alone has its pitfalls. Not all of those over sixty-five years of age have had the same experiences.

The world they live in has been changing even as successive waves of individuals reach that age. Still there may be some merit in using chronological age as a broad base for ideas about family life in the United States. Years have passed since the day that older couple sat in my office and I have grown much more aware that marriages can end at any time in the life cycle and for myriad reasons. Adding to my insight was that my own marriage ended after forty years even though I was not yet of retirement age. Suddenly being a sixty-year-old woman who wanted out of her marriage did not seem so strange. I was that woman. At about the same time, several of my friends and colleagues decided to end long-term marriages and more and more clients entered therapy with this as their agenda. Each situation was unique, of course, although there seemed to be some common explanations or, at least, some common threads running through the different explanations. That first couple I had seen was not unique in finding their goals incompatible. It is now well recognized that many couples find that the life-cycle changes associated with aging, and particularly retirement, bring conflicting goals about how to live life and differing ideas about finances. Often postretirement couples don't know how to reach consensual choices for what they urgently perceive to be their last years of life.

Even so, the majority of those categorized as elderly usually do not divorce over these issues but live out the rest of their lives. Some may be unhappy in their lives, but believe that they have little choice. Some believe that divorce has become too easy, and that many couples lack commitment. To many of the younger generations, however, that kind of tenacity may be viewed as sad, provided there are viable options to enduring an unhappy marriage until death.

Unfortunately, little is known about such couples. Research studies and clinical literature are scanty on the topic of gray divorce. Possibly this is because the best estimates of the percentage of the over-sixty-five population currently divorced or separated is only about 8.3 percent (U.S. Bureau of the Census, 2002). Nonetheless, the approximately three million men and women in this group need to be better understood. The number of couples past the age of sixty-five who initiate divorce may currently be small but it is growing. One estimate is that since 1970, the rate of divorce among the elderly has increased three times as fast as the rate of growth of the older population as a whole (Dychtwald & Flower, 1990). Much of the extant literature describes the plight of many older women who have been divorced before entering their later years. This research largely is centered on the issues of poverty, loneliness, elder care, sustaining family support, and scarce community services.

The "Bridge Group"

Another group of older individuals is not typical of the majority because this group has proven more willing to either live out remaining years alone or to look for a new partner. The actual ages of these individuals may be less important than whether they hold traditional values about marriage and divorce, what their work histories have been, and what the future holds in terms of options for more satisfying lives without their current partners. Some of these couples are financially able to divide their assets and have established full lives that are not totally dependent upon each other. A growing number of older women are in a much better financial condition than more traditional women who are dependent upon spousal support. They have resources of their own, including their own retirement benefits. Moreover men and women who decide to continue working past customary retirement ages may actually be able to recoup their losses within a few years of a divorce. They have financial resources, ongoing paths to meaningful social support, and more opportunity to remarry—if that is their choice.

The group of "bridge crossers," along with the first wave of the "baby boomers" close on their heels, includes those whose children are grown and usually do not require financial support. Both partners are likely to have been in the labor force and, more than ever before, they may have savings and a retirement plan, even if it is only a Social Security check. Those who are still working may have several years left to earn since both men and women are beginning to work past the traditional retirement age, particularly if they enjoy their jobs and need the money. Even though most of the men will remarry, the majority will have no more children to support. For the women in this group, the downside of divorce can still remain a distinct possibility if they have limited income of their own or if that income is based primarily on spousal support. In addition, women know they are less likely to remarry, if that is their goal. Some studies have disclosed that a large number of these women are realistic about the shortage of potential husbands and have made plans for being single. If they remain single, they will have plenty of company since older women currently make up the fastest growing group of singles in America, partly from widowhood, but in increasing numbers from both earlier divorces and later-life divorce. Many of these women have personal resources from their own work life that enable them to pursue activities that add to their personal well-being making singlehood far more preferable than an unsatisfactory marriage.

Many of my friends and I are in this group which bridges the current older, traditional generation and those who are in the first cohort of baby boomers described later. We neither typify the value of "making your bed and lying in it" nor are we totally in tune with an emphasis on individuality and "deserving happiness." We and members of our group are "marginal" in that we are not completely acculturated into the new ways of thinking but do not feel stuck in the old value system either. Consequently, many of our cohort—especially women—have stayed in long-term marriages while wrestling with the dilemmas of marginality, especially those involving values and finances. However, increasing numbers have come to realize that they can take care of themselves and it is not uncommon for their children, who often are more comfortable with the idea of divorce, to encourage them to move on before they, themselves, have felt ready. In fact, it is often older women who decide to leave and initiate dissolution proceedings. I have found that, when husbands are the ones who have made the decision to part, frequently it is when they have found a new partner. They also have discovered that, because of the wife's assets, the divorce settlement would not be as devastating as they had imagined. In many ways, however, it seems that the wives—as a result of greater resources for independence in this age group—have made more changes in their ideas about divorce than older husbands have. Men have traditionally been the "leavers," especially when they have found a new partner. Older women rarely leave for another relationship. Now, however, women in the "bridge group" seem to be deciding that being single is preferable to the marriage they have been enduring.

Many members of the "bridge group" can articulate a compelling rationale for the decision to divorce. They cite the added years they expect to live. They explain that many marriages may run their courses before they are ended by death. They may appreciate the institution of marriage, but not with the same partner. As one friend told me, "I'll have a fifty-year celebration but the total will have been with three men. The first was a college 'interlude,' the second was the father of my children, and the third is to grow old with." It seems more likely that multiple marriage (serial monogamy) will be the case for men than for women because women outnumber men at every stage of the life cycle. Because this population gap influences which gender is the least likely to remarry, it may make sense to replace the notion of "his marriage" and "her marriage" (Bernard, 1982) with a new topic for research and clinical practice—"his divorce" and "her divorce."

The Baby Boomers: What Lies Ahead

In contrast to the limited material written about divorce in the older generation and almost none about the "bridge crossers," a wealth of information exists about what is happening now and what is expected in the future from the wave of baby boomers who are set to enter old age. The oldest of this group have just recently celebrated their sixtieth birthdays. This means that those born in 1946 will be entering "old age," as the U.S. Bureau of the Census defines it, in 2010. The last group of "boomers," born in 1964, will be sixty-five in 2029. Therefore, beginning in 2010, and continuing for eighteen years, nearly eighty million men and women (approximately 28 percent of the population) will bring with them into old age their well-established value systems which have changed the economic, political, and family conditions of America: A belief in being intellectually and socially individualistic (Smith & Clurman, 1997). They are known for trying to make the most of life's choices. Personal fulfillment is important to them and often includes leaving what may be a stultifying job or relationship for more satisfying and growth-producing situations. They have already been active in reconfiguring traditional marriage and sexuality. They have grown up with divorce as a reality in their lives and many of them have already been divorced and remarried; some more than once. They have witnessed family members, neighbors, friends, and even their children terminate marriages. They have seen enough divorced couples, most of whom had children, to be convinced that there is "life after divorce." They have seen that the results of divorce are not always dire and totally destructive.

In fact, a popular belief permeating much of this generation is that a good divorce is better than a poor marriage.

A large proportion of the baby boomers have cohabited more than once, often between marriages and frequently bringing along their children. Very often this is a replacement for remarriage, which has decreased in the past few years. Older couples already make up a sizeable proportion of the nearly ten million cohabiting partners even though their value systems would seem to mitigate against it. The baby boomers generally are expected not to have such inhibitions, especially when remarriage might mean giving up benefits such as pensions and decreased Social Security in old age.

The sheer numbers of those who are soon to be classified as "old" challenges us as family therapists to prepare for what lies ahead. Because they are so numerous and cover an age span of nearly two decades, some demographers find it useful to separate the older boomers (born 1946-1955) from the younger ones (born 1956-1964). Each group can be compared to the other and also to those cohorts both older and younger than they are. From this comes the information that their divorce rate is almost double that of the currently old, although the younger boomers' rate is slightly higher than for the older boomers (U.S. Bureau of the Census, 1972, 2002).

These thoughts are not without debate. Several gerontologists have cautioned against assuming that baby boomers are so unique that they will somehow revolutionize aging in our society. They have urged caution in predicting the future, particularly in work and politics (Corman & Kingson, 1996). There is not even agreement about divorce within this cohort, and whether to expect that divorce will be more common among the elderly in the years to come. Some predict that those who wished to divorce have already done so or will fall into the pattern that characterized their own parents of settling for what they have. Still others believe that the greater independence of women will push the rates higher. However, even if the divorce rate does not actually go up, the numbers of those who divorce surely will be greater simply as a consequence of the growing percentage of elderly.

CONTEXTUAL PROBLEMS OF "GRAY DIVORCES"

Each couple's experience of their marriage and their thoughts about ending it are to some extent unique. It depends on who each of them are, how they fit together psychosocially, and also on the values, beliefs, resources, and sanctions of the larger world in which their marriage is embedded. In this regard we think of subcultural factors embodied in nuclear and extended families, communities, states, and nation. I have mentioned intra- and extrafamilial attitudes about divorce between the elderly as I have described the successive waves. The reader can also think of how such divorces might be regarded in their own social and, perhaps, church communities. I want to elaborate on some of these.

Contemporary Challenges

Those who currently divorce in old age, and those who have done so in the past, are most likely going against the marriage standards with which they grew up. Therefore, they may feel isolated from social support because they will be a distinct minority among others of their generation who are either still married or have been widowed. Many of their generation have values that make them reluctant to end their marriages (Smith & Clurman, 1997). The majority view is that marriage is a lifetime commitment, based on central cultural values such as duty, loyalty, "hanging in there through thick and thin," personal sacrifice, and teamwork. Divorce, therefore, is "giving up" or a "personal failure." That generation is also prone to see their children's divorces as self-centered, especially when unhappiness is given as the root cause. Those adults involved in "gray divorce" must have the strength to do what so many of their chronological peers decry.

In addition to well-ingrained value systems, the financial realities of divorce for older, retired men and women may be forbidding (e.g., AARP, 2003). They most likely will be living on fixed incomes. Tax and spousal support complications and increasing health costs suggest that they will be unlikely to maintain the same standard of living they had when married. Moreover, reluctance to divorce is often connected to how few elderly women have spent enough time in the labor force to have earned adequate retirement benefits (Lester, 1991). These women may be reluctant to give up the security they have worked so hard to attain within their marriages. Many men of this generation are deterred from divorce by laws that will obligate them to support their former partner and to share any resources they have accumulated.

Many elderly couples stay together out of fear of being alone in their later years (Antonucci, 1994). This apparently is strongest where elderly individuals perceive an absence of friendship support by blood relatives and non-kin (Pilusuk & Minkler, 1980), experience what their current social relationships provide is inferior to what they have received in the past (Dykstra, 1990), or believe that being socially linked is more important than being self-sufficient (Dykstra, 1990). Overall, the social resource needs of the older person and his or her fears of being alone depend in part of the individual's existing contacts, state of health, and psychology of the person (Pilusuk & Minkler, 1980).

A final contemporary complication may be the attitude of family therapists themselves. The couple to whom I referred early in this chapter seemed to me to have mixed motives. This case occurred nearly twenty-five years ago when the couple's age cohort almost never divorced, so I must confess that my perspective was biased in the direction of helping them try to sustain their marriage. Clearly, my own values were also being served.

Challenges to Come

Many problems divorced couples faced in the past will still be a part of the future of therapy. However, because of their vast numbers, some unexpected problems may arise for the divorced baby boomers as they age. Some of these are only beginning to surface in the literature of demographers, for example, concern about Social Security and the number of the recipients relative to those making payments. This concern makes the rest of us wonder about caregiving arrangements in general: So many will need to receive support from a much smaller younger generation.

Some eighty million elderly parents may be looking to a generation of only fifty million for care. Researchers already have found that those who have been divorced get less care from their children than either still-married or widowed elderly do. Getting remarried actually seems to make matters worse since these older men and women receive even less help from their own children and virtually none from stepchildren (Pezzin & Schone, 1999). Baby boomers usually gave that care to their own parents, even being labeled as the "caught-in-the-middle" generation, and many optimistically hope that the same care will be returned. Yet some studies of the baby boomers' children indicate that many of them harbor resentment about their parents' generation and are not eager to step up to what is sure to be a burden spread among a thin population of helpers. Some 40 percent of baby-boomer children spent time in a single-parent home and many of them are semi-alienated from one or both parents. Still others have seen the effect of their parents' divorces on their own marital lives, so they do not feel inclined to give the kind of help that may be needed.

Surveys have indicated that the increasing life span will extend the time period in which old-age health problems such as aches, pains, senility, cardiovascular conditions, and broken bones will need attention. In addition, health experts are predicting that alcohol and drug problems, especially abuse of prescription and over-the-counter drugs, will rise (Patterson & Jeste, 1999). The baby-boomer generation has a history of more drug usage than previous generations because many of them were teens and young adults in the 1960s when drug use was something "everyone had to try." Many still favor certain drugs to alleviate pain, stress, anxiety, and even boredom and a few pick up the habit again later in life to become late-onset drug or alcohol abusers.

In a study recently completed by Emory University, a large percentage of baby boomers showed current symptoms of both physical and mental problems with many having great probability that they will develop serious illnesses in the future (Keyes, 2003). Mental health experts have predicted that these data, along with the sheer numbers of baby boomers alone, may swell the elderly mentally ill to about fifteen million by 2030 (Halpain, Harris, McClure, & Jeste, 1999). Research already has found that stress as a result of divorce, remarriage, stepfamilies, and single parenting, often leads to both physical and mental health symptoms in adults and children (Amato, 2000). While most recover to live productive lives, many are left with scars that affect them the rest of their lives. As a result of the high numbers of divorces and remarriages among the baby boomers, health experts warn that the United States can expect a national crisis in mental health care for the elderly within the next two decades. This is compounded by the inadequate infrastructure, lack of funding for health care (especially mental health care), and especially the shortage of trained geriatric mental health care professionals (Halpain et al., 1999).

TREATMENT ISSUES

Many years ago, George Levinger (1966) proposed that those seeking divorce fall into two major categories: (1) negative attraction to the current spouse or current marital situation in general; and (2) attraction to something or someone outside the marriage. I have translated this to mean that some are running from the marriage and some are running to an alternative that seems preferable. Both of these seem to require a major reality check for any couples contemplating divorce. I believe that this is especially true for contemporary elderly couples and the "bridge group." At the heart of what I want to accomplish in our time together is to explore their values systems and their expectations and to provide this reality check. An overview of their values and resources can be especially significant because these men and women are so different from each other and from the preceding generations. They are breaking new ground for their generation and, as with all who change more traditional ways for those that seem better suited to their unique social contexts, they may feel pulled at from both the current older generation to keep things as they have always been and the younger generation who urges them to "be happy." Also, because these clients are marginal in so many ways, it is important to look into those areas that they may have overlooked or minimized.

One such area that later divorcing couples may minimize is how the usual involvement of others in their relationship takes on added meaning because of the length of time that extended family and friends have been a part of their family system. Several examples come to mind in which a woman has grown extremely close to her husband's sister or cousin or in which a husband reports that a brother-in-law has been his best friend since college days. Friends of the couple, who have shared a lifetime of experiences with them, often feel caught in the middle and are saddened by the loss of couple companionship. These relationships are sometimes severed over loyalty issues to a blood relative. One or both divorcing partners end long-term relationships in addition to ending the marriage. Reorganization of extended family and friendships as well as grief work over losses is often the focus of therapy as an aid to accommodating such changes.

Although it is important with all divorcing couples to probe to see how mutual the desire for divorce really is, it may be even more crucial with those who are bridging the generations. It is not uncommon for one partner to hold a value system that is not embraced by the other. A unilateral decision which impacts one's partner so completely is one of the most difficult situations faced in the therapy room. Often this seems to occur when an older spouse is faced with a younger one who may have more alternatives to staying in the marriage and may have ideas about divorce that are less traditional. Several years ago, John Crosby (1989) edited an anthology to which several authors of this book contributed. We wrote about what to do when one partner wants out and the other does not. At the time, I had worked with far more couples in which the decision to part was one-sided than mutually agreed upon. This also seemed to be the case with the other authors and still holds true in my practice today. I concluded the chapter I wrote by saying:

> "The best of all possible resolutions to the complex problem of non-mutual divorce is, of course, that one of the partners will change his or her mind. Either both will agree to save the marriage or both will agree that a divorce is the only solution." (Lasswell, 1989, p. 190)

Sometimes, in these very painful situations, the only way that I can gauge whether my services have been helpful is if we end our talks with the partners agreeing on the best way to proceed.

AUTHOR'S REFLECTIONS

How many marriage and family therapists are trained to work with the older population and how many will it take in 2011 when the boomers enter the old-age bracket? As a professional group we have a gap to fill since marriage and family therapists will be expected to give this care. For example, organizations that train and certify therapists can require of their members appropriate education and experience working with the elderly. Scholarships and awards can be given to those who specialize in geriatric care. Programs at national meetings can emphasize the urgency of what will be needed. Special issues of professional journals can be commissioned to focus on the problems at hand. The good news is that those who are trained to work with geriatric mental health problems will not lack for jobs whether those jobs are related directly or indirectly to the needs of the enormous number of elderly baby boomers. The real question is how soon can we be ready?

REFERENCES

AARP (2003). *Boomers at midlife: The AARP life stage study, wave 2.* Washington, DC: AARP.

Amato, P. (2000). The consequences of divorce for adults and children. *Journal of Marriage and Family, 62,* 1269-1287.

Antonucci, T. (1994). A life-span view of women's social relations. In B. F. Turner & L. Troll (Eds.), *Women growing older: Psychological perspectives* (pp. 239-269). London: Sage.

Bernard, J. (1982). *The future of marriage* (2nd ed.). New Haven, CT: Yale University Press.

Corman, J. M., & Kingson, E. R. (1996). Trends, issues, perspectives, and values for the aging of the baby boom cohorts. *Gerontologist, 36,* 15-26.

Crosby, J. (Ed.). (1989). *When one wants out and the other doesn't: Doing therapy with polarized couples.* New York: Brunner/Mazel.

Dychtwald, K., & Flower, J. (1990). *Age wave: How the most important trend of our time will change your future.* New York: Bantam Books.

Dykstra, P. A. (1990). *Next of (non)kin: The importance of primary relationships for older adults' well-being.* Amsterdam/Lisse: Swets & Zeitlinger.

Halpain, M. C., Harris, M. J., Mclure, F. S., & Jeste, D. V. (1999). Training in geriatric mental health: Needs and strategies. *Psychiatric Services, 50,* 1205-1208.

Keyes, C. (Ed.) (2003). *Flourishing: Positive psychology and the life well-lived.* Washington, DC: American Psychological Association.

Lasswell, M. (1989). The divorce dance: Doing therapy with polarized couples. In J. Crosby (Ed.), *When one wants out and the other doesn't: Doing therapy with polarized couples* (pp. 175-190). New York: Brunner/Mazel.

Lester, G. H. (1991). Child support and alimony: 1989. *Current Population Reports, Series P-60, No. 173.* Washington, DC: U.S. Department of Commerce, Bureau of Census.

Levinger, G. (1966). Sources of marital dissatisfaction among applicants for divorce. *American Journal of Orthopsychiatry, 36,* 803-807.

Patterson, T. C., & Jeste, D. V. (1999). The potential impact of the baby-boom generation on substance abuse among elderly persons. *Psychiatric Services, 50,* 1184-1188.

Pezzin, L. E., & Schone, B. S. (1999). Parental marital disruption and intergenerational transfers: An analysis of lone elderly parents and their children. *Demography, 6*(3), 287-297.

Pilusuk, M., & Minkler, M. (1980). Supportive networks: Life ties for the elderly. *Journal of Social Issues, 36*, 95-116.

Smith, J. W., & Clurman, A. (1997). *Rocking the ages: The Yankelovich report of generational marketing.* New York: Harper Business.

U.S. Bureau of the Census. (1972 & 2002). *Marital status of people 15 years and older.* Washington, DC: Author.

Appendix

Summary of the Career and Publications of William C. Nichols

Education

Bachelor of Arts (AB), University of Alabama
Doctor of Education (EdD), Columbia University
Postdoctoral Graduate Work, University of Colorado (National
    Science Foundation Fellowship, Anthropology)
Postdoctoral Internship, Merrill-Palmer Institute (Detroit)

Licenses/Certifications

American Board of Professional Psychology (ABPP)— Diplomate,
    Clinical Psychology (Board Certification) Number 3210
Association of State and Provincial Psychology Boards—Certificate
    of Professional Qualification in Psychology Number 3211
National Register of Health Service Providers in Psychology
Clinical Psychologist (Michigan), License Number 857,
    Independent Practice, 1969—
Marriage and Family Therapist (Michigan), License Number 26,
    Independent Practice, 1968—
Marriage and Family Therapist (Florida), License Number 1144,
    Independent Practice, 1987-1999
Marriage and Family Therapist (Georgia), License Number 662,
    Independent Practice, 1991—
Approved Supervisor (American Association for Marriage and
    Family Therapy, 1971—

Positions

University of Georgia
    Adjunct Professor, Child and Family Development and Graduate
    Faculty

When Marriages Fail
© 2006 by The Haworth Press, Inc. All rights reserved.
doi:10.1300/5562_21

Family Therapy Archives, Chair, Advisory Committee
Certificate Program in Marital and Family Therapy, Advisory
    Committee
University of Georgia Center for Continuing Education
    Instructor and Curriculum Reviser-Consultant , 1993-1997
    Post-Degree Program in Marital and Family Therapy, 1993-1997
Independent Practice and Organizational Consultation, Atlanta,
    Georgia, 1992-1997
    The Family Workshop, Atlanta, 1994-1997
Independent Practice and Organizational Consultation, Tallahassee,
    Florida, 1989-1991
Florida State University
    Interdivisional Doctoral Program—Marriage and Family
        Therapy, Adjunct Professor, Family Therapy, 1989-1991
Metropolitan Guidance Center, Tallahassee, Florida, Clinical and
    Training Consultant, 1991
Governor's Constituency for Children (Florida)
    Department of Health and Rehabilitative Services and
        Department of Administration, Executive Director, 1987-1989
Independent Practice, Birmingham, Michigan, and Grosse Pointe,
    Michigan
    Clinical Psychologist, Marital and Family Therapist, 1976-1987
University of Detroit
    Adjunct Professor of Psychology, 1977-1984
University of Wisconsin-Stout
    Visiting Professor of Marital and Family Therapy, 1978
Marriage and Family Center, Grand Rapids, Michigan, Clinical and
    Training Consultant, 1977-1978
Northfield Clinic, Southfield, Michigan, Consultant, Psychiatric
    Clinic, 1977-1981
Phoenix Center, Sterling Heights, Michigan, Consultant, Substance
    Abuse Clinic, 1981-1982, 1985-1987
Grosse Pointe Nanny Academy, Grosse Pointe Farms, Michigan,
    Instructor (Part-time), 1987
Florida State University
    Professor and Clinical Director, Marriage and Family Therapy,
        Interdivisional Doctoral Program, 1973-1976 (tenured)
Independent Practice, Grosse Pointe, Michigan, Clinical
    Psychologist and Marital and Family Therapist, 1969-1973
Advanced Behavioral Science Center, Grosse Pointe, Michigan
    Associate Director (part-time), Foundation, 1969-1972
Eastern Michigan University, Ypsilanti, Michigan
    Visiting Lecturer (part-time), 1970-1971

Merrill-Palmer Institute, Detroit, Michigan
  Psychotherapy Faculty, Post-Doctoral Training Program, 1965-1969
Samford University, Birmingham, Alabama
  Professor of Sociology, 1963-1965
University of Alabama in Birmingham, Birmingham, Alabama
  Assistant Professor of Sociology, 1960-1963

Professional Affiliations

American Association for Marriage and Family Therapy
  Fellow, Life Member, Clinical Member, Approved Supervisor
  President, 1981, 1982
  President-Elect, 1979, 1980
  Past President, 1983
  Board of Directors, 1969-1972; 1979-1983
  Founding Editor, *Journal of Marriage and Family Counseling,*
    1974-1976 (now *Journal of Marital and Family Therapy*)
  Editorial Advisory Board, JMFT, 1984-
  Editor, *Family Therapy News*, 1986-1991
  50th Anniversary Program Advisory Committee, 1991
  Task Force on Social/Family Health, Ethics and Policies, 1992
  Select Committee on Publications, 1985
  Task Force on Recognition, Regulation, and Legitimation, Chair, 1984
  Honors Committee, 1985-1986
  Task Force on CHAMPUS, 1983-1986
  CHAMPUS Advisory Committee, 1990-1992
  Insurance Committee, 1980
  Professional Standards Review Committee, 1979
  Continuing Education Committee, 1979
  Long Range Program Committee, 1976-1980
  Accreditation Committee, 1976-1978, Chair
  Training and Standards Committee, 1971-1973; Chair, 1974-1976
  (Changed to Committee on Accreditation, 1974)
  Program Committee, 1975, 1981, 1982
  Long Range Planning Committee, 1971-1972
  Research and Education Foundation, Board of Directors, 1992-1994
American Family Therapy Association (Charter Member)
Association of Marital and Family Therapy Regulatory Boards
  MFT Examination Advisory Committee to AMFTRB and
    Professional Examination Services, 1989-1992

American Psychological Association, Fellow
   Peer Reviewer, CHAMPUS Panel for Psychologists, 1978-1984
   Division 43 (Family Psychology, Fellow), Division 12 (Clinical)
American Psychological Society, Fellow
International Family Therapy Association (Charter Member)
   President, 1999-2001
   President-Elect, 1997-1999
   Past-President, 2001-2003
   The International Connection, Editor, 1996-1999
   Publications Committee, 1996-1999
Georgia Association for Marriage and Family Therapy
   President, 1996
   President-Elect, 1994-1995
   Task Force on Vendorship, 1993-1995
National Council on Family Relations
   President, 1976-1977
   Past-President, 1977-1978
   Vice-President, Publications, 1979-1980
   Board of Directors, Executive Committee, 1969-1978; 1979-1980
   Editor, *The Family Coordinator* (now *Family Relations*), 1970-
      1975
   Associate Editor, *The Family Coordinator,* 1967-1969
   Editorial Board, *Journal of Marriage and the Family,* 1976-1980
   Constitutional Implementation Committee, 1972-1973
   Finance Committee, 1972, 1976
   Publications Committee, 1969-1975; Chair, 1979-1980
   White House Conference on Children and Youth, Delegate, 1970

Publications

Editor and Editorial Boards

Editor, *Contemporary Family Therapy,* 1986-
Editor, *The International Connection,* 1996-1999
Editor, *Family Therapy News,* 1986-1991
Founding Editor, *Journal of Marriage and Family Counseling,*
   1974-1976 (now *Journal of Marital and Family Therapy*)
Editor, *The Family Coordinator,* 1970-1975 (now *Family Relations*)
Associate Editor, *Journal of Divorce and Remarriage,* 1976-
Associate Editor, *The Family Coordinator,* 1967-1969
Editorial Board, *Family Systems Medicine,* 1982-1996
Editorial Board, *Journal of Couple & Relationship Therapy,* 2002—
Editorial Board, *Journal of Family Psychotherapy,* 1984—Associate
   Editor, 1998—

Editorial Board, *Journal of Marital and Family Therapy*, 1984-
Editorial Board, *Journal of Marriage and the Family*, 1970s-1980s
Editorial Board, *Sage Family Studies Abstracts*, 1978-1998
Editorial Board, *Topics in Family Psychology and Counseling*, 1990-1992
Editorial Board, *International Journal of Family Therapy*, 1977-1985
Editorial Board, *Journal of Family Psychology*, 1986-1990
Editorial Board, *Successful Private Practice*, 1991
Editorial Board, *Grassroots*, 1992

Books and Manuals

(2004). Nichols, W. C. (Ed.). *Family therapy around the world: A festschrift to Florence Kaslow*. Binghamton, NY: Haworth Press.

(2000). Nichols, W. C., Pace-Nichols, M. A., Becvar, D. S., & Napier, A. Y. (Eds.), *Handbook of family development and intervention*. New York: John Wiley & Sons.

(1996). Nichols, W. C. *Treating people in families: An integrative framework*. New York: Guilford Press.

(1992). Nichols, W. C. *The AAMFT: Fifty years of marital and family therapy*. Washington, DC: American Association for Marriage and Family Therapy.

(1992). Nichols, W. C. *Treating adult survivors of childhood sexual abuse*. Sarasota, FL: Professional Resources Press.

(1986). Nichols, W. C. *Marital therapy: An integrative approach*. New York: Guilford Press. (Selected by Behavioral Science Book Service, Family Therapy Networker Book Service, Jason Aronson's Family Therapy Book Club)

(1986). Nichols, W. C., & Everett, C. A. *Systemic family therapy: An integrative approach*. New York: Guilford Press. (Selected by Psychotherapy and Social Science Book Service)

(1974). Nichols, W. C. (Ed.). *Marriage and family therapy*. Minneapolis: National Council on Family Relations.

(1974). Nichols, W. C. *Marriage and family counseling: A legislative handbook*. Claremont, CA: American Association of Marriage and Family Counselors. (First in the field)

(1975). Nichols, W. C. *Marriage and family counseling: A manual on accreditation*. Claremont, CA: American Association of Marriage and Family Counselors. (First in the field)

Book Chapters

(2006). Nichols, W. C. Family-of-origin therapy. In T. L. Sexton, G. Weeks, & M. Robbins (Eds.), *Handbook of family therapy: Theory, research, and practice* (Vol. III) (pp. 83-100). New York: Brunner/Routledge.

(2006). Nichols, W. C. Continuing professional growth. In R. H. Coombs (Ed.), *Continuing professional growth: Preparing for comprehensive and licensing exams* (pp. 569-587). Mahwah, NJ: Lawrence Erlbaum Publishers.

(2006). Nichols, W. C. The first years of marital commitment. In M. Harway (Ed.), *Handbook of couples therapy*. New York: John Wiley & Sons.

(2004). Nichols, W. C. Integrative marital and family therapy treatment of dependent personality disorders. In M. McFarlane (Ed.), *Family treatment of personality disorders: Advances in clinical practice* (pp. 173-204). New York: Haworth Press.

(2001). Nichols, W. C., & MacFarlane, M. Family therapy and mental health: Historical overview and current perspectives. In M. M. MacFarlane (Ed.), *Family therapy and mental health: Innovations in theory and practice* (pp. 3-26). Binghamton, NY: Haworth Press.

(2000). Nichols, W. C., & Pace-Nichols, M. A. Family development and family therapy. In W. C. Nichols, M. A. Pace-Nichols, D. S. Becvar, & A. Y. Napier (Eds.), *Handbook of family development and intervention* (pp. 3-22). New York: John Wiley & Sons.

(2000). Nichols, W. C., & Pace-Nichols, M. A. Childless married couples. In W. C. Nichols, M. A. Pace-Nichols, D. S. Becvar, & A. Y. Napier (Eds.), *Handbook of family development and intervention* (pp.171-188). New York: John Wiley & Sons.

(2000). Nichols, W. C. Integrative marital therapy. In F. M. Dattilio & L. J. Bevilacqua (Eds.), *Comparative treatments for relationship dysfunction* (pp. 210-228). New York: Springer.

(2000). Nichols, W. C. Family systems therapy. In S. W. Russ & T. Ollendick (Eds.), *Handbook of psychotherapies with* children and families (pp. 137-152). New York: Kluwer Academic/Plenum Publisher.

(1999). Nichols, W. C. Integrative family therapy. In A. M. Horne (Ed.), *Family counseling and therapy* (3rd ed.) (pp. 539-564). Itasca, IL: Peacock Publishing Co.

(1999). Nichols, W. C., & Lee, R. E. Mirrors, cameras, and blackboards: Modalities of supervision. In R. E. Lee & S. Emerson (Eds.), *The eclectic trainer* (pp. 45-61). Galena, IL: Geist & Russell.

(1998). Nichols, W. C. Integrative marital therapy. In F. M. Dattilio (Ed.), *Case studies in couple and family therapy* (pp. 233-256). New York: Guilford Press.

(1996). Nichols, W. C. Persons with antisocial and histrionic personality disorders in relationships. In F. Kaslow (Ed.), *Handbook of relational diagnosis and dysfunctional relational patterns* (pp. 287-299). New York: John Wiley & Sons.

(1991). Nichols, W. C. Interventions in context. In T. Nelson & T. Trepper (Eds.), *101 family therapy interventions* (pp. 112-113). Binghamton, NY: Haworth Press.

(1990). Nichols, W. C. Tear down the fences: Build up the family. In F. W. Kaslow (Ed.), *Voices in family psychology*, Vol 1 (pp. 177-191). Newbury Park, CA: Sage Publications.

(1989). Nichols, W. C. A family systems approach. In C. R. Figley (Ed.), *Treating stress in families* (pp. 67-96). New York: Brunner/Mazel.

(1989). Nichols, W. C. Problems and needs of children. In M. Textor (Ed.), *The divorce therapy handbook* (pp. 61-76). New York: Jason Aronson.

(1988). Nichols, W. C. An integrative and psychodynamic approach. In H. A. Liddle, D. C. Breunlin, & R. C. Schwartz (Eds.), *Handbook of family therapy training and supervision* (pp. 110-127). New York: Brunner/Mazel.

(1988). Nichols, W. C. Polarized couples: Behind the facade. In J. F. Crosby (Ed.), *When one wants out and the other doesn't: Doing therapy with polarized couples* (pp. 1-21). New York: Brunner/Mazel.

(1985). Nichols, W. C. Family therapy with children of divorce. In D. A. Sprenkle (Ed.), *Divorce therapy* (pp. 55-68). (Simultaneous publication in Volume 1(2), *Journal of Psychotherapy and the Family*)

(1984). Nichols, W. C. Foreword and contributor. In V. D. Foley & C. A. Everett (Eds.), *Family therapy glossary*. Washington, DC: American Association for Marriage and Family Therapy.

(1980). Nichols, W. C. Stepfamilies: A growing family therapy challenge. In L. R. Wolberg & M. L. Aronson (Eds.), *Group and family therapy* (pp. 335-356). New York: Brunner/Mazel. (Reprinted in D. R. Bardill & A. Kilpatrick [Eds.] [1981; rev. ed., 1983], *Family therapy: A relational-systems view*. Lexington, MA: Ginn.)

(1977). Nichols, W. C. Counseling the childless couple. In R. F. Stahmann & W. J. Hiebert (Eds.), *Counseling in marital and sexual problems* (2nd ed.) (pp. 134-145). Baltimore: The Williams Wilkins Company.

Editor of Special Issues of Journals

(2004). Nichols, W. C. Guest Editor, Special double issue, *Journal of Family Psychotherapy,* Family therapy around the world: A Festschrift in honor of Florence W. Kaslow.

(1997). Nichols, W. C. Editor, Special issue on family therapy in South Africa. *Contemporary Family Therapy, 21*(2).

(1996). Nichols, W. C. Editor, Special issue on family therapy in Israel, Part 2. *Contemporary Family Therapy, 18*(1).

(1995). Nichols, W. C. Editor, Special issue on family therapy in Israel, Part 1. *Contemporary Family Therapy, 17*(4).

(1995). Balch, W. H., & Nichols, W. C. (Eds.), Special issue on stories and storytelling. *Contemporary Family Therapy, 17*(1).

(1994). Nichols, W. C. Editor, Special issue on after the Wall: Families and therapy in Germany. *Contemporary Family Therapy, 16*(3).

(1993). Hardy, K. V., & Nichols, W. C. (Eds.), Special issue on critical issues in marital and family therapy education. *Contemporary Family Therapy, 15*(1).

(1991). Hardy, K. V., & Nichols, W. C. (Eds.). Special issue on emerging trends in marriage and family therapy education. *Contemporary Family Therapy, 13*(4).

(1988). Hicks, M. W., Hanson-Gandy, S., & Nichols, W. C. (Eds.), Special issue on coping with victimization. *Contemporary Family Therapy, 10* (4).

(1988). Nichols, W. C., & Deissler, K. G. (Eds.), Special issue on power and family therapy. *Contemporary Family Therapy, 10*(2).

(1978). Nichols, W. C. Guest Editor, Special issue on education and training in marital and family therapy. *Journal of Marital and Family Therapy, 5*(3).

Articles

(2002). Lee, R. E., Nichols, D. P., Nichols, W. C., & Odom, T. Trends in family therapy supervision: The past 25 years and into the future. *Journal of Marital and Family Therapy, 30*, 61-69.

(2000). Nichols, W. C. Integrative family therapy. *Journal of Psychotherapy Integration, 11*, 298-312.

(1992). Nichols, W. C., & Pace-Nichols, M. A. Developmental perspectives and family therapy: The marital life cycle. *Contemporary Family Therapy, 15*, 299-315.

(1990). Nichols, W. C., Nichols, D. P., & Hardy K. V. Supervision in family therapy: A decade restudy. *Journal of Marital and Family Therapy, 16*, 275-285.

(1990). Nichols, W. C. Consulting opens new doors to therapists. *The Family Psychologist, 6*(4), 34.

(1990). Nichols, W. C. Do we divorce the whole family? *Family Advocate, 13*(1), 22-23.

(1988). Gass, G. Z., & Nichols, W. C. Gaslighting: A marital syndrome. *Contemporary Family Therapy, 10*, 3-16.

(1987). Nichols, W. C. Boredom in marital therapy: A clinician's reflections. *The Psychotherapy Patient, 3*, 137-146.

(1986). Nichols, W. C. Understanding family violence: An orientation for family therapists. *Contemporary Family Therapy, 8*, 188-207.

(1986). Nichols, W. C. Sibling subsystems therapy in family systems reorganization. *Journal of Divorce, 9*(3), 13-31.

(1985). Nichols, W. C. Family therapy with children of divorce. *Journal of Psychotherapy and the Family, 1*(2), 55-68.

(1984). Nichols, W. C. Therapeutic needs of children in family system reorganization. *Journal of Divorce, 7*(4), 23-44.

(1980). Nichols, W. C. Preserving traditional families: The myth, the reality, the need. *Conciliation Courts Review, 20*(2), 55-61.

(1980). Hutchison, K., Nichols, W. C., & Hutchison, I. Therapy for divorcing clergy: Implications from research. *Journal of Divorce, 4*(1), 83-94.

(1979). Nichols, W. C. Education of marriage and family therapists: Some trends and implications. *Journal of Marital and Family Therapy, 5*(1), 19-28.

(1979). Nichols, W. C. Doctoral programs in marital and family therapy. *Journal of Marital and Family Therapy, 5*(3), 23-38.

(1979). Nichols, W. C. Notes and comments: AAMFT:AFTA. *Family Process, 18,* 99-101.

(1979). Smith, V. G., & Nichols, W. C. Accreditation in marital and family therapy. *Journal of Marital and Family Therapy, 5*(3), 95-100.

(1978). Nichols, W. C. The marriage relationship. *The Family Coordinator, 27,* 185-191.

(1977). Nichols, W. C. An end to the double standard. *Osteopathic Physician, 46*(1), 80-89.

(1977). Nichols, W. C. Divorce and remarriage education. *Journal of Divorce, 1*(2), 153-161.

(1975). Nichols, W. C. Sexuality in the midst of change. *Osteopathic Physician, 44*(9), 52-57.

(1975). Gass, G. Z., & Nichols, W. C. "Take me along"—A marital syndrome. *Journal of Marriage and Family Counseling, 1,* 209-217.

(1975). Nichols, W. C. An interview with a married couple: A comment. *The Counseling Psychologist, 5*(2), 47-52.

(1973). Nichols, W. C. The field of marriage counseling: A brief overview. *The Family Coordinator, 22,* 3-13. (Reprinted in various publications)

(1969). Gass, G. Z., Nichols, W. C., & Rutledge, A. L. Family problems in upgrading the hardcore. *The Family Coordinator, 18,* 99-106.

(1968). Nichols, W. C. Work and family life: A male dilemma. *Annual meeting proceedings, National Council on Family Relations.* Plenary address. New Orleans, LA.

(1968). Nichols, W. C. Personal psychotherapy for the marital therapist. *The Family Coordinator, 17,* 83-88.

(1965). Nichols, W. C., & Rutledge, A. L. Psychotherapy with teenagers. *Journal of Marriage and the Family, 27,* 166-170.

Works in Progress

Nichols, W. C., & Lee, R. E. Regulation, certification, and licensure: What progress have we made? What is needed for the new millenium.

Nichols, W. C. A glimpse at family therapy around the world.

Everett, C.A., & Nichols, W.C. *The teaching and learning of family therapy.*

Index

Abelsohn, D., 6
Ahrons, Connie, 7, 8, 11, 12, 14

Babcock, J., 103
Bader, E., 237, 239
Baucom, D.H., 219
Benowitz, M., 160
Beyer, R., 8
Blended families, 10-15
Bohannan, P., 4
Bowen, Lee, 5
Bowlus, A.J., 102
Bowman, S., 162
Bozett, F.W., 94
Brown, H., 11
Brown, L., 8
Brown, M., 8
Bubolz, M.M., 40
Buxton, A.P., 91, 92

Carter, A.E., 5
Cherlin, A., 10
Children and divorce, 7-8, 31, 41-48,
        91, 112, 114-118, 119-126,
        129-130, 131-133, 182-185,
        187-189, 191-192, 255-256
    and parental conflict, 125-126
    school and friends, 119-120
    separate parental households,
        120-121
Christensen, D., 14
Cognitive-behavioral therapy, 217-220,
        221-222

Cox, M., 7
Cox, R., 7
Crohn, H., 11
Crosbie-Burnett, M., 11
Crosby, John, 297
Cultural issues, 62-63

Daly, M., 103
Dispute resolution, 8-9
    mediation, 134-135
Divorce
    and baby boomers, 291-292
    checklist, 28
    coparenting, 9
    the decision to, 24-26
    joint custody, 136-137
    and men, 142, 143
    at an older age, 285-287, 287-291
    policies for, 9-10, 38-39, 41-44
    as a social issue, 4, 21-22
    statistics, 4, 145-148, 218
    statstics in Iceland, 130
    and women, 141, 247-248
Divorce dynamics, 145-148, 251-258,
        281-283, 285-287, 292-295
Divorce process, 4, 72-73, 149-152,
        195-196, 229-231
Divorce stages, 5-7, 31-32, 182-185,
        187-189, 191-192
Divorce therapy, 5
Doherty, William, 10
Domestic violence, 102, 102-104,
        159-162, 163-165
    goals of therapy, 167